Men and Social Work

Theories and Practices

Edited by

Alastair Christie

Consultant editor: Jo Campling

First published 2001 by
PALGRAVE
Houndmills, Basingstoke, Hampshire RG21 6XS and
175 Fifth Avenue, New York, N.Y. 10010
Companies and representatives throughout the world

PALGRAVE is the new global academic imprint of
St. Martin's Press LLC Scholarly and Reference Division and
Palgrave Publishers Ltd (formerly Macmillan Press Ltd).

ISBN 0–333–69083–4

This book is printed on paper suitable for recycling and
made from fully managed and sustained forest sources.

A catalogue record for this book is available
from the British Library.

10   9   8   7   6   5   4   3   2   1
10   09   08   07   06   05   04   03   02   01

Printed in Malaysia

Contents

List of Figures

Notes on the Contributors

Jill Annison worked as a probation officer and specialist social worker in the 1970s and 1980s. After obtaining an Open University degree she undertook postgraduate research, being awarded her Ph D in 1998 for her thesis *Probing Probation: Issues of Gender and Organisation in the Probation Service.*[1] Since November 1998 she has worked as Co-ordinator for the new Community Justice (Probation Studies) programme at the University of Plymouth.

Ric Bowl is Senior Lecturer in Social Policy at the School of Continuing Studies at the University of Birmingham. His teaching and research interests lie in the areas of mental health and ageing and the development of anti-oppressive practice within social work.

Alastair Christie is Lecturer in the Department of Applied Social Studies, National University of Ireland, Cork, and Honorary Research Fellow, Department of Applied Social Science, Lancaster University. He has worked as a social worker in England and Canada. He has also worked as Director of post-qualifying training at Lancaster University. His research interests include social work education, gender and professional identities and 'European' social policy and the politics of social work.

Viviene E. Cree is Lecturer in the Department of Social Work at the University of Edinburgh. Her most recent publications include *Sociology for Social Worker and Probation Officers* (2000), *Transfer of Learning: a Study*, with Macaulay and Loney (1998) and *Working with Men: Feminism and Social Work*, with Cavanagh (1996). She has recently, in partnership with Children in Scotland, begun a new research project on children affected by HIV and AIDS.

Jeff Hearn is Professorial Research Fellow in the Faculty of Economic and Social Studies, based in the Department of Applied Social Science, University of Manchester, UK, and Visiting Professor at Oslo University and the Swedish School of Economics, Helsinki. His co-edited books include *Men, Masculinities and Social Theory* (1990), *Violence and Gender Relations* (1996) and *Men, Gender Divisions and*

Welfare (1998). His authored books include *The Gender of Oppression* (1987), *Men in the Public Eye* (1992) and *The Violences of Men* (1998). He has been involved in anti-sexist activity, and researching and publishing on men, gender relations, and social welfare for over twenty years.

Stephen Hicks is Senior Lecturer in Social Work and Welfare at the University of Central Lancashire. He is co-editor (with Janet McDermott) of *Lesbian and Gay Fostering and Adoption: Extraordinary Yet Ordinary* (1999), and is a founder member of the Northern Support Group for lesbians and gay men with fostered or adopted children.

Nigel Phillips has had a varied career as a social worker and lecturer. He has been a lecturer in the Department of Social Policy and Social Work at the University of Manchester, and is currently a social work team manager in Oldham, North-West England. His publications are in the area of parents with mental health problems (with Richard Hugman).

Keith Pringle is Professor in Comparative Social Policy and Co-Director of the International Centre for the Study of Violence and Abuse at the University of Sunderland. His research interests are men's practices and social welfare, child care, anti-oppressive practice and comparative social policy. He is author of *Men, Masculinities and Social Welfare* (1995) and *Children and Social Welfare in Europe* (1998) as well as co-editor (with Margit Harder) of *Protecting Children in Europe: Towards the New Millennium* (1997) and co-author (with Margit Harder) of *Through Two Pairs of Eyes: a Comparative Study of Danish Social Policy and Child Welfare* (1999).

Acknowledgements

I would firstly like to thank the contributors who met deadlines, promptly delivered their chapters and waited patiently for the book to finally come to fruition. I would also like to thank the Department of Applied Social Science at Lancaster University where this book began and the Department of Applied Social Studies at the National University of Ireland, Cork where it was finished, for providing stimulating environments to work in. Thanks to Jo Campling and Catherine Gray for their encouragement and helpful suggestions along the way. I am especially grateful to Jeff Hearn for his help and support.

ALASTAIR CHRISTIE

To John and Mattie

Introduction: Themes and Issues

Alastair Christie

This book is about men and social work. It addresses the following questions: Where are men social workers located in the profession? When do men become social work service users/recipients (the terms 'user ' and 'recipient' are used here to emphasize the degree of choice that different individuals may have in working with a social worker)? How is social work gendered? How do men's 'presences' and 'absences' both within the profession and as actual or potential social work users/recipients contribute to the gendering of the social work profession? What are the particular issues that men social workers encounter in their work? These are just some of the questions that this book sets out to address while also raising new questions in this little researched area.

The initial idea for this project arose out of my unsuccessful search for a book that critically discussed the relationships between men and social work. Many books touch on this topic, for example, feminist writers provide analyses of men social worker's practices through their critiques of the gendered nature of social work. Writing by, and about, gay men and more recently, the development of the critical study of men provide descriptions and analyses of men's practices and gendered identities. However, it seemed to me that these three areas of work needed to be brought together in order to analyse the broad topic of men and social work. At the time of editing this book, an academic and practice based debate was taking place about whether men should or should not be employed as social workers. While this debate raises important questions, it tends to polarize opinion and does not offer spaces for men who are employed as social workers to think about how they might develop professional practice in less gender-oppressive ways.

Although the relationships between men and social work are seldom explicitly discussed in social work texts, there is considerable public debate about men as fathers, partners, and workers and as members of the wider community. There has also been much public debate about the 'revelations' in the 1980s and 1990s of child abuse by men social workers. Questions were raised about why particular men social workers commit these offences and how child abuse by men social workers could go 'undetected' for so many years. These debates raise fundamental questions about the connections between dominant constructions of masculinity, caring, violence and social work.

Social work can, in some ways, be seen as a non-traditional occupation for men (Christie, 1998a). It is seen as a 'caring ' profession and while some aspects of the work involve 'control' and 'surveillance' as much as 'caring', the emphasis on 'care' positions it as a 'feminized' profession. The majority of social workers (non-managers) are women and the majority of service users are women and children. So numerically, men, both in the practice of social work and the use of social work services, tend to be very much in a minority. Yet, men are visibly present in large numbers at higher levels of the social work hierarchy whether that be management or academe.

An overview of social work practice reveals the extent to which the work of the profession is largely taken up with responding to the consequences of men's violence whether in the public or private spheres. However, men social workers, like their women colleagues, find themselves working with mainly women and children rather than the perpetrators of violence. Men tend to be absent then as service users and very much present in the higher levels of social work management. This theme is addressed in the latter section of Chapter 1. Some of these patterns might indicate the contradictory positioning of men within social work and the potential for their presence within the profession to simultaneously transgress and reinforce gendered work boundaries. A further point of interest here is the unique requirement within social work training that all social workers be 'competent' in anti-discriminatory practice. This competence requirement means that men social workers are expected to reflect on their gendered privilege and the gendered nature of their work (alongside issues of 'race', class, sexuality and disability).

While the boundaries of gender come under question when men or women enter a 'non-traditional' occupation, the boundaries of social work are also open to question. Social work takes place in a wide variety of settings and with a variety of different groups of service users and recipients. Social work is constantly changing as a result of shifting legal frameworks and policy guidelines, the development of professional practice and changing media representations. This book addresses this diversity and change by including different discussions about men working with a variety of service users different service user / recipient groups and in changing social work settings. However, there are limitations on this diversity, for example, there is little discussion about work with people who are learning disabled and limited attention to social work in residential and day care settings. These (partial) absences may be an example of how I as editor and chapter authors may be complicit in perpetuating dominant discourses of social work which include and exclude particular groups.

While the nature of social work may be fluid, the social construction of the category 'men', also goes through changes. Many of the writers in this book draw on Connell's (1995) concept of masculinities which emphasizes multiple gendered practices and identities associated with men. The full range of these practices and identities is never fully visible. While identifying diversity, Connell also argues that there are hegemonic masculinities, i.e. particular forms of masculinity which are associated with powerful positions. Through dominant forces of masculinity, particular gendered practices and identities become institutionalized and normalized within social work practices. Dominant discourses of welfare and social work tend to provide only limited ways of thinking about 'men' which are often based on essentialist and quasi-biological models (Christie, 1998b). As a result, discussions about men and social work often get polarized into debates about 'types' of men – 'safe' men and 'dangerous men', 'criminal' and 'non-criminal' men, 'good' and 'bad' men social workers. These debates tend to shut down the potential for developing less gender oppressive practices and often reinforce the exclusion of already marginalized groups of men.

When inviting contributors to write a chapter for this book, I was conscious of a need to 'open up' debates in this area. In developing my own ideas about men and social work, I have increasingly recognized the involvement of both women and men in subverting and supporting dominant constructions of masculinity. Yet, this book includes only two chapters by women. While the book would benefit from more women contributors, I hope that the strong presence of men writing as *men* social workers and academics will begin to address men's absence in debates about the gendered nature of social work. I am also conscious of the absence of men contributors from service user/recipient groups. Perhaps this gap can be addressed in future publications in this field. The contributors draw on the work of feminists, theorists of social work, social welfare and sexuality, and men who write critically about men and masculinities. A wide range of issues and opinions about men and social work are expressed throughout the book, often conflicting, contradictory and sometimes in common.

In Chapter 1, men in social work are placed in a wide British social policy context. The discussion focuses on the ways in which discourses of welfare position men as 'breadwinners', 'nation-builders' and 'soldiers/heroes'. It is argued that *late modernity* (Giddens, 1991) has heralded social changes which give rise to new discourses of welfare. These new discourses have produced an awareness of 'risks' associated with both men's 'presence' and 'absence' in communities, families and in social work. These emerging discourses of welfare are institutionalized within gendered social work policies and guidelines and normalized within everyday practice. These new discourses highlight 'risks', but also potentially offer new opportunities for the development of anti-oppressive practice.

In Chapter 2, Keith Pringle traces his career in social work and social work education in relation to the debates about the position of men as social workers. Pringle's keynote article (1992) stimulated a debate about the abuse of children by men social workers and whether men should be employed as social workers. He argues in Chapter 2 that men have an important role to play in the provision of social welfare services, but insists that an analysis of violence by men should be central to any discussion about men in social work. Pringle goes on to identify specific recommendations for the development of anti-gender oppressive social work and preventive work that might be undertaken in social work with boys in particular.

In Chapter 3, Stephen Hicks explores questions of why men choose to work in child care social work and the particular issues for men working in this area. He also considers some of the issues that gay men encounter in their work as social workers. He argues strongly that men social workers working with boys who have been sexually abused need to be cognizant of the operation of patriarchy and hegemonic masculinities when making their professional assessments. Hicks uses case studies to illustrate his work with children and their carers/parents as well as to describe what such an approach might involve.

In Chapter 4, Jeff Hearn discusses the broad issue of how masculine dominance in social work has become institutionalized within social work organizations. He draws on research relating to men's violence to known women. Hearn argues that social workers appear to have little direct contact with men who are violent to women and notes that when social workers do have contact with men who are violent to women, it is usually as a consequence of another present-ing problem. Probation officers often work with men who are violent, however, Hearn found little evidence in his research, of probation officers working specifically with men on their violence to women. He also evaluates the 'effectiveness' of various groups which work with men who are violent. Finally, he points to some of the issues that social work agencies might consider when working with men who are violent to women.

In Chapter 5, Jill Annison describes the rapid organizational change that has occurred in the probation services during the 1990s. Annison argues that a 'smart macho' organizational culture is developing with the probation service which devalues social work knowledge and practices. While a professional social work qualification is now not a requirement for employment as a proba-tion officer, most probation officers are qualified social workers. Also, since the beginning of the 1990s most main-grade probation officers are women. Within this context, Annison analyses the posi-tion of men probation officers. In her own research, men probation officers increasingly questioned their vocational motivation to be a probation officer and identified new limitations on their professional autonomy. New administrative duties were also identified as placing probation officers under increasing stress which raised questions for men about the work/family divide. While the changes in organiz-ational culture might be expected to attract more men into the ser-vice, only 30 per cent of the first cohort of probation officer trainees are men. This suggests that there is no simple linkage between changing organizational cultures and the recruitment of probation officers and social workers.

In Chapter 6, Ric Bowl considers the position of men in the con-text of community care. He uses the concept of 'mainstream mas-culinity', drawing together feminist, Marxist and psychological theo-ries to analyse men in social work. Literature on men who care for spouses, siblings and friends is reviewed as Bowl examines men's relationships to giving and receiving care. While men's participation in caring may be limited, Bowl suggests that men's potential as car-ers is largely unrecognized. Social workers' assessments often assume that men are, at best, reluctant carers. He argues that working in community care provides men with opportunities to develop less oppressive forms of masculinity.

Chapter 7 by Nigel Phillips reviews the literature on men and men-tal health. Phillips raises questions about dominant constructions of masculinity and social constructions of mental health, focusing particularly on men and depression, severe mental disorders and suicide. He points to the sexual abuse of boys, discrimination against gay men and stress as factors which may affect men's mental health. He also argues that dominant constructions of masculinity emphasise self-reliance and restrict men's expression of emotions. This may hinder individual men social workers' and service users/recipients' ability to promote their mental health. Phillips points to how discourses of 'race' and gender combine to position men within the category of 'severely mentally disordered'.

In the final chapter, Viviene Cree describes social work education as a possible avenue for challenging dominant constructions of masculinity. Her chapter provides an analysis of the gendered nature of social work training in higher education. She describes possible strategies for change in social work education and men's practices as social workers, thereby concluding the book with some positive recommendations for intervention at the training stage which may facilitate an opening up of the categories 'men' and 'social work' into the future.

1 Gendered Discourses of Welfare, Men and Social Work

Alastair Christie

This chapter traces discourses of welfare in Britain by considering some post Second World War discourses of welfare (associated with modernity) and discourses of welfare towards the end of the twentieth century (often identified with late modernity). The main concern of the chapter is with how these discourses are gendered, particularly in relation to the gendering of men in families, as social workers and social work service users/recipients. It emphasizes the close association of men with the roles of 'breadwinner' and 'soldier/hero' in discourses of welfare in the middle of the twentieth century and the discursive production of men in relation to 'risk' by discourses of welfare in the latter decades of the century. The final section of the chapter considers the ways in which discourses of 'risk' associated with men impinge on social work practice. It also identifies the ways in which associations between men and 'risk' may contribute to men's exclusion from some social work services and raises questions about their roles in the social work profession.

Introduction

To understand the positions of men within social work as workers, or as service users/recipients, it is necessary at the outset to consider how discourses of welfare frame the categories 'men' and the profession of 'social work'. The nature of social work is constantly changing, being produced initially, through numerous, more 'established discourses', in particular, discourses of law, medicine and health. However, in the twentieth century, social work has been increasingly defined by discourses of welfare (Parton, 1996). The relationships between men and social work are complex, often contentious and also constantly shifting. Discourses of welfare emphasize certain men's practices while leaving others obscure and/or hidden. Similarly, men and men's practices are 'present' and 'absent' in particular areas of social work as workers and service users / recipients (see Christie, 1998a and Chapter 2 for a discussion of men social workers' positions in social work). In this chapter, I argue that we have come to understand men partly through post-Second World War welfare discourses of men as 'breadwinner'/'family man' and 'soldier heroes'/'nation builders'. I also trace the emergence of new discourses of welfare in a 'late modern' British society which emphasizes both men's 'presence' and their 'absence' in families, in communities and in social work.

We understand the social world through discourses which give meanings to practices, events and ideologies. Foucault (1977) described how particular discourses legitimate, institutionalize and normalize certain practices, constructing 'common sense' and /or dominant ways of understanding the social world. Discourses of welfare legitimate particular material practices with specific material effects. For example, the discourse of 'lone women parents' used by Margaret Thatcher in the late 1980s, positioned single young women as deliberately getting pregnant to 'jump' the housing queue and to gain other welfare benefits (Carabine, 1998). This led to the de-prioritization of lone mother's access to public housing by local authorities. In beginning of the 1990s, government and media attention in Britain began to focus on the position of young working-class fathers. Conservative politicians described these young men as 'feckless', as failing to financially support their children and as being reluctant to take on their role as 'head of the family' (Westwood, 1996). It is evident from these examples that discourses of welfare change over time and privilege and discourage particular forms of masculinities and femininities. Discourses of welfare are not gender 'neutral', but implicitly and explicitly gender men and women, offering them specific gendered identities and subject positions. This chapter is mainly concerned with the variety of ways in which men's identities within the social work profession are structured by discourses of welfare in the late 1940s and 1950s and in the 1990s.

If discourses of welfare are not fixed, the ways in which we understand the relationships between men, social work and the 'welfare state' are constantly changing. Fairclough (1992) argues that discourses 'contribute to reproducing society as it is, yet also contribute to transforming society' (p. 65). In this chapter, I try to keep alive this tension between the discursive reproduction of society and the transformative potential of discourse. The contested and changing nature of discourses, as well as the potential for reflexivity in Foucault's notion of self-regulation, suggests that there may be opportunities for developing less oppressive forms of social work practice through the active subversion of dominant gendered discourses of welfare. This might be aided by the development of self-reflexive practice. I return to these possibilities in the conclusion to this chapter.

Men, modernity and discourses of welfare

The term 'welfare state' was first used to describe the collection of policies implemented by the post-war Labour government in the UK (Briggs, 1961). This post-Second World War 'welfare state' has been described as exemplifying *modernity*, with the British government aspiring to manage society through a combination of social and economic policies (France and Wiles, 1997). O'Brien and Penna (1998) argue that key features of modernity are: 'differentiation', 'detraditionalization' and 'rationalization' (p. 188). The development of the welfare state is discussed below with reference to these processes.

Differentiation describes processes of classifying and categorizing the social world. Governments, through the development of the 'welfare state' ordered and attempted to co-ordinate different aspects of the society. Progress within modernity was guaranteed by the development of new forms of social regulation. The gendering of the social world, identifying particular practices and knowledges as 'male' or 'female', provided a fundamental way of classifying the social world. These forms of regulation included the social construction of dominant forms of masculinities and femininities (Skeggs, 1993).

Bauman (1991) uses the metaphor of the 'gardening state' to describe how the state within modernity, through access to technical resources, new forms of management and knowledge, attempts to differentiate the social world. He argues that '[t]he modern, obsessively legislating, defining, structuring, segregating, classifying, recording and universalizing state reflected the splendour of universal and absolute standards of truth' (Bauman, 1992, p. xiv). The welfare state can be seen as managing populations by processes of 'weeding out and "decontamination" of particular groups on the basis of "race"' Rattansi (1994). In a similar way, through gendered discourses of welfare, the welfare state regulates gender identities, reinforcing boundaries between 'men' and 'women' by defining 'appropriate' practices for men and women (mainly within families, but also in public places). Dominant discourses of welfare encourage and discourage particular gendered practices, and enforce gender divisions by 'exclusion and moral regulation' based on notions of the 'deserving' and 'undeserving' poor (Leonard, 1997, p. 19). For example, until recently, British governments have represented working-class women who care for children as not 'deserving' child-care services which would allow them the opportunity to enter the paid workforce and/or participate outside the private world of the family. More recently, working-class women are portrayed as 'deserving' child-care services, but only if they are actively participating in the paid labour force or undertaking training to enter the labour market. It is evident from these few examples that the welfare state is deeply involved in processes of classifying and categorizing the social world and, in the process, gendering it.

Detraditionalization refers to the 'displacement of established customs, habits, institutions and beliefs and their substitution by seemingly impersonal and objective systems of coordination' (O'Brien and Penna, 1998, p. 188). In pre-modern society, communal traditions provided ways of understanding the social world with individual's gendered identities being defined by local customs and practices. In modern societies, with the development of mass media/communications and national and international governmental and financial organizations, individuals' identities are often organized outside of the local context. The national 'welfare state' provided new regulations and expectations relating to the practices of men and women. In particular, the post-Second World War 'welfare state' incorporated discourses of universality in which rights and collective morals were defined in the public rather than private and local spheres (O'Brien and Penna, 1998).

A distinctive feature of the early post-war welfare state was the expansion of the state in the provision of welfare. Giddens (1994) questions the relationship between 'welfare' and 'state'. He argues that while the modern state is seen as providing welfare services in order to relieve poverty, sickness and unemployment, it is, in fact, an integral part of the process of state formation. The welfare state is less a subsequent event than an integral part of state building itself. The process of state building has been described as implicitly and explicitly gendered because it incorporates dominant constructions of masculinity and develops services which benefit men as a gendered group (Franzway, et al., Court and Connell, 1989). Bryson (1992) suggests that the 'welfare state' developed within the dominant discourses of masculinity which privileged the position of men workers, employers and politicians. Similarly, Fraser (1987) argues that the gendered nature of welfare in the United States is so distinct that, separate men's and women's welfare states can be distinguished. In Britain and the US, men are positioned as active citizens, whereas women are positioned as passive receivers of benefits.

For MacKinnon (1983), the 'liberal state coercively and authoritatively constitutes the social order in the interests of men as a gender, through its legitimizing norms, relation to society, and substantive policies' (p. 140). Hearn (1992a), while supporting MacKinnon's position, argues that elements of the state may also challenge the patriarchal nature of society. He points to the introduction of legislation on pornography and sexual harassment as examples of state challenges to dominant sexual practices. Similarly, legislation on equal pay and equal opportunities represent attempts to redress gender inequality in the labour market. The state acts in contradictory ways, however, it is necessary to take a critical approach to apparently progressive policies and legislation which may, in the end, be a means of gaining and maintaining state legitimacy. Liddle (1996) complicates the simple gender dichotomy when he argues that the process of state formation not only reinforces boundaries between dominant constructions of masculinity and femininity but also encourages hierarchical rankings of different forms of masculinity. The state, in particular the welfare state, can be viewed as breaking down local 'traditional' practices and establishing complex and hierarchical practices for men and women in relation to other social factors such as class and 'race'. It is not always clear, however, whether these developments have progressive implications with regard to the categories 'women' and 'men'. It is possible that they represent forms of re-traditionalization which appear more progressive, but appropriate feminist politics as a means of legitimating the state itself.

Rationalization describes the 'substitution of objective criteria and standards for subjective preferences and desires' (O'Brien and Penna, 1998, p. 188). Modernity was founded on the belief that the application of reason and rationality would overcome ignorance, superstition and disorder within society. This rationality is often associated with dominant constructions of masculinity (Seidler, 1994). Instead of a God-given social order, human reason was seen as identifying the foundational knowledge on which social order could be based (Howe, 1994). The application of reason, in particular through scientific, and later professional knowledges, was expected to produce a new order social world free from poverty. Social welfare was seen as a product of the application of reason and science to the social world (Penna and O'Brien, 1996). However, it was recognized that this new social order was a contingent and vulnerable one and hence required regulation (Parton, 1996). Rattansi (1994) argues that the fear of chaos and recognition of rapid social change were the main driving forces behind the developing notion of a 'rational', 'ordered' society.

Social workers and other professionals have historically used a variety of 'rational', scientific knowledges, in particular psychology, to ensure the 'appropriate' gendering of their own practices and the practices of service users. Because they operate in the spaces between the public and private lives of individuals/families (Philp, 1979), they are authorized to intervene in the private lives of individuals/families based on some notion of the public good. This liminal professional position between the public and the private can have a powerful regulating role in relation to gender identities and gendered practices. While some social work practices challenge dominant constructions of gender, social workers are often involved in the implementation of policies and legislation based on pseudo-scientific knowledges which reproduce a gendered public/private dichotomy. In the next section of the chapter, I look at how the Beveridge Report, published immediately after the Second World War, prioritized particular practices for men. The Beveridge Report differentiated between the practices of men and women by providing a 'rational' plan which built on principles of universality.

The Beveridge Report – men as 'breadwinners', 'family men', 'nation-builders' and 'soldiers/heroes'

The Beveridge Report on Social Insurance and Allied Services (1942a) provided a 'blueprint' for 'slaying the five giants' of 'Wants,

Disease, Ignorance, Squalor and Idleness', by developing a system of income maintenance based on: family allowance, comprehensive health-care provision and full employment (Hill, 1993). The aim of Beveridge's social insurance scheme was 'to abolish want by ensuring that every citizen willing to serve according to his powers has at all times an income sufficient to meet his responsibilities' (1942a, p. 165). The Report provided an outline basis for a social insurance scheme based on liberal collectivist values. The Report assumed two parent families maintained by the husband's wage. Benefits were to be available on the basis that men citizens took up employment and remained employed. If unemployed, men were expected to actively pursue employment and avoid idleness. Work and the elimination of idleness were seen as prerequisite to tackling poverty with men being placed under a moral obligation to seek and maintain employment.

The post-war government was faced with the problem of creating employment for the large number of returning soldiers. The government responded by invoking discourses of the traditional 'family', which encouraged women to give up full-time employment in order to provide jobs for men returning from the armed forces (Harlow, 1996). This new gendered settlement safeguarded men's employment and re-positioned women as belonging within the home, an approach which largely achieved support across the political parties. The state had controlled many areas of social and economic welfare during the war. The 'success' of the command economy during the war suggested that the state could manage the post-war economy, shifting from a 'war-time' state to a 'welfare' state. This shift was supported by the development of bureaucratic administration and professionalization which included the growth of the profession of social work (Clarke, 1996). Williams (1989) suggests that the post-war welfare state helped to establish a new set of relationships between the *family*, *work* and *nation*. Below, I discuss how post-war discourses of welfare in the Beveridge Report (1942a) and the subsequent legislation, positioned men as 'breadwinners' and 'family men' and as 'nation builders' and 'soldier / heroes'

Men as 'breadwinners' and 'family men'

The Beveridge Report (1942a), as noted already, positioned men and women as having unique and complementary characteristics. Men were represented as workers, citizens, soldiers and ex-soldiers, all active in the public arena as the sole, or main 'breadwinner' for their families. Women were defined, largely within the private space of the home, as carers of children and other adults, and dependent on men's financial resources (Bryson, 1992):

> The state in organising security should not stifle incentive, opportunity or responsibility; in establishing a national minimum it should leave room and encouragement for voluntary action by each individual to provide more than the minimum for *himself* and *his* family.
>
> (Beveridge, 1942a, emphasis added)

Drawing on specific discourses of welfare, Beveridge privileged a particular family form which Pascall describes as the 'Beveridge family' (1997b, p. 294). In 1932, Beveridge had questioned whether women's financial independence was compatible with family life (Oakley and Rigby, 1998). In the 1942 report, he clearly suggested that men should assume financial responsibility for *all* other members of the family. The discourse of men as 'breadwinners' positioned men as having a duty to assume financial responsibility for family members. This discourse also legitimated men's patriarchal position to exercise legal and informal control over women and children (Pascall, 1997a). His patriarchal position is partly legitimized by the use of the possessive pronoun to denote the husband/father as having a relationship of possession to *his* family.

Benefit rates were set at subsistence level or below, in order to ensure that the welfare state did not discourage individual men's enterprise, or their responsibility as family 'breadwinner'. At the same time, the benefit system did not challenge men's position as family 'breadwinner' by providing women with an alternative source of income, apart from the family allowance. In cases where men were not able to provide a 'family wage', the welfare state assumed a role in helping men to financially provide for their families which was seen as their (the men's) moral duty. Women were positioned as financially dependent on men, relying on the good will of their husbands and/or the charity of the state. In return for economic support, men were able to able to gain physical and emotional care, 'labours of love' (Finch and Groves, 1983), for themselves and other members of their family, from women. Finch and Groves (1983) have demonstrated that policy-makers undervalue women's work in the home and that community-care policies developed in the 1990s have increased the burden for women carers.

Beveridge's welfare state provided social insurance to men, but only limited cover for women. Married women were able to opt out of the scheme relying on their husband's contribution. Married women who contributed to the National Insurance scheme received benefits at a lower rate than married men or single people (Finch and Groves, 1983). As a result, married women seldom received benefits in their own right and remained dependent on men (Millar, 1996). The marriage contract became the main determinant of their social status as dependent adults.

Within the social work profession, which became integral to the workings of the welfare state, psychological theories supported discourses of men as 'breadwinner'. Some of these theories argued that the psychological health of children was dependent on mothers remaining at home with their children. For example, Bowlby's (1951) theory of 'maternal deprivation' stressed the importance of continuous contact between mother and child for the welfare of children. This theory justified minimal social provision for children under five (Riley, 1983). Theorists minimized the significance of fathers' relationships with children implying that it did not extend beyond that of financial 'provider'. It is, perhaps, not coincidental that these theories were developed at a time when a large number of children were growing up without fathers because they had been killed or injured during the war (Lewis, 1985). By the 1960s and 1970s, discourses of welfare had incorporated other psychological theories which emphasized the importance of contact with fathers for children. For example, Rutter (1972) suggested that boys in particular, were likely to have psychiatric disorders if their father had died or was mentally ill. These psychological theories suggested that men had an important role as fathers, especially in relation to their sons, yet, the nature of the role of fathers remained vague (Williams, 1998).

Although Beveridge envisaged men as carrying the 'heroic burden of the male breadwinner' (McNeil, 1991), it is questionable as to how far the 'Beveridge family' ever existed, or how much it was just a myth based on particular middle-class stereotypes of the 'ideal' family. While the 'Beveridge family' can be considered largely mythical, it is an amazingly tenacious element in discourses of welfare. By the end of the twentieth century discourses of welfare continue to represent men as the main 'breadwinner' earning the 'family wage' (a wage that is expected to provide for the financial needs of all family members). Vogel and Pahl (1993) argue that the concept of the 'family wage' is a misleading one because it implies that all family members equally share in the family wage. They found that although couples might share their joint income, this income is not available to all members of the family in the same way. While women's incomes account for an increasing percentage of family income towards the end of the century, men continue to have more say over how the family income is spent which includes men retaining personal spending money Millar (1996). The discourse of the man 'breadwinner' disadvantages women, but also fails to recognize the contribution of children to the general welfare of families and to joint family wage (Marsh and Arber, 1992). Children frequently contribute to the family wage and welfare through their work inside and outside of the home.

When European welfare states were categorized by Lewis (1992) in relation to men's positions as 'breadwinners' in the 1990s, she described Britain and Ireland as 'strong male-breadwinner countries', France as a 'modified breadwinner country' and Sweden as a 'weak male-breadwinner country'. In the UK and Ireland, the low pay of work traditionally associated with women, the often 'precarious' position of women in temporary and part-time work, and the lack of adequate child care provision, ensure the continuance of the 'strong male-breadwinner' model (ibid.). While the heroic myth of men as 'breadwinners' continues to be supported through discourses of welfare, the myth is becoming increasingly detached from the everyday experiences of men, women and children. Men's ability to act as 'breadwinner' is increasingly compromised by labour and housing policies and by changes in structures of families in the late 1990s (Pascall, 1997b).

The dominance of the free market towards the end of the century has resulted in the employment of men and women becoming less secure with a dramatic increase in jobs in the services sector favouring women employees. At the same time, the extension of house ownership has placed increasing demands on household's incomes. Women have become increasingly well qualified and active in the paid labour market: in 1979, 64 per cent of women were 'economically active', this had increased to 72 per cent by 1994 (Pascall, 1997a). Despite the increasing numbers of women entering the labour market in the latter decades of the century, discourses of welfare, as well as the actual provision of welfare services, continue to reproduce their position as the primary carers of children and other adults. Women in the 1990s were negotiating dual roles and a double burden. While European and UK equality legislation had been introduced, Pascall (1997b, p. 295) argues that the Thatcher/Major legacy of welfare policies based on the male 'breadwinner' model remain largely intact. (Policy developments of the new Labour government are discussed later in this chapter).

Men as 'nation builders' and 'soldiers/heroes'

Through the development of the welfare state, Beveridge sought to promote 'Britain', partly by the exclusion of particular groups and partly by the improvement of the so-called British 'race'. 'Race', 'nation' and 'empire' are deeply embedded within Beveridge's view of the welfare state (Lewis, 1997). In this section, I bring 'race' and gender together in a discussion of how racialised discourses of welfare privilege particular forms of masculinity.

Beveridge followed leading British socialists, such as Beatrice Webb, Sidney Webb, H.G. Wells and John Maynard Keynes, in supporting eugenic policies aimed at promoting a more healthy and efficient nation by 'improving the genetic stock' (Freedland, 1997). The welfare state was to provide health and welfare programmes which would help to 'preserve white superiority and ensure imperial survival' (Leonard, 1997, p. 22) in countries such as India. The welfare state was expected to secure the welfare of the British both at 'home and abroad'. Although the Beveridge report was based on universal and humanitarian principles, it 'rested on the most narrow kind of racial and sexual chauvinism' as Black men and women were positioned differently from White men and women by its ethos and policies (Cohen, 1985, p. 88).

While White British men were seen to be concerned with defending and ruling the empire as well as promoting 'British ideals', White British women were represented as responsible for the reproduction of British nation – the 'white woman's burden' (Dale, 1986).

> In the next thirty years *housewives as mothers* have a vital role to do in ensuring the *adequate continuance of the British race* and of British ideals in the world.
>
> (Beveridge, 1942a, para. 117, emphasis added)

In fostering the preservation of the 'British race', Beveridge looked back to Marlborough, Cromwell and Drake as the 'best of our breed' (Beveridge, 1942b, quoted in Cohen, 1985, p. 89). Here Beveridge seeks to reinvent the 'British race' by referring to White, military, male, 'heroes' of the distant past, as exemplary, noble, British citizens. The Report can be read in these terms as representing a conservative, racist imperialist and patriarchal vision of the welfare state. Such sentiments were invoked again in 1981, when Enoch Powell (Former Conservative government minister and Ulster Unionist MP) used a military metaphor to define 'Britishness' by suggesting that in the final analysis, a man's nationality could only be tested by his willingness to die for his country (Dawson, 1994). Dawson (1994) notes that the construction of a heroic, military masculinity excludes any reference to women. Beveridge's heroic men lived in a world of men, independent of women, defending their country against the foreigner and promoting British imperialism. Such idealized heroic representations of the soldier/hero need to be distinguished from the 'lived' experience of British soldiers. At the end of the Second World War, Beveridge was quick to replace men's role as heroic soldier, with that of heroic 'breadwinner' who single-handedly supported his family and thereby contributed to the reproduction of the national stock.

Beveridge was not alone in his concern for the 'British race', even Richard Titmuss, the well-known social policy academic, pointed to the falling birth rate in post-war Britain and expressed concern for the future of 'white peoples'. Titmuss argued that the 'white peoples' had a responsibility to protect and spread western culture and knowledge to less 'evolved' countries such as India (Jacobs, 1985). Such arguments helped to justify the development of a National Health Service which was seen as safeguarding the continuance of the British White 'race' by reversing the falling birth rate in the post-war years.

The post-war Labour government addressed its labour shortages by harnessing a variety of sources of surplus labour, including the labour of ex-POWs and service men from other European countries. The Black workers who came to the UK from the West Indies in the late 1940s and early 1950s, were less welcome because of racist assumptions about the quality of their work and because, as British citizens, they were not so easy to deport or direct towards particular areas of employment. While, in principle, universal welfare services were available to the new Black workers, their access to these services was denied or the services were not flexible enough to meet their particular needs. Although Bevan claimed that the National Health Services were to be available to all, by the 1949 National Health Service Act, access to particular services were restricted. For example, free medical treatments were removed for people who were not an 'ordinarily resident' in the UK (Jacobs, 1985). Black people had to face discrimination at all levels including employment, housing, education, health and social services. According to Cohen (1985), 'the black working class were relentlessly pushed to the end of the queue, being allowed only the worst that society had on offer and even that very begrudgingly' (p. 11). Within post-war Britain, Black migrants were viewed as competing against the White working-class, for limited resources.

Black workers were increasingly viewed as 'problems' and 'scroungers'. The services that were provided, tended to overtly regulate the lives of Black men and women. Black men were over-represented in mental health and probation services and Black boy children were over-represented in children's homes. Men positioned in marginal locations in the labour market and with limited access to housing could hardly be seen as comfortably occupying the category of 'breadwinner'. Beveridge's discourses of welfare positioned men in general as 'breadwinners', but excluded particular groups of men, such as Black men. In this way, discourses of 'race' can be seen as cutting across the gendered assumptions within welfare state policies. Men whose access to medical treatment is curtailed because they are not be 'ordinarily resident' in the UK, who are over-represented in mental health services and within the criminal justice system are pushed outside of the category of 'soldier/hero'. Their relationship to the nation state is structurally undermined at many levels and their masculinities are constructed in opposition to the heroic masculine British 'White' national or citizen.

Men, 'late modernity' and emerging gendered discourses of welfare

An ongoing debate at the end of the twentieth century centres on the nature of social change. This debate has focused on whether we are living in 'new times' (Bauman, 1992), or whether there has been a distinct break with the past and we are living in a distinctly different, 'post-modern' age (Lyotard, 1984). Giddens (1991) argues that instead of representing a distinct break with the past, western society in the last decades of the twentieth century can be characterised as being in the final stages of modernity, i.e. *late modernity*. He suggests that we have entered a period of late modernity when discourses of welfare have become more contested and fragmented. The hegemony of the post-war Beveridge welfare discourse is undermined by the emergence of new discourses of welfare. Giddens argues that one of the features of late modernity is the discovery of 'new risks' many of which challenge some of the apparent certainties of modernity. These 'new risks' are often associated with the presence and absence of men in communities, in families and as social workers and service users. The more fragmented discourses of welfare, characteristic of late modernity, complicate the subject positions of 'breadwinner' and 'nation builder' and indeed the category 'men' which underpinned post war discourses of welfare in Britain.

In Giddens' *late modernity*, the welfare state has increasingly come under critical scrutiny. Instead of being seen as emancipatory and empowering, the welfare state is increasingly regarded as restricting human freedom and at worst, oppressing individuals and groups. The breakdown of the welfare state is based, according to Giddens, on three fundamental social changes. First, *the labour market and patterns of work have changed*. The welfare state was based on aspirations of full employment for men. However, this patriarchal assumption is being challenged by growing unemployment among men and the increasing participation of women (albeit in part-time and casualized work) in paid labour force. These changes render the myths of the heroic, male 'breadwinner' and the 'family wage' increasingly difficult to sustain. Some see the post-industrial phase of capitalism as having led to the collapse of the 'world of the family wage' (Fraser, 1994). Fraser argues that new gender orders have developed which are characterized by unstable employment and more diverse family forms. The emergence of these new gender orders has prompted public discussion about the position of men, often in form of debates about 'new men' and the role of fathers (see discussion later in this chapter).

The second change outlined by Giddens relates to the undermining of the nation state by an *increasingly globalized economy*. Welfare policy is increasingly being decided outside the nation-state. For example, the New Labour government signed Social Chapter of the Maastricht Treaty in 1997 thereby adopting European Union based social policy. In the future, European legislation and models of welfare may increasingly influence British social policy and much of EU policy emphasizes equality issues, particularly in relation to gender. While globalization encourages *supra*national governmental forms, such as the European Commission and European Parliament, globalization also promotes the development of new regional governments and policies (Giddens, 1998). The re-emergence of regional and community-based politics in the late 1990s may also result in the re-emergence of men's political power at regional and community based levels.

Thirdly, Giddens argues that *new risks* have been discovered in late modernity, for example, global warming, HIV/AIDS and nuclear disaster. Governments can no longer assume that careful balancing of economic and social policies will guarantee citizens' welfare against these new risks. As well as 'new risks', the welfare state is expected to deal with increasing demands relating to 'known risks'. Beck

(1992) suggests that we are now living in industrial societies where scientific (including social scientific) knowledge has become a two edged sword, providing solutions while also creating problems. The growth in professional knowledge has led to the (re)discovery of poverty, child abuse, child sexual abuse, drug misuse and domestic violence. Social workers are expected to address and even control this spectrum of risks. The discourses of risk with which the welfare state and more specifically the social work profession are most associated include: risk to children and women (mainly form men's physical and sexual violence); risks to society (persons and property also largely associated with men's deviance); risk to community cohesion (often associated with female lone parent families and with men's absence from the family and the community).

The breakdown or transformation of the welfare state is marked by new discourses of welfare which produce changing relationships between family, work and nation. Below, I argue that discourses of risk are integral to discourses of welfare towards the end of the twentieth century. I focus on particular discourses of risk that associate men's presences and absences within communities, families and social work with risk.

Men's presences and absences in communities

The New Labour government in the late 1990s advocated the development of a 'Third Way' which Giddens (1998) describes as a shift away from the 'old' left and the 'new' right. In the context of 'stresses on the welfare state', Giddens (1998, p. 2) argues for the development of political idealism around achievable aims. He sees the postwar welfare consensus as discredited. Changes since the early 1970s, including globalization, technical change and the development of the 'New Right' with its reliance on the market fundamentalism, its hostility to 'big government', its moral authoritarianism and acceptance of inequality, have contributed to a displacement of the values of social democracy. Giddens notes that the 'Third Way' 'is an attempt to transcend both old-style social democracy and neo-liberalism' (ibid., p. 26). I am mainly concerned here with that aspect of the 'Third Way' which addresses 'new individualism' and which emphasises that we accept responsibility for our choices and their consequences. Giddens sees this as being conducive to self-fulfilment (Giddens, 1999). Central to this political doctrine are the expansion of democracy at local and national level, and the revitalisation of civil society. One means of achieving this is to attempt to tackle social problems at a local community level:

> Britain cannot be a strong community, cannot be one nation where there are so many families experiencing a third generation of unemployment, when so many pensioners live in crime-ridden housing estates, are afraid to go out and when thousands of children play truant.
>
> (Tony Blair in Ward, 1997, p. 8)

This government's interest in 'strong' communities is informed by the work of Etzioni (1993, 1995) and, in particular, his concept of communitarianism. Communitarianism encourages the re-assertion of civic values and new forms of ethics developed by communities rather than by the market or the state. Etzioni argues that in these 'strong communities' men will be active as citizens and fathers. While the term 'communitarianism' might suggest a focus on communities, Etzioni's primary concern is with the 'family' which he views as the basic building block of strong communities. When men are absent from communities and families, it is argued that social problems arise, including everything from gang warfare to a general lack of moral responsibilities.

Etzioni (1993) suggests that in the USA, the increase in lone parent families and families in which both parents work, has resulted in most American children suffering from a 'parenting deficit'. He cites 'easy' divorces as the main cause of the break up of the 'traditional' American family and the rapid increase in lone parent families. He also points to the growth in consumerism as accounting for the increasing number of families where two parents are in paid work. The argument is that consumerism encourages parents to prioritize disposable income and work over contact with their children and 'family life'.

Etzioni's vision of communities draws on essentialist notions of gender, with men and women having largely biologically determined positions within the family and lacks any critical gender analysis (Fraser and Lacey, 1993). For example, in Etzioni's (1995) critique of 'easy divorces', he suggests that 'above all, we should cancel the message that divorce puts an end to responsibilities' (p. 14). Fraser and Lacey (1993) suggest that from the evidence of who cares for children after divorce, women's parental responsibilities, instead of coming to an end following divorcee, are increased. Etzioni's link between 'parenting deficit' and lone parents reflects an anxiety in relation to the role of fathers which manifests itself in the assertion that families need to be fathered (Campbell, 1997). This discourse centres on the importance of reintroducing fathers to families in order to control the behaviour of *young men* in particular. Social order and control are strongly associated with men's presence in families.

Etzioni paints a romantic and conservative picture of the 'community' implicitly referring to a 'golden age' when children lived in two parent heterosexual families and child-friendly communities. By seeking to re-invent communities, he disregards the experiences of groups and individuals who have been marginalized and discriminated against in these idealised patriarchal communities (Fraser and Lacey, 1993). Etzioni, like Beveridge, adopts a mono-cultural concept of society (Williams, 1994), failing to recognize how 'community solidarity' often excludes groups and individuals and reinforces the demarcation between the positions of men and women (Clarke, 1996). Campbell (1995) sums up Etzioni's communitarianism as 'more or less misogyny and old fogeyism' (p. 49). She argues that the emergence of communitarianism 'enables "respectable", white mainstream masculinity to exempt itself from critique ... of masculinities that make life a misery in hard pressed places' (Campbell, 1995, p. 49). When the British New Labour government argues for 'strong communities', it draws on discourses of welfare that privilege men's presence in communities and disregards the consequences for women, children and other men.

The management of 'new risks' by recourse to a communitarianism that focuses on parenting, particularly the role of fathers, and implicitly pointing the finger at working mothers does little to challenge the gendered work of community production and maintenance. The call for men's presence in the family ignores the many complex reasons for their absence (when absent). There is also an implicit view that 'mothering', the means by which more and more children are parented, is not adequate. Below, I consider the renewed emphasis on the family in discourses of communitarianism which were prevalent in debates about the implementation of the Child Support Act in Britain.

Men's presences and absences in families

The addressing of 'new risks' through communitarianism, focuses on men's absences and presences in families as well as local communities. Politicians' public statements about the importance of fathers and discussions about the Child Support Act in the UK encouraged a public debate about men's positions in families. Tony Blair asserted that the 'family' is central to modern society and argued that the New

Labour government 'will uphold family life as the most secure means of bringing up our children. They should teach right from wrong. They should be the first defense against anti-social behaviour' (Blair quoted in MacAskill and White, 1997, p. 1). The implication is that two parent families are central to the moral well-being of British society. This discourse is marked by class, for example, Murray (1994, also see 1990) argues that in the United States there is an emerging 'underclass' in which fathers are generally 'absent'. Even when fathers are present in the 'underclass', they are often unemployed and/or misusing drugs and alcohol and therefore not able to provide the appropriate financial and moral lead (Murray, 1994). Without the presence of a 'good' father, he argues that boys are going to be inadequately socialized into their role as men and are likely to turn to crime. He suggests that the traditional nuclear family is the only arrangement that can ensure the welfare of men, women and children. Campbell (1993) critiques Murray's work as anti-feminist because he reinforces patriarchal relationships between men and women by emphasizing the presence of men in the family, largely denying the work undertaken by women as carers. Murray directly attacks lone women parents by suggesting that welfare benefits should be withdrawn from them and that more lone women parents should consider giving up their children for adoption (Wallbank, 1997). He also questions whether extended families, often associated with 'ethnic minority' communities are able to promote the welfare of children (ibid.). Both Blair and Murray's analyses see modern society as needing to be underpinned by a two-parent family in which men, particularly working class men, are present as fathers. But what, in particular, are these present fathers seen as providing?

Horn and Bush (1997) argue that the absence of a 'committed, responsible and loving father' is currently the greatest threat to American society. Similarly, Halsey (1993) in Britain, argues that not only are fathers good for families, but also that families have a civilizing effect on men. He suggests that men who aren't fathers are likely to take on other, often destructive, ways of proving their manhood. Men's separation from families is linked to riots on working-class housing estates, where Halsey argues, young men are discouraged from taking on adult responsibilities, such as fatherhood and marriage. Mature manhood and fatherhood are conflated in these discourses which represent social order as reliant on the reproduction of mature 'family men'. There is also the implicit suggestion that women, as wives, do the work of 'civilizing' men, shifting this responsibility away from men themselves and onto women.

Groups like *Families Need Fathers* established in the UK in 1974 (see Wallbank, 1997) argue that fathers, as well as their children, 'suffer' when fathers are absent from families. They suggest that a particular phenomenon – 'Parental Alienation Syndrome' – can develop between fathers and their children when fathers are absent. This alienation arises when the children's mothers encourage them to have negative attitudes towards their 'absent' fathers. The group suggests that this 'syndrome' can result in children's poor school performance and general anti-social behaviour. In this way *Families Need Fathers* construct 'absent' fathers and children as the 'real' victims of the separation/divorce. It is the mothers who are represented as bringing about this form of alienation.

Discourses of welfare have tended to describe fathers in stark terms as either good or bad, absent or present in families. Williams (1998) suggests that that discourses of welfare earlier in the century, had created similar dichotomies had been 'fit' and 'unfit' mothers. Both Collier (1995) and Wallbank (1997) argue that the concept of the 'absent' father is unhelpful because fathers may live with their children and yet may provide little emotional or financial support for their welfare. On the other hand, fathers, who do not live with their children, may be actively involved in the care of their children. The labels 'residential' and 'non-residential' fathers may be more helpful in distinguishing between fathers who do and do not live with their children (Wallbank, 1997). However, these distinctions raise questions about the significance of fathers' contact with their biological children and what men's contribution to children's welfare might be? Oakley and Rigby (1998) suggest that there is no clear evidence that the presence of a man in the home is an advantage to women and children. From their research on families with low birth weight children in which men were 'absent' and 'present', they argue that it is patriarchy that is bad for women, rather than the presence or absence of men per se. Collier (1995), Wallbank (1997) and Oakley and Rigby (1998) emphasize the ways in which patriarchal gender relations are obscured by discourses of fatherhood and risk in the late 1990s. The discussion so far suggests that discourses of welfare in the 1990s represent men's presence and absence within the family in relation to risk. Their presence gives cause for concern about violence or abuse, while their absence is represented as having long-term negative effects on boy children in particular. By focusing on the ways in which men are absent and present in discourses of welfare, there is a danger of reinforcing the polarized gender stereotypes on which these rely. Writers, such as Collier and Wallbank offer more complex readings of men's relationships to their family/children which direct our attention to factors beyond risk. These readings were precipitated by the introduction of the Child Support Act in Britain.

The Child Support Act is a controversial piece of government legislation which attempted to reassert men's role as fathers within families. The Act required that absent fathers be named and contribute financially for their children's upbringing. It was passed in 1991 and by April 1993 the Child Support Agency (CSA) began to implement the legislation. The rise and fall of the Child Support Agency added to public debate about the absences and presences of men in families. In February of 1993 the James Bulger Tragedy in Merseyside raised the temperature of the debate about the connections between lone parents, absent fathers and children's anti-social behaviour. This case involved the abduction (from a Liverpool shopping centre) and killing of a young boy (aged two) by two young boys (aged ten). In July 1993, John Redwood (then Secretary of State for Wales in the Conservative government) is reported to have said, while visiting a socially disadvantaged housing estate, that lone parents were 'one of the biggest social problems of our day' and that 'if someone is old enough to father a child, he should be old enough to bring it up'. He suggested that fathers should be reinstated in families where they should provide the 'normal love and support that fathers had offered down the ages' (*The Times*, 3 July 1993 reported in Collier, 1994, p. 18). The ambiguous theme of 'back to basics' associated with 'family values', was the prime focus of the Conservative Party Conference in the autumn of 1993. Conference delegates blamed lone women parents and 'absent fathers' for rising criminality among young men, family breakdown and urban disorder (Collier, 1994).

These 'feckless fathers', who the Conservative government had identified as absenting themselves from families and rescinding on their financial responsibilities towards their children, were often traditional Conservative Party supporters. In response to public pressure, the Conservative government made the first amendments to the Child Support Act in January 1995. These amendments resulted in assessments on cases that did not involve the payment of state benefits being deferred and maintenance payments being limited to no more than 30 per cent of fathers' incomes (Westwood, 1996). The discourses surrounding the legislation and the amendments to it represented men in terms of their financial responsibilities. A father's contact with his children was evaluated in terms of his ability to financially support them. This discourse, when extended to all men, was challenged by those middle-class men who resented state intervention in their lives. The amendments positioned the unemployed and working-class fathers as needing surveillance in meeting their fatherly duties. The Child Support Act and discourses surrounding it, like most welfare discourses, position working-class men, or 'under-class men, as failing to meet their moral and financial duties. These developments in the implementation of the Child Support Act reflect Murray's communitarian concern in the USA with what he sees as a emerging 'underclass' of absent fathers. The Child Support Act can be seen as instrumental in producing and reinforcing such classed formations of masculinity.

Other suggestions about formalizing the position of fathers in families came from the Institute of Public Policy Research which developed the idea of the 'child commitment contract' (Grant, 1998). In the UK, half of all marriages do not last to see the children into adulthood and half of all fathers lose contact with their children within two years of the divorce (ibid.). This 'child commitment contract' would clarify the men and women's long term responsibilities for the care of children, inside and/or outside of marriage. The notion of father's rights was increasingly being asserted in response to a perceived imbalance in the rights of mothers and fathers. The very idea of fatherhood is at stake in these discourses and policy initiatives, which, more than anything else, are marked by an anxiety about the role of fathers in contemporary British society. This anxiety shifts in discourses of welfare from fathers' presence and absence and back again, thus contributing to the very instability of the fatherhood that they could be seen as are attempting to counteract. The following section considers how discourses of social work represent men in terms of their presences and absences.

Men's presence and absence in social work

Locations of men in the social work profession

Since at least the 1970s, a number of authors have identified the gendered patterns of occupational segregation in social work (for example see Walton, 1975; Wilson, 1977; Howe, 1986; Lyons *et al.*, 1995 and Christie, 1998a). Hearn (1982) describes social work as a 'semi-profession' and argues that men as workers and managers within the semi-professions have quickly moved into managerial and specialist posts where they publicly monitor activities that were formerly undertaken by women in private. Hearn (1987) identifies how semi-professions construct and maintain particular forms of masculinity and how welfare institutions, such as residential homes and schools, attempt to explicitly develop 'manly' qualities in young boys. Men are seen as having a variety of motives for entering social work. These may include wanting to develop more ' "liberal" models of masculinity' (Hearn, 1987, p. 144), but also a desire to benefit from rapid career promotion in organizations where relatively few men are employed.

During the 1980s, feminist writers such as Hanmer and Statham (1988), and Dominelli and McLeod (1989) who investigated the positions of women in social work, raised questions about the 'presence' and 'absence' of men as social workers. Hanmer and Statham (1988) identified how the promotion of men resulted in women being excluded from management positions in social work agencies. They also raised concerns about how men social workers may reproduce gendered stereotypes, such as 'learned helplessness' in their work with women service users and workers. Dominelli and McLeod (1989) while describing similar concerns, argued that men could be supportive of women and develop less gender oppressive practices.

Justifying men's presences and absences in the social work profession

During the 1980s and 1990s, a series of child abuse 'scandals' raised further questions about the role of men in social work and the relationships between child abuse and men's violence. Hearn (1990) suggested a number of strategies for men social workers working with men service users which might prevent child abuse. These include the idea that men social workers actively work against men's violence. Pringle's (1992) article entitled 'Child sexual abuse perpetrated by welfare personnel and the problem of men' started a debate in the 1990s about the employment of men as social workers (see Chapter 2). In this article, Pringle argued that men should not be employed as social workers in child care because of the prevalence of child abuse by men. He argues that, 'a degree of restriction on the role of men [social workers] is likely to reduce the levels of sexual abuse in the care systems significantly' (Pringle, 1992, p. 16).

While Pringle has modified his position (see Chapter 2), there has been an increasing public and professional awareness of the risks of employing some men in social work. The Warner Report (Department of Health, 1992) was published after Frank Beck, the former manager of Leicestershire's children's homes, was sentenced to five life sentences for abusing approximately two hundred children over thirteen years (D'Arcy and Gosling, 1998). This report makes many useful recommendations on the recruitment, selection, management and support of staff. The report also acknowledges that a minority of staff, 'overwhelmingly male' (p. 20), abuse children in children's homes, but fails to make recommendations specifically related to men workers. A more recent government report, *Lost in Care* (Department of Health, 2000) was published after a three year inquiry into the abuse of children in children's homes in North Wales. *Lost in Care* makes 72 recommendations to improve the quality of care provided in children's homes, but, like the previous report, fails to provide any gendered analysis of abuse by men workers and avoids making gender specific recommendations. While the actions of particular men do not justify the exclusion of men from social work, they do raise questions about the selection and monitoring of social workers, men's social work practices and the relationships between men, masculinities and social work.

It is sometimes assumed that men, because of their gender, have unique qualities that can benefit the users of social work services. For example, they are seen as making up for 'absent' fathers (Ruxton, 1992; 1993), as working more effectively than women with 'unruly' boys (Jensen, 1995), as providing a 'gender balance' within teams (Ruxton, 1993; Jensen, 1995; Christie, 1998c) and as improving the working conditions of women (Jensen, 1995). Individual men may be able to provide a valuable service to women, men and children, but this is not guaranteed on the basis of their gender. The discourses of welfare discussed earlier in this chapter position men as fathers with financial responsibilities. When it comes to discourses of social work, men's presence as social workers with responsibilities for children is often contradictory and complex. On the one hand, men workers are seen as a potential threat to children, while on the other hand, they may counteract a deficit of male role models. Essentialist notions of women being natural carers tend to raise questions about men's presence in a 'caring profession' such as social work. Discourses of risk enter again to identify men's presence as 'dangerous' and indeed the amount of convictions of men social workers in the 1990s demonstrate that there is some foundation for these fears. Nonetheless, these discourse highlight the danger of homogenizing the categories 'men' and 'women', reinforcing gender stereotypes, and closing down possibilities for the profession as well as for the care of children.

Men service users/recipients of social work

When it comes to service users or recipients, most men are involuntary social work clients. Men are over-represented in the criminal justice system (Brake and Hale, 1992) and in specific areas within the mental health system (Busfield, 1996). However, men are far less visible as carers of adults and/or children. Arber and Gilbert (1989a) describe men as 'the forgotten carers' arguing that men carers are largely ignored by policy makers. These 'forgotten carers' usually care for their spouse. Men who care for their spouses often report personal rewards and a positive sense of identity as carers (Fisher, 1994). There is little research evidence to indicate that men care for other adults, apart from their spouses. However, caring for men with HIV/AIDS has opened up new opportunities for men to care for other men (Pringle, 1995). Parker and Seymour (1998) found that men as carers were both 'invisible' and 'ultra-visible: '[t]hey became invisible when the gender assumptions by welfare workers excluded them as a potential source of informal care' (p. 191). Yet, 'those men who *are* identified as carers may be "ultra-visible" due to the gendered nature of most caring tasks' (p. 191). Discourses of welfare and social work, for the most part, represent men as either passive recipients of care or resistant recipients of control and not as active providers of care.

Milner (1992) found that fathers are systematically excluded from the child protection system, with social workers often taking the place of absent fathers and primarily monitoring women's ability to care for their children. The ambiguous nature of fatherhood results in social workers having unclear expectations about the roles of fathers in caring for children. Social workers often have differing expectations of mothers and fathers, resulting in the responsibilities of fathers being minimized (Milner, 1996). Marsh (1987) suggests that social workers tend to marginalize the father's position in families. This marginalization of fathers by social workers may increase when child abuse has occurred in the family. Social workers often fail, for example, to involve non-abusing fathers in discussion about their children (Roberts, 1998). As yet, there is little information and research on social work with non-abusing fathers (Trotter, 1997). However, evidence of professional ambivalence in relation to fatherhood is not surprising given the fragmented and contradictory discourses of family welfare and the particular anxieties that mark discourses of fatherhood in the 1990s. When the 'breadwinner ' role is of less significance, as in many social work cases, then the father often becomes absented altogether. There seems to be an absence of discourses within which to make sense of his presence and to imbue fatherhood with positive value outside of financial responsibilities.

Barker (1994) found that men lone parents were often unaware of services that were available. Even when they were aware of these services, they were often reluctant to contact social services for support. While it is unlikely that lone fathers are actively discriminated against by social workers, Jo Adams (1996) found that social workers assumed that women would be better able to meet the needs of children. Like men who cared for their spouses (see above), men lone parents were both 'invisible' and 'ultra-visible'. There are still relatively few lone fathers, yet these men tend to remain relatively isolated within their own communities and become visible only when they are identified by social services and participate in services for lone parents (Adams, 1996). Hence, the overt assumption of the feminized role of caring, or even lone parenthood, 'visibilizes' fathers, because they are assuming what is seen as a non-masculine relationship to their children.

In the arena of child protection, there is a lack of procedures for working with fathers who want to be active in providing childcare and evidence that fathers are often reluctant to work with social workers. Milner (1996) suggests three ways in which men exclude themselves from participation in child protection services: mitigation, expressions of remorse and intimidation. Men are able to argue they have mitigating circumstances, claiming that it was not their intention to be violent towards the child or that they were not able to control their emotions. Secondly, expressions of remorse can minimize the seriousness of the incident and third, men can use threats of violence to avoid contact with social workers. These responses on men's behalf may not be the full story. It is possible that social workers may also be involved in excluding men from the service. O'Hagan and Dillenburger (1995) describe child care social workers' avoidance of men as an 'pervasive and endemic problem' (p. 197). They suggest that social workers tend to disregard the violence of men to women and children. They provide examples of cases where the exclusion of men from social work assessment has resulted in the death of a child. The social workers avoided contact with the men who were violent, partly because of practice orientation. Similarly, Edwards (1998) found that social workers', and other professionals' low expectations of fathers' involvement in child care led to men being both 'absent' and 'absented' from contact with social workers.

Concluding comments

In this chapter I have traced some of the changing discourses of welfare which position men in a range of ways since the expansion of the welfare state in the post-war period. The welfare state has explicitly and implicitly positioned men as 'breadwinners', 'nation builders' and 'soldiers/heroes'. Despite shifts in discourses of welfare in late modernity, these discourses remain central to the identities of many men who regard themselves as British. The late modern masculine hero in peacetime is probably more likely to be a pop star or sportsman than a soldier but still represents a Britishness based largely on notions of a 'White' 'race'. The discourse of 'breadwinner' also produced an idealized heroic image of men who provide for their families, positioning women and children as dependent on men. While the myth of men as 'breadwinners' may be increasingly hard to sustain in the context of an increasingly globalized and service-based economy, this discourse is never far from the surface of many of the Labour government's policies on child care and work at the millennium. As discourses of welfare become fragmented in late modernity, discourses of 'breadwinner' represent the 'breadwinner' in both masculine and feminine terms as relating to both women and men. Yet discourses of care, child-rearing and housekeeping seem more resistantly feminized.

Some new discourses of welfare have emerged then in the late modernity, characterized by changing labour markets, globalization and a new awareness of risk. In this chapter, these new discourses of welfare have been described under the headings of men's 'absences' and 'presences' in communities, families and in social work. These new discourses of welfare involve a new concern with men and their roles in society beyond politics and the workplace. Welfare discourses in late 20th century Britain are framed by binaries, producing men as either 'absent' or 'present', 'good' or 'bad', 'safe' or 'dangerous'. These simple binary categorizations limit possibilities of change by producing essentialist notions of gender, work and care. Debates about the positions of men in social work in particular have drawn on essentialist, quasi-biological models of gender suggesting that men have unique gender characteristics which make them suitable or unsuitable for employment as social workers. Men social workers are represented as either compensating for 'absent fathers' and/or representing potential risks to children and women.

Since the 1980s, there has been an increasing recognition of men's violence and abuse and many revelations of the propensity of some men social workers to perpetrate violence and abuse. There has also been as a shift in the structure of the labour market towards more feminized service-orientated work which has undermined men's dominant role in the labour market. Both of these changes have produced a heightened anxiety around fathers and men undertaking caring work and they may also have impacted on the social work practice of men social workers and social work responses to men service recipients.

The social work profession is expected by governments to deal with many of society's 'social problems'. However, within late modernity there is a growing awareness of new risks, of professionals' inability to find solutions to existing risks and that professional 'solutions' often create new risks. Contemporary discourses of welfare which focus on 'risk' place men at the centre of their concerns. Men are represented paradoxically, as both sources of risk and offering the potential to reduce risk by their active presence in families and communities. I have not addressed the implications of this focus on men for women other than to note that there is a potential repositioning of women in dependent relationships to men, as in the case of the Child Support Act. I have, however, noted the circumscribed nature of these discourses of welfare, which are less concerned with men's involvement in caring and domestic tasks than with their physical presence and financial contribution to family welfare.

The new Labour government's interest in politics of the 'Third Way' may be an attempt to 'break the mould' of post-war, left/right politics but is contributing to a reassertion of men's positions within communities and families. This political approach emphasizes the development of 'strong' communities built around the two parent, heterosexual family. The development of a reflexive social work practice will involve cognizance of the discursive (re)production of families, men, women and children through social work and how social work policy and practice are influenced by, for example, 'Third Way' politics. It will involve 'working' critically within and against these discourses as well as against the re-assertion of 'fixed' gender positions. One way of beginning might be to ask: what is at stake in the current resignifying of masculinity as both risk and solution to risk? The very invocation of the categories 'men' and 'women' is always in danger of reinforcing gender stereotypes. Reflexive practice, while demanding such deliberation also involves action. Social workers need to use discourses and categories strategically to achieve goals such as the welfare of children, women and men service users. Questions also need to be asked about the contemporary anxiety around fatherhood and how this status might be positively occupied in a variety of ways beyond that of 'abuser', 'breadwinner' or 'hero'. Because the social work profession is located so centrally at the nexus of the public and the private, gender identities are always being negotiated through social work practice. Men's presence in social work, precisely because of the gender contradictions it raises, offers an important site of reflexivity for both women and men social workers.

2 Men in Social Work: the Double-edge

Keith Pringle

As a key actor in stimulating the debate about the employment of men as social workers in child care services, Keith Pringle offers an autobiographical account of how he came to this debate and outlines his current thinking on this issue. Arguments *for* the employment of more men in social work are critically discussed most notably those put forward by the European Network on Childcare Studies in the area of social psychology and on men's violences to women are reviewed to identify evidence about men's practices. Pringle develops his own model for addressing the issues raised by men in social work by bringing together work on anti-oppressive practice and on the critical study of men and masculinities. His concern here is to put oppressive power relations at the centre of the analysis. The final section of the chapter looks at models of anti-sexist practice that might be taken up by men social workers. It also considers strategies for enabling men's positive contributions to the social work profession.

Introduction

This chapter echoes some of the issues raised by Christie in Chapter 1 but focuses more specifically on the role of men in social work. The debate originated in concerns about the sexual abuse of service users, especially children, by welfare personnel. However, as I shall demonstrate, the issue of men's role now extends far beyond the parameters of that original debate.

In my own writing about men and social welfare I have welcomed, and continue to welcome, the prospect of more men entering the 'caring professions' including the profession where I actively practised for twelve years, social work (Pringle, 1995, 1998). However, in that writing I have also sought to place this positive approach within a realistic context by pointing out the problems which the presence of men as practitioners within welfare agencies may create.

Among the potential problems of employing men in social work are (Pringle, 1995, pp. 18–36, 214–19):

(a)   Men workers may collude (consciously and unconsciously) with, and thereby reinforce, the oppressive practices of some men service users.

(b)   Men working in welfare settings (even those committed to anti-oppressive objectives) may divert resources away from the positive initiatives developed by female colleagues, particularly those services developed to meet the needs of women or girls.

(c)   Similarly, men workers may colonize and/or annex positive work developed by female colleagues.

(d)   Through vertical and horizontal job segregation and the operation of what has been termed 'organization sexuality' (Harlow, 1996; Hearn, 1996b), men may develop and maintain oppressive gender relations.

(e)   Men who are welfare workers may use their personal and structural positions of power to abuse service users in a variety of ways. I have argued that one of the most obvious, most frequent and most heinous examples of this phenomenon is the sexual abuse of people using social work services.

The object of this chapter is to review the research and debates which originally arose out of this latter issue. As we shall see, those debates now encompass a much wider field of enquiry relating to the broad topic of men in social welfare and social work generally

Much of this chapter will focus on child care social work. There are several reasons for this focus. First, it is the area of social work where I spent the vast majority of my years in social work practice. Secondly, it is also the field of social work where most research has been carried out about the abuse of service users and around which the British debate on the specific issue of abuse by professionals has centred. However, it needs to be stressed at the outset that the issues thrown up by this debate offer a challenge to the social work profession in all service user areas.

Autobiographical account of the author's interest in the abuse of service users by social work professionals

The immediate origins of the debate in Britain have their roots in the 1980s. I believe it is really important to think about these roots because such a consideration throws into perspective some of the main issues of the debate. I now want to use my own professional history as a 'barometer' of those times.

When I trained to qualify as a social worker in 1979–81 we never addressed the issue of child sexual abuse, whether inside or outside welfare systems. In many discussions with other social workers since then, I have a clear impression that in this respect my training course was typical of courses across Britain at that time.

From 1986 through to 1991 four female colleagues and myself at Barnardos developed a fostering service specifically for young people who had been sexually abused. Increasingly, our experiences in terms of what we saw and of what the young people told us about their lives led us to develop principles of practice which were pre-dominantly and explicitly feminist and pro-feminist (Davies *et al.*, 1987; Kidd and Pringle, 1988; Pringle, 1990). Our writing at that time expressed some of the personal anguish and professional isola-tion which adoption of feminist and pro-feminist approaches entailed for us (Helm *et al.*, 1993). Part of our story involved the increasing numbers of children referred to the Barnardos project who told us of previous abuse at the hands of social welfare staff and foster carers in various other social welfare agencies. Another part of our story at that time was our effort to engage agencies in addressing such cases: efforts which were sometimes met by a degree of professional resist-ance in those agencies.

By the end of the 1980s we had found other texts and other com-mentators who, based on peoples' lived experience, were providing effective analyses of what was happening and on ways to move for-ward in the area of child sexual abuse (e.g. Finkelhor *et al.*, 1986; Kelly, 1988). These linked closely with our own professional experi-ences and helped us to develop effective ways of assisting children who had been sexually abused.

In 1991 for a variety of reasons, some of which related to being a man working in the field of sexual abuse (Pringle, 1992, 1993), I left mainstream social work practice for teaching and researching in social work/social policy. One of my objectives thereafter was to try to open up a public debate about this recurrent phenomenon of peo-ple (mainly men) abusing children within welfare systems. Virtually nothing was written in British social work circles about this issue, except briefly in the social work press whenever some 'scandal' hit the headlines. This happened with increasing regularity in the early 1990s. Moreover, what I observed in those situations was local authorities repeatedly responding with the same 'nostrums' while scandal piled on scandal: more training for staff; better selection of staff; use of police checks; improved management structures; strategies by which children could be helped to say 'no' or could report abusers. Elsewhere (Pringle, 1992, 1993, 1994, 1995) I have argued that such strategies have their place but that they are unlikely in themselves to make a major impact on the safety of children.

The trend in advocacy of such strategies culminated with the Warner Report (HMSO, 1992) following the Frank Beck case in Leicestershire. This prestigious, and apparently thorough, report repeated the same old responses to the problem of sexual abuse committed in welfare settings. Moreover, the report was also remarkable for wholly ignoring one of the most salient features of sexual abuse both within and without welfare systems: the preponderance of men and boys as perpetrators (Pringle, 1993). Instead, the Warner Report seemed to cast around in its recommendations for some formula by which the problem might be solved such as psychological profiling of staff – even though the main body of the report itself found no current evidence to support the value of such profiling (Pringle, 1993, pp. 248–9).

In contrast to the Warner Report, by 1992 I was suggesting that more effective strategies for significantly reducing the incidence of sexual abuse in professional care systems could be developed precisely by focusing on the fact that most perpetrators were men or boys (Pringle, 1992, 1993). At this stage I advocated, for the purposes of debate, consideration of a range of potential strategies: including provision of training to assist men not to abuse (see Pringle, 1990, for an analysis of just such a training programme); and limiting or excluding men from some areas of professional childcare work (Pringle, 1993, p. 254). In opening up these issues, I was careful not to take a firm personal position on what was 'the right thing to do', primarily because (like most other people in the field) I was still trying to think through these difficult issues.

The positive outcome from this work was that a debate did indeed ensue concerning the issue of men in professional childcare about which, until then, there had largely been a deafening silence (Carter, 1993; EC Network on Childcare, 1993; Chandler, 1993; Pringle, 1994; Ruxton, 1994). Moreover, the debate continues (Chandler and

Dennison, 1995; Dodd, 1995; Pringle, 1995, 1998; Jensen, 1996; Owen et al., 1998). I now want to outline the main contours of that debate as it exists at the millennium.

Current debate about men's employment as social workers in child-care services

The first, and most important, point which needs to be made is that concern over the sexual abuse of children in the welfare services is probably higher now than it has ever been in both public and professional circles. In the summer of 1996 the Government established both a judicial inquiry into events in some North Wales care services and a national Children's Safeguards Review covering out-of-home placements including residential care, boarding schools and foster care (Community Care, 20–6 June 1996, p. 1). In announcing this Review, the Health Secretary said that it had 'become clear from court cases and criminal justice investigations that the scale of abuse and of abuse risks was higher than generally appreciated' (ibid., p. 1). This recognition and the inclusion of foster care within it was a major achievement, though some might argue a tragically belated one.

Having said this, the issue of gender did not become a central focus of the report which was the outcome of this review entitled '*People like us*' (Utting, 1997). Moreover, it is ironic that at this very time the pressure to involve men more intensively in professional childcare services had become greater than ever before, particularly from the EC Network on Childcare (1993, 1996). Indeed, the Network proposed a target for the next ten years of men constituting 20 per cent of workers in childcare services across the European Union (1996, p. 6): latest figures from the 1991 census suggest men currently account for 2 per cent of staff in 'childcare and related occupations' in the United Kingdom (ibid., p. 31). So the debate that this chapter surveys is as pertinent as it has ever been.

It seems to me that since the debate around the place of men as workers in child-care services emerged, some commentators have developed arguments which have been very useful in helping all of us to move forward in our thinking, while others have appeared to adopt approaches which are less helpful. Let me address the latter first of all.

For the most part, those contributions which have been of only limited value tend to recycle old arguments which have already been deconstructed. For instance, Ruxton (1994, p. 16) appears to use the

well-established fact that some women commit sexual abuse as a reason for taking much of the focus away from the position of men in
the debate. Of course few would deny that women are responsible for
perpetrating some child sexual abuse. Even those who emphasize the
gendered nature of such abuse most strongly, such as Liz Kelly
(1991) and myself (Pringle, 1992, p. 9), have never sought to deny
this fact. The point is that a proportionately large amount of child
sexual abuse is committed by men or boys both in society as a whole
(Finkelhor *et al.*, 1990; Kelly *et al.*, 1991) and in a wide range of welfare settings (Finkelhor *et al.*, 1988; Fanshel, 1990; Rosenthal et al.,
1991; Benedict *et al.*, 1994) – the latter phenomenon being particularly striking when one considers the relatively small number of men
working in many of these settings (Pringle, 1992, 1993, 1994).

While tackling the abuse of children in professional care from a
gender perspective may not completely eradicate that abuse, such an
approach may significantly reduce sexual abuse and prove far more
efficacious than the standard strategies which enquiry after enquiry
has recycled to little or no effect. Recent initiatives announced by the
Government and noted above may simply give us 'more of the same'
rather than tackling the gender dimension head-on.

Many of the old familiar arguments certainly continued to reappear
in publications of the European Network on Childcare. Let us take for
example one of their most relevant documents, *Men as Workers in
Childcare Services* (Jensen, 1996). Here Jensen argues that involving
men in such services will benefit in a variety of ways children, parents, gender relations, the equal opportunities profile of the labour
market and men themselves. Of course, involving men in childcare
services can have very positive outcomes for all concerned, but only
if the issue of men's sexual violences is positioned centrally in discussions about how men's involvement is to be achieved. I would argue
that the evidence of the Network on Childcare's publications suggests
that they did not make this issue of men's violences sufficiently central (EC Network on Childcare, 1993; Jensen, 1996).

This unwillingness to place the subject of men's violences in a central location when discussing childcare issues is also common in
much of the US literature (see, for example, Hood, 1993; and
Marsiglio, 1995). Indeed, as Jeff Hearn notes (1996a), the centrality
of men's violences has been absent from recent writing on men and
masculinities more generally, especially that produced within the field
of 'men's studies'.

As far as the Network on Childcare is concerned, their relative lack
of focus on men's sexual violences may well be partly a result of their

adoption of perspectives on child abuse prevalent in western and northern continental Europe. As I have argued elsewhere (Pringle, 1996, 1998; Harder and Pringle, 1997), the awareness of child sexual abuse in those countries often seems to be less sharp than it is in Britain. Although British perspectives may insufficiently address issues of men's violences, at least the widespread existence of child sexual abuse is relatively acknowledged. Of course it could be argued that the lower profile of child sexual abuse in other countries might be due to lower prevalence rates than in Britain. However, it seems more likely that this reduced profile is the outcome of less readiness to acknowledge the problem for complex cultural, political, socio-economic and religious reasons. For instance, I have argued (Harder and Pringle, 1997; Pringle, 1998) that the greater commitment to principles of social solidarity which exists within the institutions of other west and north European countries compared to Britain may paradoxically produce more unwillingness to acknowledge the existence of widespread social ills, such as sexual violence.

A review of international child sexual abuse prevalence rates by David Finkelhor (1991) suggested that variations in rates were attributable primarily to methodological differences between national studies rather than cultural differences between countries – and that those national studies adopting the most rigorous methodologies tended to produce the highest prevalence rates across the board. Whatever the explanation, the relatively low priority assigned to the topic of men's sexual violences in the publications of the Network on Childcare to some extent reduced the value of the network in moving forward the debates around the role of men in welfare work with children.

By contrast, I want now to focus on the work of some commentators who have helped to develop a more sophisticated and useful approach to the issues we are addressing in this chapter. Although some of these commentators have written from divergent perspectives, their work points in a similar direction.

First, let us consider gender-based analyses of violence based on empirical data from various social psychology studies relating to men's violences to women generally (Archer, 1994; Pringle, 1995, ch. 5). The work of Ann Campbell (1993; Campbell and Muncer, 1994) emphasizes men's largely instrumental use of sexual violence and helps to explode myths around the allegedly uncontrollable nature of violence. Campbell also places the issue of men choosing to use violence as a strategy centre stage and draws attention to the crucial role that peer group experiences play in this aspect of male socialization. A similar point is made by Paul Pollard (1994) also drawing on social psychology perspectives. He links such influences to wider societal endorsements of men's sexual violences, 'rape-supportive cultures' as he terms them, which pervade western societies. Indeed, some social psychology material has been especially valuable in highlighting the relative 'normality' of men's sexual violence, i.e. most rapes are committed by 'psychologically normal' males (Pollard, 1994; Pringle, 1995, p. 97); a perspective supported by studies indicating that a significant proportion of men believe that it is acceptable to carry out sexual assaults on women and children, with the fear of being caught as the main deterrent for not carrying out such assaults (Fisher, 1994; Pringle, 1995, pp. 170–1). Some social psychology studies reinforce the view that men's sexual violence should often be regarded as being at least as much about the expression of power dominance over women, children and other men as about sex per se (Pollard 1994). They also indicate that for some, perhaps many, men sex and the abuse of power are routinely linked to their daily relations with women (Briere *et al.*, 1994; Pollard, 1994; Pringle, 1995, p. 96). This social psychology research echoes views on the nature of men's sexual violences which have a much longer history in the writings of feminist commentators (e.g. Kelly, 1988; Jeffreys, 1990; Segal, 1990). However, many feminist/pro-feminist analyses and gender-focused social psychology studies do not fully acknowledge the complexity of men's sexual violences towards children. After all, the majority of men and boys do not commit sexual violence towards children. How are we to explain this if we rely on theories of general male socialization to analyse the generation of men's sexual violences?

Moreover, such sexual violence involves other relations of domination in addition to gender. For instance, it is surely no coincidence that we have growing evidence of sexual violence being experienced by people (of both genders) who are elderly, who are disabled or who have been subject to mental distress (Pringle, 1995, ch. 6). It is also significant that current research indicates that most abusers of boys are functioning as heterosexual men in the remainder of their social and personal lives (McMullen, 1990). As Pam Carter says in an important contribution to the debate (1993, p. 105):

> It is the various ways in which masculinity is woven into the web of power within welfare organisations which must be addressed. This involves examining the powerless position of children in public care. This

web of power involves the social relations of class, patriarchy, heterosexuality and racism.

Age and disability should also be added to Carter's list of power
dimensions relevant to an understanding of child sexual abuse. The
latter phenomenon can thus be seen as primarily the outcome of
oppressive relations of power permeating our society: and those
power relations are associated with the dynamics of racism, classism,
heterosexism, disablism, and ageism as well as sexism.

In order to address the complexities demanded by Carter I draw on
two, generally compatible, sources. One is those perspectives based on
principles of *anti-oppressive practice* (AOP) (see, for instance, Dominelli,
1988; Dominelli and McLeod, 1989; Ahmad, 1990; Thompson,
1993). The other source is those recent analyses of power relations
provided by a number of commentators providing a *critical approach
to men and masculinities*, for instance Connell (1987, 1995) Hanmer
(1990), Stoltenberg (1990), Hearn (1990, 1992b, 1996a, 1996b),
Morgan (1992) and Cornwall and Lindisfarne (1994). Perhaps the
most substantial contributions in this area have been provided by
Connell and Hearn.

Mark Liddle's re-working of Connell in specific relation to sexual
abuse has made an important contribution to the critical study of
men in social work (Liddle, 1993), as has Connell's own more recent
writing (1995). For Liddle, the value of Connell is not only the
detailed link the latter makes between structural relations of power
and individual behaviour but also the connections he forges with 'the
emotional and other complexities which seem to occasion matters of
sexual desire and attachment'. Liddle attributes this range of linkages
to the fact that Connell analyses gender relations by focusing on three
sets of structures together: the division of labour; the structure of
power; and, most important of all from Liddle's point of view, the
structure of cathexis which relates to the social construction of sexuality and practices of sexual desire.

Liddle convincingly demonstrates how in Connell's model the
differences between men and women in terms of structures of
desire are compatible with a greater propensity in men to engage
in abusive sexual relations. These differences correspond quite
closely to characteristics which I identified in my earlier work
(Pringle, 1992) as being more typical of men: 'the need for control,
the inability to express emotions other than anger, and a tendency to objectify the world'. In the context of Connell's model we can
identify these as characteristics of hegemonic masculinities. Liddle

(1993) notes that in the creation of such masculinities several themes are writ large: imperious sexual desire plays an important role and is strongly linked to a sense of personal adequacy and success; numerous conflicts and uncertainties over dependency and personal adequacy remain which may be resolved by satisfaction of sexual desire.

In terms of the present discussion, several important practical implications flow from such an analysis based on AOP perspectives and critical studies of men. First of all, it suggests once again that choice is a central feature of men's violences: men choose to abuse and not to abuse. The element of choice opens upon the real possibility, though of course not the guarantee, of change in men's behaviour. In other words, there is no determinism in this analysis: no man has *to* commit sexual violence.

Secondly, it helps us to appreciate the very complex way in which multiple variables (structural, interpersonal, personal and intrapsychic) inter-react dynamically over both space and time to produce men's sexual violences at any given moment. Several other practical implications then flow from this perspective. For a start, it means the sheer complexity of potential variables involved in the generation of sexual violences makes the possibility of ever developing valid screening profiles of abusers nothing more than a simplistic fantasy of policy-makers who are looking for a 'quick fix' to this horrendous problem. Another crucial implication of this analysis is that effective action to counter men's sexual violences needs to take place at all those interacting 'levels' (Pringle, 1995, ch. 9) or 'domains' (see Robert Adams (1996) for a discussion of the concept of 'domains') embraced by Connell's model ranging from the structural to the intrapsychic.

A third and central implication is the impossibility of understanding and then countering sexual violences except within the frame of an even wider set of social divisions generated by oppressive power relations associated with what Connell calls hegemonic forms of masculinity. To confront men's sexual violences entails confronting those wider social divisions of which men's violences are an organic part. Challenging sexual violence has to be placed within the broader anti-oppressive project both inside and beyond social work, a project which again requires action at what can be conceptualized as a series of levels or domains. Such a perspective clearly opens out the debate about the role of men in countering oppressions and abuses on to a wider plain.

Developing models of anti-sexist practice for men social workers

In many respects social welfare agencies often reflect and reinforce the oppressive features of the society to which they belong rather than countering them (Pringle, 1995, p. 206). Men working in social work agencies have a particular responsibility to engage in challenging those oppressive structures of power from which they may benefit directly or, at the very least, derive what Connell describes as a 'patriarchal dividend' (1995, p. 79). Indeed, the very process of men working together (and with women) to challenge such power relations is itself a central pre-requisite of any meaningful transformation of gendered power relations.

I have suggested elsewhere (Pringle, 1995) that men social workers who are seeking to develop anti-sexist practice need to work at a number of different levels. These include:

- work with, and upon, one's own behaviour;
- individual work with men or boys;
- groupwork with men or boys;
- creating change at local, agency and community levels;
- change at societal levels.

In terms of the second and third items on that list, I have also described the specific tasks which need to be focused on regarding men's work with men within social welfare (Pringle, 1995, chs 7–9; 1998, pp. 226–7). To a large extent those tasks are the same in work with abusers and in work with men service users more generally. The differences would be that in working with abusers these tasks would be particularly focused and the way in which they would be dealt with would be more confrontational. However, my contention is that such tasks need to be addressed one way or another wherever men social work workers with service users who are men or boys. The tasks are as follows:

- assisting men and boys to acknowledge their own capacity for acting oppressively;
- making explicit the links between men's oppressive acts and oppressive structures permeating society;

- countering societal attitudes which reinforce men's oppressions (myths about women, 'real men', violence, control, racism, heterosexism);
- recognizing how peer group activities can reinforce men's tendency to oppress;
- devising strategies to avoid situations where oppressive behaviour is most likely;
- helping men to look at their own masculinity and to re-consider the forms of masculinity they want to develop in various aspects of their lives.

I need to emphasize that these themes are equally relevant to men who are welfare workers themselves both in terms of their initial training and their ongoing staff development.

Salisbury and Jackson (1996) have provided what is, in most respects, a good example of how such a programme of action can be developed within an education setting at the levels of individual, group and institution, less so at community and societal levels. Other examples can be found in the regular journal *Working with Men* and in two books which share the same title (Cavanagh and Cree, 1996; Newburn and Mair, 1996). What is notable in all these sources is that there are relatively few examples of men's practice as it relates to social work itself. Particularly in the journal *Working with Men*, there are numerous contributions from the fields of education, community work and health but noticeably few from social work.

The discussion so far critically considers why it is necessary that more men work in the welfare services including social work. It is not simply about making the pressures of 'care provision' less focused on women, nor the idea that some men in caring professions may thereby encounter experiences which can help them transform their masculinities in a more positive fashion. I would suggest that the inclusion of men in social work is primarily advantageous because men in this profession (as elsewhere) have a particular responsibility to challenge those relations of power from which (to lesser or greater extents) they benefit. If men in social work and welfare try to broadly change the ways they live their masculinity as I have suggested above, that in itself should over time have an impact on the relatively more narrow issue of abuse perpetrated by professionals. Moreover, some standard strategies such as police checks are no doubt useful even if their efficacy is clearly limited.

A more focused gender-oriented approach is also necessary for the safety of children. In line with the more complex models derived from

Connell's work, I have recently (Pringle, 1994, 1995, pp. 185–92) outlined a strategy framework for deciding what level of limitation may be appropriate for the practice of men in child welfare settings on a case by case basis. I argue that each welfare setting needs to be assessed for the degree of potential risk, and safety, to children along a number of criteria such as: chronological and developmental stage of the children in that setting; other restrictions placed on children's ability to communicate when they are distressed, including the nature of their environment; whether the children have a previous history of abuse in their lives; levels and nature of staffing in the setting; messages from the children themselves, where possible, as to what makes them feel safe in that situation.

Such criteria should then offer some indication as to what is appropriate behaviour by men in that setting so as to make children relatively safe there. The restrictions on men's practice in many situations will be quite minor: for instance, an awareness about the problems of using touch as a means of communication or when it is appropriate for men to work alone with children. The number of situations where so many 'risk' factors coincide that it may be appropriate to limit or exclude men's practice from specific tasks will be very small.

I should add that the idea of placing some restrictions on men's practice, depending upon the nature of each specific situation, may be of benefit to men workers as well as to children, although I do not disguise the fact that my primary concern is the welfare of the children. It is very uncommon for a child to deliberately make up false allegations of sexual abuse (Salter, 1988). On the other hand, some children who have previous abuse in their life histories may on occasions misinterpret 'innocent' behaviour by a carer as being part of a process of abuse – for instance, if that behaviour was part of a 'grooming' strategy used by their perpetrator in the past to lead up to abuse. In these situations, the kinds of approach I am advocating may be protective not only for the child (my primary consideration) but also for the man social worker.

These tactics will not, as I have indicated earlier, stop child sexual abuse completely: my hope is that they may significantly reduce it – certainly more effectively than many of the standard recommendations in the continuing flow of child care scandal enquiry reports, useful though some of those recommendations are. Some readers might feel that the strategies I am advocating are too draconian, too negative. To this I would reply that experience suggests that men who want to abuse children, and sometimes adults, may well target those jobs and locations where access is easiest (Hunt,

1994; Irving, 1996) – and this may include social work agencies. The stream of welfare scandals and the government's focus on them speak for themselves: it would be naive to believe that such abuse was a feature of the 1970s and 1980s and that it is not a major problem as we enter the new millennium.

Conclusion

In this chapter I have sought to trace the development of a debate around the place of men in social work and social welfare. While much of that debate originally focused on the issue of sexual violence in welfare settings, it has quite rightly broadened into a discussion of men in social welfare as a whole: to those power relations associated with hegemonic forms of masculinity which are so central to welfare organisations; and the responsibility of men in welfare agencies to do something about them.

So men do have an important and positive role to play in social welfare. On the other hand, we must not allow the issue of men's violences to slip from the centre of our analysis. Consequently, in the last section of the chapter I have reminded readers about the problems of men working in welfare and, in particular, the continuing issue of sexual violence perpetrated by welfare workers against service users. Finally, I have tried to demonstrate that there are strategies by which men may be involved in this field for very positive purposes whilst also maximising the safety of the service users with whom they work.

3 Men Social Workers in Children's Services: 'Will the *Real Man* Please Stand Up'?

Stephen Hicks

In this chapter, Hicks describes the experiences of men, and in particular gay men, who are working in children's services. He argues, using three case studies, that men social workers can develop positive working relationships with children and parents. Hicks identifies an absence of analysis of men's sexual violence in research on male survivors of sexual abuse. He does not argue that men social workers should become 'role models', but that they have particular responsibilities to challenge men's sexual violence and to question dominant forms of masculinity.

Introduction

What is the role of men as social workers in child-care services? Do men have anything to contribute to services for children? Should men be child care social workers? These are some of the questions I address in this chapter, which is concerned with the position of men who are social workers for children and their families. I argue that men do have something to offer as social workers for children, and that they should have a place in such welfare services. But the position of men in child care is not unproblematic, and I ask what men have to contribute, before going on to consider two practice issues in more depth. These are, first, the particular dilemmas facing gay men who choose to work with children and, second, the role that men have in working with boys who have survived child sexual abuse. I argue that the way in which 'masculinity' is theorized within social work, particularly in the two practice areas mentioned, tends to rely on stereotypical and hegemonic views which assert the place of 'real men'. These views rest on the assumption that any sexuality other than the heterosexual is inappropriate for workers in child care, and the concept of the 'male role model' which is used to reconstruct 'proper' masculinity in boys who have survived sexual abuse.

The chapter looks at what is involved for men in being a social worker for children, including issues concerned with child protection and men's violence. I also give two case studies taken from my own work. In the second section, I look at the position of gay men working with children, and in the final section I focus on working with boys who have survived child sexual abuse. This final section includes a survey of literature about male survivors, and a case study from my own work. The case studies, and many of the ideas in this chapter, are taken from my experiences as a social worker in children's services.

What do male social workers do?

Working with children, I frequently found myself to be the only man at case reviews, planning or referral meetings. Sitting in a review in which I was the only man reminded me that I had chosen to work in a non-traditional occupation for men (Williams, 1993; Christie, 1998a). Research on men who do 'women's work' has shown that they are far less likely to aspire to work in such fields in the first place, but that if they do then they may be suspected of not being a *real man* (Williams, 1993, pp. 2–3).

Most people are less used to seeing men working with young children, and they may actively construct a man as 'soft', 'nice', 'unusual' or even 'gay', in order to make sense of the situation. Many of the women – mothers of the children – with whom I worked, told me that they were not used to men who did child care, or actively listened to them. Instead, often the women were themselves survivors of men's sexual, physical or emotional violence. They had every reason to distrust me as a man, and to distrust me with their children. However, I believe that my statements of 'outrage' at their violent treatment by other men, my declared opposition to such violence, and my re-framing of the abuse as being a consequence of men's violence, helped us to build a working and trusting social work relationship.

Here then is a positive contribution that I think men can bring to child care social work, but it necessitates an *active* opposition on their part to all forms of men's violence. It is men, usually heterosexual men, who commit most sexual violences towards women and children (Archer, 1994; Hearn, 1990, 1996a, 1996b, 1996d), so it is particularly important for male social workers to acknowledge their own gender may be something which provokes fear or distrust.

Like most child-care social workers, much of my caseload involved working with women and their children, and only rarely, men. Bowl (1985) argues that this is a central dilemma, because, if male workers want to bring about change in men's violence, then they need to engage with men as 'clients'. Further, Milner (1996) notes that social work often fails to engage with men, particularly in the arena of child protection. In my practice, however, I found that most social work time in children and families is taken up with child protection work, most of which involves responding to the effects of abuse by men and sometimes women. This is necessary in order to protect children, usually the most vulnerable and powerless in such situations. In addition, active engagement with abusive men is often very difficult to achieve because such men avoid contact with social workers, or may be violent towards them. Therefore the 'policing ' of men's violence is a key, but often unacknowledged, role in all child protection work (Wise, 1990, 1995). It is helpful for male social workers to think about ways in they can challenge men's violence on the job, rather than focus solely on the need to engage men as 'clients'.

A part of my caseload involved preventative work with 'families'. I use the word in inverted commas because it was, for the most part, work with women and their children. Many women living in situations of poverty, and struggling with day-to-day child care, have been left by, or are recovering from the violences of, men. I worked with women clients on what they saw as priorities (benefits, housing, nursery places, immigration advice, health issues, and therapeutic work for their children), but included on the agenda opportunities to discuss violence by men. This latter area is often painful, distressing to discuss and involves longer-term work. Further, it is often important to sort out more practical issues such as housing and finance, before this work can be done. Some women and children may, of course, choose not to talk about such experiences with a male social worker. However, the issue must not be avoided and the most appropriate outcome may be to refer women and children to more specialized agencies.

Case Study 1

How can casework help women to challenge men's violence?

Jane is a single white mother, caring for her three small children, aged two, four and seven. In the past there have been allegations of neglect in relation to her care of the children and their names have previously appeared on the Child Protection Register. I was asked to work with Jane on her ability to parent her children. I began life history work with Jane, and it emerged that her previous partner had been physically, sexually and emotionally violent towards her. Jane rarely talked about this, and tended to blame herself, taking on total responsibility for the neglect of the children.

I asked how Jane felt about working with a male social worker and was able to build a good relationship with her, in which she felt able to talk about the abuse she had experienced. By re-framing her abuse as violence from a man, Jane began to reconsider her experiences. She began to recognize abuse in many of her past relationships and we began to look at ways in which she might develop relationships in the future. This work provided important information when considering whether the children had been neglected.

I have argued that men should challenge male power within social work, but I am aware that this choice is not made by all male social workers. Men can and do choose to continue to exert inappropriate and abusive power within social work settings, be that over women, other men or children. Men dominate managerial positions (Carter et al., 1992; Harlow, 1996), and indeed agency responses to men's violence are just as much gendered as those of individual men (Hearn, 1996a).

Within social work teams, and especially in meetings, men may dominate the agenda, space and time, using the justification of 'professionalism' and 'having your say'. This is often part of a masculinist work culture, in which men must prove themselves by what they say in public rather than what they do in their everyday practice (Hearn, 1992a, p. 207). Male social workers may collude with sexism, leaving this unchallenged, and may hide behind claims to support 'equal opportunities', what Arshad (1996) calls the 'anti-sex-ist sexist' (p. 153):

> the most undermining type of male social work colleague. This is the man who is knowledgeable about gender issues, who uses the language of equality but whose attitudes and behaviour towards women continue to be discriminatory and oppressive.
>
> (Arshad, 1996, pp. 153–4)

Indeed some social work practice may be based upon stereotypical male gender roles. Examples include notions of male 'role models' for boys (discussed later in this chapter), ideas about who ought to be the carers of children, or allowing self-appointed men to speak for entire service user communities. Bowl (1985) makes the point that not all men within social work can, or want to, aspire to this 'ideal' hegemonic masculinity (1985, p. 18). Of course there are some men within social work who are 'positioned' and 'constructed' by others in ways which do not always allow them to occupy such powerful positions: 'racism, both individual and institutional, ensures that Black men do not have the same relations to patriarchal, capitalist hierarchies as white men' (Arshad, 1996, p. 149). Gay social workers, similarly, are rarely viewed in the same way as heterosexual men, and it is to such divisions of *men* that I now turn.

What divides men? the case of gay men in children's services

There are some particular dilemmas for gay men who work with children, and these revolve around the view that to be 'gay' is not to be a *real man*. It is here that the concept of the 'male hegemonic mas-culinity' (Carrigan *et al.*, 1985) may be helpful.

Carrigan *et al.* (1985) argued that 'masculinity' is a political order, with some forms being socially dominant or *hegemonic* (1985, p. 552). They define hegemonic masculinity as 'a particular variety of masculinity to which others – among them young and effeminate as well as homosexual men – are subordinated. It is particular groups of men, not men in general, who are oppressed within patriarchal sexual relations, and whose situations are related in different ways to the overall logic of the subordination of women to men' (Carrigan *et al.*, 1985, p. 587). While they argue that the dominant model of masculinity may only correspond to the characteristics of a small number of men, most men are complicit in sustaining this model

(1985, p. 592). This complicity is available to all men, regardless of race, sexuality or disability. This is a vital point, for I am not suggesting that all gay men are always 'oppressed'. Gay men can, and sometimes do, choose to oppress women (Stanley and Wise, 1993, p. 87) and benefit from sexism. But it is overwhelmingly heterosexual white men who are advantaged by, and actively construct, hegemonic masculinity.

Within social work, this has particular consequences for gay men in children's services. One of the key ways in which this works is through the suggestion that it is gay men, rather than heterosexual men, who represent a sexual risk to children. Gay men are seen as potential child abusers in a way that heterosexual men are not (Berry, 1987; Hicks, 1996). This poses problems for those of us that choose to work with children.

A report by Sone (1993) highlighted the fact that both lesbian and gay social workers face discrimination at work, and have to make choices about whether to come out. Within services for children, gay men felt immediately under pressure because of suspicions about their motives for choosing this area of work (Sone, 1993). Ferris' (1977) survey of social services committees, although carried out some time ago, found that 13 authorities would not employ gay men in residential, child care or learning disability work. He reports that many gay male workers felt constrained to conceal their sexuality because of such prejudice, and notes that three authorities specifically mentioned 'the fear of sexual involvement with children as a reason for discrimination against homosexuals' (Ferris, 1977, p. 19).

What are the implications of this for those of us who choose to work as 'out' gay men in social work with children? I did not choose to come out to every single child and parent I ever worked with, but I applied for my social work position as an openly gay man. While some people viewed this positively, I think others were threatened by it because gay men are often seen as either one of two extremes, 'soft, nice, and caring' or 'an abuser and sexual risk'. Many gay men who go into work with children are 'soft, nice, caring' people, but they are also viewed as not *real men* because of this. They are also often considered a sexual risk to children (Berry, 1987), and such ideas lead to discrimination at work (Ferris, 1977; Sone, 1993) and in the development of services, for example, gay men not being assessed as potential foster and adoptive parents (Hicks, 1996, 1997).

Gay men who work in children's services, therefore, have to make daily decisions about whether to be out or not. What is most interesting to me is that, when we do come out, we may be viewed as not *real men*, yet at the same time posing the kind of sexual risk that mainly *real men* pose to children. This view is often held not just by service users, but also by social workers or managers, who consider openly gay men to be 'unprofessional' (Hearn and Parkin, 1987). Gay men may be the lie that tells the truth about men in child care, pointing to contradictory notions of gender in child protection and the failure to take men's violences seriously. By this I mean that it is often the sexualities of gay men that are targeted as 'inappropriate', 'deviant', 'risky' in work with children, and yet the sexualities of heterosexual men, largely responsible for sexual violence, are normalized, invisible, absent from analysis.

Working with boys who have survived sexual violence

I now want to go on to discuss work with boys who have survived child sexual abuse. Male social workers may find themselves being asked to undertake therapeutic work with boys because they are seen as being a 'positive male role model'. This has been my own experience in working with a number of boys who have come through both physical and sexual abuse. I was sometimes asked to do such work because I could be a 'positive male role model' for such boys. The assumptions behind this are that (i) these boys needed to learn to re-trust men; (ii) they needed to see that not all men abuse; and (iii) they needed a worker to help them with any gender confusion they might have. Underlying these assumptions is the belief that boys who have been abused by men are likely to want to reject their own 'masculinity'.

As a social worker, I did engage positively with such therapeutic work and I believe that such work can be beneficial to boys who survive sexual abuse. However, I remain concerned about the assumptions behind the 'male role model' notion. I question whether a male worker, or any other man, will by virtue of his gender automatically provide a positive therapeutic experience for a boy who has survived abuse. Futher, I suggest that if male social workers are to engage with such therapeutic work, then they need to have considered issues of sexual violence and male power (Kelly, 1988; Hester *et al.*, 1996). This work should should also challenge the homophobia often experienced by male survivors (Queer Press Collective, 1991). For example, male social workers should actively resist the reinforcing of conventional power relations in the therapeutic situation, since there is a danger that the 'male social worker – boy survivor' dynamic might actually mirror that of the abuse.

male social worker	—————	male child
man	—————	boy
male abuser	—————	male victim

Figure 3.1   *'Mirrored' power dynamics*

My other concerns about the assumptions behind the 'male role model', are linked to more general questions about uses of 'therapy' with the survivors of sexual abuse (Armstrong, 1996). The 'therapy industry' can be dangerously anti-political at times, seeking to defuse any real challenges to male power and men's sexual violence (Kitzinger and Perkins, 1993). Why should the survivors of such sexual violence be expected to work towards re-trusting all men? Why should they be expected to work towards an acceptance of men and to 'forgive' their abusers? If a boy is experiencing 'gender confusion', why should we be so concerned to rectify this? It appears that therapeutic approaches can be used to protect male power, promote heterosexuality and reinforce traditional gender roles.

An interesting critique of the 'male role model' theory is also provided by Hainsworth (1996). She suggests that the arguments made by male social workers doing boys work, that such boys need them as 'role models', may actually be about preserving men's power in certain areas of work (p. 174). Like my own arguments here, Hainsworth says that whether a 'male role model' is positive or not depends upon the man, and that this is not necessarily challenging male power or abuse (p. 175). She points out that most boys are saturated every day with 'male role models', many of which are violent or aggressive and do nothing to challenge the kind of sexual violence that those who have survived abuse experience (p. 179). Any man who wishes to do social work with boys who have survived sexual violence ought to consider these points very seriously, as they seem to me to be key aspects of such work.

The literature on male survivors of child sexual abuse

In this section, I review some of the major texts dealing with male survivors of child sexual abuse. My aim here is to provide a critical analysis of such texts, and to ask whether they are helpful for male social workers who are going to be doing direct work with boys who have survived sexual violence.

The work of Hunter (1990) is mainly concerned with therapeutic issues and the process of 'healing' for boys who survive sexual abuse. In that sense, the text is representative of the 'therapy industry' and Hunter (1990) positions himself as 'expert' on dealing with such cases. He suggests that abuse is 'worse' for boys, and indeed the book's subtitle, *The Neglected Victims of Sexual Abuse* reinforces this message (pp. 5, 37). Hunter's view is that, because we are far less used to understanding men as victims, this means that the abuse of boys is regarded less seriously or that they are seen as 'willing participants' in it (p. 37).

While Hunter does acknowledge that most sexual abuse is perpetrated by heterosexual men, his text does not engage with the issues of men's sexual violence (pp. 22, 34). Indeed he is keen to emphasize that women may also perpetrate abuse, to the point where women are disproportionately represented as abusers (pp. 34, 37, 40). Some boys are sexually abused by women, but like many of these texts, Hunter uses this as a way to present an anti-feminist account and refuses to engage with the issue of who mainly perpetrates sexual violence (i.e., men) and how this is supported and accepted within traditional heterosexual masculinity and the continuum of male violence (Kelly, 1988, 1996).

Hunter is also keen to emphasize the 'male role model' idea in suggesting that a male therapist is probably best:

> I am reparenting the client, teaching him about manhood. Rituals concerning manhood are very useful in helping my client to claim his manhood...I have met with my male survivors in a wooded setting, around a fire, and used stories to teach about manhood...I think men learn about being men best from other men.
>
> (Hunter, 1990, p. 127)

This sounds as though it comes straight from the 'primitive/Wild Man' concerns of 'Iron John' (Bly, 1991), and it suggests that, if only these boys had been strong enough to be *real men*, then they might have fended off the abuse. What Hunter's approach does not engage with is the system of male power and violence that is a part of the continuum of sexual violence perpetrated by men (Kelly, 1988). Rather, Hunter is concerned that male survivors of sexual abuse need to learn to become *real men* once more. Presumably the subtext here is to try to ensure that such boys do not 'become' gay, but rather that they should be 'normalized' into heterosexuality.

Gonsiorek (1994) is particularly dismissive of feminist models of child abuse. In passing, he acknowledges that it is largely due to feminism that the issue of child sexual abuse has been put on the agenda (p. 22), but he then goes on to say that feminist understandings of sexual violence as a form of male oppression tend to minimize numbers of male victims and female abusers (p. 22). Essentially, Gonsiorek views feminism as too political, a 'cause' which he sees as anti-therapeutic (p. 22). He suggests that political activism in challenging abuse deflects from the needs of individual survivors requiring clinical care (p. 23). Gonsiorek also suggests that feminist models overemphasize the devastating effects of surviving abuse, not allowing for those people who are only minimally affected (p. 4). Instead, he suggests a continuum of effects from virtually none to the most psychologically devastating (p. 55).

This is objectionable on two grounds; first, many feminists have been keen to emphasize the 'non-victimization' of survivors and do not exaggerate devastating effects (Kelly, 1988). Second, Gonsiorek (1994) is confusing 'effects' of sexual violence with 'coping'. All sexual violence has devastating effects, but some people cope with it extremely well while others certainly do not.

Gonsiorek (1994) also suggests that feminist responses to abuse treat survivors who do not agree with their political aims in an infantilizing and pathologizing way (p. 24), and that feminism is as responsible as the patriarchy for the silencing of male survivors (p. 46). How can this be so? How can a political agenda that is concerned with challenging male power silence the victims of that power? Yes male survivors are silenced by the need to be a *real man*, to be strong, for fear that people will think they are gay, but all of these are conditions of male power, not of feminism. Gonsiorek does not like the feminist agenda because it is concerned with opposing male power, and also because it is concerned with activism for change. His preferred option is individual therapy for survivors, which he sees as client-driven rather than 'theoretical' (p. 35). Again he emphasizes that women can also abuse (p. 41), and in terms of whether boys are abused as much as girls he suggests a 'near gender parity of victim prevalence' (p. 55).

Mendel (1995) similarly finds feminist approaches less applicable to male survivors (p. 82). He holds feminism responsible for the underreporting of female abusers (p. 25), and he goes on to make the distinction that the 'fundamental underlying factor, however, is not gender but power' (p. 94). Why should he say this? Feminist approaches understand that it is both gender and power intersecting that are fundamental to sexual violence (Kelly, 1988; Driver and Droisen, 1989; Hester *et al.*, 1996). Etherington (1995) also suggests that the feminist model is used too widely (p. 22). She says that feminism has not accounted for female abusers (but see, for example, Kelly, 1991, 1996), and that the patriarchy not only betrays women but also men. Once more an interesting concept of the effects of the patriarchy is used here; Etherington (1995) says that men are prevented from discussing their abuse by patriarchal expectations about being a *real man*, strong, coping, self-defended, heterosexual (p. 144). Yet she does not engage with men's sexual violence and its role within the patriarchy (Kelly, 1988). In a strange inversion, then, patriarchy is what oppresses male survivors rather than having anything to do with sexual violence in the first place.

It is not enough simply to identify 'patriarchy', 'masculinity' and 'homophobia' as oppressive to male abuse survivors in this way. I agree that men are prevented from disclosing their abuse for fear of being seen as weak, not a *real man*, or gay. But we need to ask how such concepts also actively contribute to male power. It is the system of male hegemonic power (Carrigan *et al.*, 1985) which holds that men should be strong, dominant and heterosexual, and this is upheld by many men who have much to gain from its continuance. But isn't sexual violence towards women, towards children, towards boys, towards some other men a part of that system? Doesn't the system of male power and sexual violence need to be actively resisted and challenged? Of course my answer is yes, and this is why I believe that male social workers can do just that in their work.

The literature reviewed here (Hunter, 1990; Gonsiorek, 1994; Etherington, 1995; Mendel, 1995) is largely anti-feminist, however suggesting that feminist models cannot be applied to male abuse survivors. But like Kelly (1988, p. 22), I believe that notions of male power can be applied to men's sexual violences towards boys and other men. So why should the existing literature be so keen to put feminism down? Is this a part of an anti-feminist backlash? (Faludi, 1991). Much of the literature comes from the powerful 'therapy industry' (Armstrong, 1996), which emphasizes the individual therapeutic needs of survivors, in which boys and men who survive abuse are helped towards 'forgiveness' of their abusers (Etherington, 1995, p. 316; Mendel, 1995, p. 213). Some male therapists are also keen to argue that survivors need 'male role models' in order to rediscover their masculinity, or a 'correct' masculinity (Hunter, 1990, p. 127).

There is a limited literature for working with male survivors. Two self-help volumes (Lew, 1988; Grubman-Black, 1990) provide useful insights into working with boys who are sexually abused. However, most of the literature attempts to deny the issues of gender power, to 'divert challenge to male authority' (Armstrong, 1996, p. 263). I do not believe that this is the way forward for male social workers who work with boys who have been sexually abused. Feminist approaches can be applied to such work with boys but these do not ask boys to forgive their abusers, trust all men, or re-develop their identities as *real men* (Kelly, 1988, p. 187).

Case Study 2

Direct work with a boy who survived sexual abuse

Liam is 10 years old and has recently been acting aggressively at home. His mother refers him for social work help and explains that Liam has never talked about the fact that he was sexually abused by his step-father.

I agreed to do some direct work with Liam, and planned to make use of his interest in drawing and painting. I met with Liam and he agreed to work with me for ten sessions. We started with some life-story work (Ryan and Walker, 1985) which Liam used to introduce his negative feelings about his step-father. We went on to do work on emotions, which helped him to discuss his anger about the abuse.

After this, I did some disclosure work with Liam and he felt able to tell me what had happened to him, as well as describing another incident of stranger-assault in a local park. Liam lost interest in the sessions after about eight, telling me that he had appreciated being able to talk but that he had 'had enough'. I gave him the artwork he had done to keep.

My gender was a key issue in my work with Liam. Liam reacted very strongly to some adult men, whose faces reminded him of the 'angry face' of his abuser, and I had to check out with him that this was not the case with me. Lew (1988) is helpful in providing ideas for thinking through the setting, basis and power issues within such work (pp. 195–202), and I discussed such issues with Liam. I was keen not to 'replay' the abuse of power he had experienced. Like most survivors, he partly blamed himself for the abuse and I tried to reframe this with him. For male social workers embarking on such work with boys, I think a serious consideration of the issues I have raised is vital. Just going into such work as a 'male role model', as a *man*, is not good enough.

I am arguing for boys to be helped to work through their feelings about, and to discuss the abuse they have experienced. 'Being able to talk about it' may actually be the key here, as many boys have never disclosed the abuse before. But disclosure is difficult work and must *not* be forced. I do not see the 'reconstruction of masculinity' or the 'retrusting of all men' as appropriate foci for work with boys who have been abused, and have argued against these.

Conclusions: what can men contribute as social workers for children?

I have suggested that men are in the minority of child-care social workers, and I expect that this will continue to be the case. Child-care social work is simply not given proper recognition by most men presently, and many men who go into such work may be seen as 'suspect'. Yet those men who do work with children often have a disproportionate influence within such services. They are far more likely to occupy management positions, or may use daily exertions of power by dominating meetings and 'doing sexism' at work (Wise and Stanley, 1990).

I have argued therefore that a key role for male social workers, and one which I believe was central to my practice, is to challenge men's (sexual) violence 'on the job'. This cannot be done within child protection services solely by calls to engage men as 'clients'. But it can be done by challenging men's attitudes towards women and children, by not colluding with sexism and by questioning some women's perceptions of male abuse as being 'their own fault'.

I have given two examples which suggest social work's concerns about gender relations and the need to assert the place of *real men*. First, male hegemonic practice is challenged in social work services for children by the mere presence of gay workers. Gay men may be actively constructed by others as 'soft', or 'sexually threatening' and even sometimes to be sexually harassed by other men. Further, within social work with boys who have survived sexual violence, the use of male workers as 'positive role models' betrays anxieties to reassert 'proper' masculinity. However, there are plenty enough *real men* out there already, responsible largely for most forms of emotional, physical and sexual violences. Social work does not, and should not, need to be concerned to be 'reconstructing' *real men* in this way, and male social workers have a key role to play in challenging men's violences wherever they occur.

Acknowledgements

I would like to thank Alastair Christie, Steve Myers, Julia Sohrab and Paul Tyrer for reading and commenting upon earlier versions of this chapter.

4 Men, Social Work and Men's Violence to Women

Jeff Hearn

In this chapter, Hearn considers men's violence to women within the context of patriarchal gender relations. Findings from his research on men who have been violent to women highlight specific practice issues for social workers, probation officers and workers in 'men's programmes'. The research identifies how little direct contact social workers had with men who were violent to women. To illustrate his arguments, Hearn describes five cases in which men who were violent to women had direct contact with social workers. The research also found that while probation officers had more contact with men who were violent to women, there was relatively little work done by probation officers with these men specifically on their violence to women. Hearn argues for the development of more pro-active approaches by social workers and probation officers to working with men on their violence. However, this development cannot depend solely on the motivation of individuals or groups of workers, but needs to be supported within agencies. In the final section of the chapter, Hearn identifies issues that agency policies need to attend to if this type of work is to be appropriately supported.

Introduction

In recent years there has been increasing development of a critical focus on men and masculinities. The inspiration for this has come from feminist work, gay and queer work and men's responses to feminism, along with a variety of other critical perspectives. These initiatives have been significant in political, academic, media, policy and professional domains. Feminist work has particularly involved attempts to understand how men reproduce power over women; gay and queer work has focused on men's same-sex and diverse desires and the critique of dominant forms of sexuality, particularly heterosexuality; pro-feminist work has connected feminist and gay analyses with men's personal experiences, political priorities and academic analyses in responding positively to feminism.

In this chapter the critical focus on men is turned to the actions and activities of men in and around social work, both as social workers and service users. Special attention is given to the problem of men's violence to women. In discussing this, I draw on recent research that I have conducted on men who have been violent to known women (that is, women already known to the men concerned) and the responses made (or not made) by welfare agencies to that violence.

Gender dominance and the problem of men

Gender relations in the UK at least can still be characterized by dominance and subordination, by men's dominance and women's subordination. It is in this context that the problem of men persists (see Hearn, 1992a). The problem of men is both very simple and rather complex. While men and masculinities continue to be associated with power and control, men and masculinities are just as variable as women. Another aspect of the problem of men is that while there are clearly all manner of changes in process, there is also a profound state of no change, in the sense that many arenas of power remain in the control of men.

The forms that gender dominance take are also complex. They include gendered economic exploitation, whereby the value of women's labour is not fully rewarded; gendered political and personal oppression, whereby people, along gender lines, are discriminated against, ignored, neglected, degraded, or harmed, to reduce them to less than human (Hearn, 1987, p. xiii); and gendered violence and violation. Importantly, exploitation and oppression can continue without the direct use of physical violence and even without a direct awareness of experiences of violation. Within this context, particular associations of men and masculinities with power create specific political and personal problems in the form of pain, damage, distress, and indeed violence for women and children.

Men's gender dominance is complicated by resistance and social change in these patterns; by the cross-cutting of age, class, disability, ethnicity, race, religion and sexuality; and by the full range of contradictions, ambiguities and paradoxes that persist intrapersonally, interpersonally, collectively and structurally. Thus, for example, men's association with power also creates problems for men themselves (Thompson, 1995). Men who are themselves in social, medical or psychological difficulty may live that experience through a relation, or attempted relation, with power. Indeed the very power and control of both some men and men generally create problems for other men, and for each other (see Hearn, 1987). These combinations of pain, damage and distress to others, and power and difficulty for men themselves constitute many of the problems dealt with by social work.

Men, social work and social welfare

Men's relations to social welfare, as service users or potential service users, are diverse (see Pringle, 1995; Hearn, 1998c). Sometimes these involve care from others, as in the case of men who suffer from addiction, ill health, depression, disability and so on; sometimes the need for control, as with the problem of men who use violence; and sometimes the avoidance or absence of contact from care and/or control. Men may be reluctant to use services that provide assistance around health, emotional crises, and mental well-being. They may be absent from receiving care; they may be absent from agency contact when they directly or indirectly cause problems for others, for example, child care and child protection (Milner, 1992, 1993, 1996; O'Hagan and Dillenburger, 1995; O'Hagan, 1997). Furthermore, all of these kinds of relations can occur at the same time with particular individual men and welfare agencies.

While social welfare problems may or may not be 'caused' by being men, the experiences of them is likely to be mediated by gender, by being men (Gershick and Miller, 1995). Men may cause harm and damage for both others and in time themselves by virtue of their power and control, even when they are themselves relatively powerless within the context of societal power. Interestingly, patriarchal relations can persist and be reproduced through the combination of men's control of welfare, men's need for care and control, and men's avoidance of control and/or control.

All these issues are important for men and for changing men in and around social work. For example, the long-standing debate on 'care and control' in social work can be redrawn in terms of men's different relations to welfare and indeed different forms of masculinities. This entails an understanding of the position of men in society, in terms of both men's collective power, and the differences between different groups of men and different individual men (see Hearn, 1999). Additionally, Social Services social work and probation work both have their own particular characteristics and local challenges, in terms of men in agencies and men in contact or potentially in contact. Social work in Social Services Departments has become increasingly focused around child protection in recent years. This raises the question of whether this is a model that should be extended to other spheres, for example, men's violences and abuse to women.

Probation has traditionally been a relatively larger employer of men than the Social Services Departments (see Chapter 5 for a discussion on the employment of men and women probation officers). It also operates within the context of the criminal justice sector, with its male-dominated culture, and the associated law and order debate. While the Probation Service and probation officers may have had more autonomy than Social Services Departments and social workers, probation have in recent years been subject to much closer control with tighter budgets and less discretion for individual officers. On the other hand, there are signs of increasing interest within the Probation Service on focused work with men who have been violent to known women in the form of men's programmes.

In order to change men in social work, both as social workers and service users, it is necessary to look carefully at the particular situation within different agencies. It involves working from the existing gender structure of agencies, and developing an analysis of that structure. Different possibilities for changing men exist where, for example, men are in a majority, a minority, or are evenly represented with women. Such basic gender structures affect the possible strategies for changing men. At its simplest, the allocation of work to men is affected very largely by the proportion of men present in a particular agency. Similarly, the gender structure of agencies is also a major determinant of relations between women and men there. Men in social work agencies who are concerned to change need to examine the particular structures, tasks and culture of those agencies and work with women on a collaborative process of change. Within different agencies, there are many ways for men to change – as workers and practitioners, managers and users (see Hearn, 1990, 1995a,

1995c, 1995d). Indeed men in social work agencies themselves can adopt different orientations to the work in hand: these can again include caring, controlling, and avoidance. One of the most important social problems that men social workers can attempt to care about, control or avoid is men's violence to women. This remains the clearest demonstration of men's power and dominance over women.

Men's violence to women

Men's involvement with social work agencies as the creators of harm and damage to others is most obviously so with the question of men's violence and abuse. Men remain the specialists in the doing of violence and violent crime. About 84 per cent of all recorded crime is by men; about 97 per cent of those in prison are men; a quarter of all men are convicted of an offence by the age of 25; and two-thirds of all male offenders are under 30 (Cordery and Whitehead, 1992).

Men's use of violence and abuse has often been ignored or even implicitly condoned. This is especially so with regard to men's violence to known women. While Social Services Departments have a statutory duty in relation to children in danger of violence, abuse and neglect, this does not apply to women who are in similar danger from violence by men. Men's violence and abuse clearly causes pain, damage and distress to those receiving the violence and abuse. It may also lead to or be associated with damage to the man himself, in the form of depression, use of drink or drugs, and occasionally institutionalization.

The problem of men's violence to women is now clearly and well established. There is now a large literature in the form of official records and statistics, social science and policy surveys, and victim/survivor report studies that chronicles the extent and pervasiveness of men's violence to women (see Dobash and Dobash, 1992). As Edwards (1989, p. 214) notes: 'The safest place for men is the home, the home is, by contrast the least safe place for women.' It has been estimated from recent British national and regional surveys that between 10 and 25 per cent of British women have been a victim of violence from a male partner (Smith, 1989; Mirrlees-Black, 1994; Mooney, 1994, cited in Dobash et al., 1996, p. 2). However, even these estimates should be treated with caution, as they do not take full account of rape, sexual harassment, coercive sex and pressurized sex, as well as emotional, psychological and other abuses.

At the same time there has been a substantial development of policies against such violence – internationally, nationally and locally – prompted by feminist politics and action research. Much of this has quite rightly focused on the provision of women-centred services in the state, community and voluntary sectors. Key initiatives have included criminal justice system reforms; the support of victims/-survivors; the establishment of the women's refuge and rape crisis movements; the provision of safer housing alternatives for women and children; and the attempt to create safer public spaces.

The last 30 years have thus seen major advances in the publicisation (Brown, 1981) of men's violence to women, primarily through feminist theory and practice. This period has also been one in which men and masculinities have been problematized. Yet while many aspects of men and masculinities have been put under the spotlight, the problem of men's violence to women has not generally been the main focus of attention in this problematization. The need to focus critically on men and men's power and the problem of men's violence to women have been made apparent by feminist theory and practice, yet this work has, not surprisingly, made its main priority the giving of support to women, the hearing of women's voices, and the improvement of women's lives. Accordingly, much remains to be done in spelling out the implications of feminist and critical studies on men for: the analysis of the problem of men's violence to women; the critical deconstruction of men's violence and violent men; and changing men to reduce, stop and abolish men's violence to women; and the education of men against violence to women.

In particular, the implications of men's violence to women for social work and probation work have often been left unclear. Both Social Services Departments and Probation have not, at least until recently, made this problem, and especially men's violence to known women, a high priority, even though many of the other problems that they may deal with may be connected and even derive from that violence. Much of the initial research on this was based on investigations of the work and files of social workers and probation officers (Leonard and McLeod, 1980; Maynard, 1985; Swain, 1986). This demonstrated the relative lack of attention to the problem of violence in the interventions and indeed the recording of many social workers. There have also been broad based surveys of the range of agency responses to women who have experienced violence from men (for example, Mama, 1989; McWilliams and McKiernan, 1993). There are increasing indications of growing interest in the development of policy and practice in both Social Services Departments and Probation that works directly on this problem (for example, Burnham *et al.*, 1990; McColl, 1991a, b; ACOP, 1992/1996; Gillespie and Lupton, 1995; Potts, 1996; Mullender, 1997). However, research on the contact or lack of contact that men who have been violent to known women have with social workers and probation officers is still relatively unusual. Indeed discussion of the direction of such professional intervention, particularly by men, also remains relatively underdeveloped.

Research on men who have been violent to known women

The remainder of this chapter addresses the problem of men's violence to women, drawing on a three-year (1991–4) study that I have directed on men who have been violent to known women (Hearn, 1995b, 1996e, 1998b, 1998c). The project has been linked to, but separate from, the project on women's experiences of violence by known men (Hanmer, 1995, 1996, 1998; Hanmer *et al.*, 1995). Both have used the same basic methods and methodology, although many of the issues raised have of course been different between the two projects.[1]

The project on men has been unusual in that it has directly faced the question of interviewing men who have been violent to known women. Sixty men were interviewed, sometimes more than once, from a number of sources: following arrest by the police; from men's programmes; via probation officers; from prisons; from various welfare agencies; as well as men who were not currently in contact with agencies. The first part of the interview consisted of an account of the man's story of the violence he had done, what had happened subsequently, how he understood why he had been violent, the reactions and responses of family, friends and agencies. The second part of the interview was a pre-coded questionnaire, which covered the man's and the relevant woman's biographical details, patterns of social support, responses from agencies, and measures of the man's well-being, his self-esteem and sense of control of his future. This was an application to men of Mitchell and Hodson's (1983) social psychological study of 60 battered women in the United States. At the end of the interview men were asked for their permission to do follow-up interviews and consulting of their case records with the agencies that had had dealings with them or their 'case'. These were followed up in every case, that is 40 men gave 116 permissions which led to 130 agency follow-up contacts. Policy information was also collected from agencies through separate policy interviews, postal and other contacts with agencies.

This research has provided a wealth of material on what men think and say about their violence to women, and what agencies do in response to men's violence. Here I focus primarily on those men's contacts with Social Services and so-called voluntary sector social work agencies, the Probation Service, and men's programmes.

Social Services

The most important general conclusion from this research on men who had been violent to known women was the relatively low level of contact with Social Services Departments in relation to their violence to women. Only 8 of the 60 men reported contact with Social Services Departments or Voluntary Social Work Agencies. This low level of contact did not increase with greater violence. Of the 24 men who reported more than 15 assaults or murder, only 3 reported contact with Social Services or voluntary social work agencies. This very limited amount of contact contrasted with the much greater level of contacts reported with, for example, doctors and GPs. Of 55 men who had had agency contact in relation to violence, 29 reported contact with GPs, and 8 with hospitals in relation to their violence.

There are at least two major issues to be examined here. First, there is the question of the low level of contact and how men's violence to known women needs to be a more central part of Social Services work. Second, there are lessons to be learned from the contacts made. There are a number of ways of considering and explaining the low level of contact of men who have been violent to known women with Social Services agencies. Indeed, this is of course possible in terms of all the activities and functions of Social Services, including: child protection and preventative work with children; community care; mental health and psychiatric work; medical social work; work with people with disabilities, impairments and learning difficulties; work with older people. Other activities and functions may include work in relation to addiction; women fleeing violence; welfare rights; advocacy, representation and counselling.

In practice, Social Services Departments in recent years have become increasingly focused on child protection, work with people with disabilities and mental health problems, and work with older people. Thus the most obvious explanation is that work on violence to women is not a high priority for Social Services. This might be thought to be the case with the prioritisation of child protection work, and the increasing concern with the management of care in the community. Work around men's violence to women may often involve women who are defined as 'able-bodied' and 'healthy', even if their health and body has been impaired and even disabled by men's violence. As such, these women may be often defined as not needing specific assistance as people with disabilities or elderly people may be. The damage of violence by men is characteristically distinguished from other physical and mental impairments.

The specialization on child protection in Social Services Departments clearly reflects broader movements in the prioritisation of certain potential welfare recipients over others. This has both ideological and financial elements. It tends to lead to a distinction between 'dangerous'/'non-dangerous', 'deserving'/'undeserving' people, families or situations, with the later in each case not receiving assistance (for example, women experiencing violence). This neglects the fact that many people in the 'dangerous' or 'deserving' categories may also be experiencing, or have experienced, violence.

These distinctions may also obscure the fact that child abuse is also usually violence to women, and violence to women is also child abuse, when children are present in the home or relationship. Thus, although child abuse is usually distinguished from violence to women, child protection intervention can often be intervention against violence to women, and intervention against violence to women can often be child protection intervention. There remain many different connections between violence to women and child abuse (Bowker et al., 1988; Mullender and Morley, 1994).

The limited involvement with Social Services might be thought of as to be partly the result of the way that the sample was recruited. However, as noted, even men who reported a long history of violence to women did not usually report contact with Social Services Departments in relation to the violence. Indeed, where contact was reported with social workers, this was not necessarily with local authority social workers, but also, in some cases, with voluntary sector social workers. In addition, there is a large number of other professionals and workers doing work that is similar at least to part of the tasks of social workers and social services, particularly in the counselling aspects of social work. These include Relate counsellors, GPs, psychiatrists, psychotherapists, nurses, group counsellors and therapists, whether they are focusing on violence itself, addiction, or some other issue, as well as probation officers, following either conviction for violence to women or some other offence. It is as if local authority social services and social workers are surrounded by a mass of other agencies that may provide aspects of social work to men who have been violent to known women. In this context, Social Services can be something of an empty centre to this ring of agencies, other than where specific allegations of child abuse are being investigated.

While the issue of men's violence to known women can be relevant in all aspects of the work of Social Services, the specific involvement of men in this work is much more problematic. When Social Services Departments offer support and services to 'women fleeing violence' or women who have experienced violence from known men, the primary intention is to do work separate from the man. This still leaves open the question of the place of direct work with men who have been violent. On the one hand, while the absence of men users from work with women may be welcomed, the absence of men's contact with Social Services is problematic. This is especially so if it simply means that men persist with their violence or move on to be violent to another woman in a different relationship. Thus, in terms of the work of Social Services Departments, men may both need to be resisted in order to change the situation of the women and children, and need to be assisted to stop the violence and prevent future violence to that or other women. These two, and in many ways contradictory, tasks may of course become entangled with all manner of other considerations and potential difficulties and demands – for example, addictions, mental health, disability. They may also become intertwined with the man's own violation as a boy. This was clearly an issue for several men in the research. In some cases, men considered that their earlier violation accounted for their current violence to women (very much in keeping with cyclical and learning theories, and disregarding the problems of such theories in relation to gender); in a few of these, they suggested that it was the emotional process of confronting their violence that had led them on to explore their feelings about their own childhood experiences. There are difficult issues here of how experience, explanation and excuses can become mixed with and confused with each other.

This brings us on to the specific reports of the Social Services agency workers who had contact with the men. Of the five men who gave permission for follow up interviews with Social Services, one yielded no records on either the client index or the Child Protection Register, despite the man's own admission of contact with Social Services and indeed his conviction and imprisonment for murder. Of the others, three men had contact with social workers in relation to children, and the other man was had a contact of a more general nature. Three of the men had contacts with Social

Services Departments, one had contact with a Voluntary Social Services agency and one had contacts with both.

One of the men was referred to the research from a Family Centre. This man had a number of children who had been in and out of local authority care. While there was a risk of permanent removal of the children, Social Services work included weekly home visits by the social worker and visits to the family centre. The children in the family were continually on the threshold of being taken into care. In this context violence 'between the parents' was described as a minor focus of the intervention, as each tried to blame the other for the 'family's failure'. The social worker saw any incident of aggression or violence as relevant, as this had had an effect on 'family functioning'. Any such row was seen as affecting the care of the children and as an avenue for blame. While the man had been prosecuted for assault on his wife and had spent some time in a probation hostel, the concern here was with the effect of the context of violence 'between the parents' on the children.

Another man was referred to the research from the voluntary social work agency. He was also involved with the Social Services Department because his 'mentally handicapped' stepson was in care with the Social Services Department, and living at home on trial. Social Services were thus involved in the supervision of the placement. The work was focused on reviews of this placement, together with some concern for child protection in relation to other children in the man's family. The violence that Social Services knew of involved the man's assault on his wife, his arrest, her hospitalization and then his release on bail to look after the children, as his wife was in hospital receiving medical treatment for her injuries. This was at the suggestion of Social Services, as they did not feel that the children were in danger, even though the voluntary social work agency who supervised most of the family were not happy with this. The man was convicted for the assault and given a nine-month suspended sentence. In the research he also reported that he had been violent to the women on more that 15 occasions. According to him, the question of his violence was not addressed by the local authority social worker.

The voluntary sector social work agency continued to supervise the rest of the family, while Social Services maintained statutory supervision of the stepson. The violence to the woman was not a focus of Social Services work, and indeed it was affirmed by the social worker that violence from a man to a woman is never one of Social Services responsibilities. The social worker concerned did, however, contact voluntary anti-violence men's programme, which the man attended for one session and found to be 'a waste of time'.

The voluntary social work agency worked with the family members in a variety of ways. These included:

- working alongside family members and helping them decide what they wanted to do;
- supporting the wife in taking legal action, advising and counselling her;
- letting the man know that the social worker would support the woman if he was violent to her, i.e. help her find a place to stay if she wanted to leave;
- looking at the circumstances in which violence had occurred with both of the partners, so they could both try to change the situation to prevent these circumstances arising again.

The man became more willing to discuss the issue of his violence when he was facing legal proceedings. The overall outcome was reported by the voluntary sector social worker as an improvement in the relationship between the man and the woman, and as far as the agency knew, the stopping of the physical violence, though some problems remained, and there was a great improvement in the care of the children.

A fourth man's involvement with Social Services followed concerns about the 'failure to thrive' of his wife and child. Following separation, the man alleged that his wife was not providing adequate care for their child. The court granted care and custody of the child to the man, with access granted to his wife. Home Care Services were also involved in assisting the man to care for the child. Care and custody was granted to the man even though Social Services knew that his wife had left following considerable violence by him to her. Subsequently, after allegations of the man's neglect, physical abuse and sexual abuse of the child, a Care Order was made and the child was removed from his care and placed with foster parents. Social Services were aware of his assault on a subsequent female cohabitee, and that he had verbally abused and threatened social workers. While his file was marked as that of a 'dangerous client', there was no specific work undertaken in relation to violence, other than monitoring the safety of the child. Any broader work that might have been done was seen as dependent on the client's own wishes as to whether to deal with the violence. The man was convicted on two charges of Actual Bodily Harm, fined and placed on probation.

The fifth man who lived with his wife and two children referred himself to a voluntary social work agency because he wanted help with health problems, drinking and marital problems. The man brought the issue of violence onto the agenda in his contact with the agency. He reported in the research that he had been violent to the women on more than 15 occasions. The specific social work intervention eventually broke down, the woman left, and the man was placed on remand for grievous bodily harm to the women. This was a unique example of an attempt at intervention without child protection being the key issue, and even though violence was not the primary problem he presented.

There are a number of general issues that arise from this discussion of social worker contact with men who are violent to known women:

1. The need to relate child protection work and work on men's violence to known women.
2. The need to consider men's violence to known women in other sectors of Social Services work other than child protection work.
3. The need to consider men's violence to known women as a priority for social work intervention in its own right.
4. The need for focused work with men who have been violent to known women while maintaining and developing support for women.
5. The need for accurate recording on men's violence to known women.
6. The need to develop interagency work.

The Probation Service

The Probation Service and probation officers became involved with men who have been violent to known women in a number of ways within the full range of activities of the Service. In particular, they include the making of Pre-Sentence Reports to Court, Community Supervision, the management and staffing of Hostels, the work of the Probation teams in Prisons, supervision of men on life sentence, through care, the management and staffing of sex offenders programmes, family court welfare work, liaison with other agencies and so on.

Seventeen men gave permissions to the research for follow-up interviews with probation agencies about their violence to women. Fifteen interviews were conducted with probation officers, along with three postal responses. All those men who were referred from Probation Officers gave permission for follow-up interviews with the Officers. Other interviews were conducted in relation to men who had been referred from other sources. Clearly, in every case of referral of men from the Probation Service, the relevant Officer was aware of the men's violence to known women, whether or not this was the reason for their current contact. The criteria for referral from Probation were themselves interesting. Men who were currently in the midst of crisis because of their violence to known women were generally excluded, just as were men where the problem was too distant in the past or appeared to have been 'solved'. It was men who had been violent in the near past that were generally seen by the Officers as most appropriate for referral to the research.

Having said this, the amount of ongoing direct work by probation officers on the problem of men's violence to known women was found to be disappointingly low. Indeed, in one case, the man was referred for the research interview, because such work was not being done, and it was thought by the probation officer that the interview might help the man address the problem. Another Officer said they were pleased to have the chance to talk through the case, as they had not had that opportunity to do so within the Probation Service, as the man was not a lifer.

Sometimes the involvement of the Probation Service is relatively short term. In one case the involvement spanned just three weeks, from appearance in the Magistrates Court on charge of Section 47 Assault Occasioning Actual Bodily Harm. As a result of the bail condition, the man entered a bail hostel, until he was given a conditional discharge, when he returned home. However, a major complication in this case was that his son had been placed in care after sexually abusing his younger sisters. This did not appear to be explored by the Probation staff.

One Officer reported that the man's violence to the known woman was apparently and formally the focus of the probation contact, but that, in effect, this was not the case, as other matters had taken up their time during the Supervision of the Court Probation Order. In another case, it was revealed that, except for the Court Report of the initial offence of affray, there was no mention of violence to women in the case records and no discussion of reports of violence. Yet the original Court Report included the observation that the man had admitted to being violent to his wife on numerous occasions. Furthermore, the Court Report presented the violence as a product of his alcohol misuse. Following his attendance at six sessions of an alcohol education group, the report from the group noted that the original offence had stemmed from 'aggravation at home' – an unfortunate and ambiguous turn of phrase. Despite the apparent lack of attention to the problem of violence to the known woman, the probation officer applied to the Court for an early discharge of the Probation Order because of his 'good progress', and this was granted.

A rather different example was of a man on a Probation Order in relation to several offences that did not include violence to known women. This led to joint work with him and his wife, to establish a joint agenda. In the course of this work, the man's violence to her came to light. However, no energy or commitment to address this was reported by the probation officer. The man had, however, recognised that he himself 'may be ducking the issue'. Even though there had been many meetings over several years between the man, the woman and the probation officer, other issues were given priority over any focus on the man's violence.

A more complex case concerns a man imprisoned for Going Equipped, Assault Occasioning Actual Bodily Harm, and Indecent Assault. The Probation Officer had difficulty focusing on the man's offending because he was in denial. The man did not define himself as violent, and was prepared to work on his alcohol problem, but not his violence. The man also moved between three prisons, further interrupting any consistent work with the Probation Service. In the last prison, the probation officer worked with the man on his personal and family history, and his self-confidence, but did not focus on the offence itself. Work against violence to women remains scant in prison, and rests upon the prisoner's co-operation.

Another complex case involved the man's imprisonment for Abduction, Unlawful Restraint, Threat to Kill, Assault Occasioning Actual Bodily Harm and Indecent Assault. An unusual feature of this case was that the probation officer knew about the situation from the point of view of the man and woman's children, by virtue of dealing with custody of one child, before becoming directly involved in the man's case. Visits to him in prison included work on violence and relationship issues, which the man himself did not define as a problem. In this way the man was forced to look at the issue of violence. He completed his parole licence successfully and returned to the community with apparent stability in his life, living separately from the woman but not from all the children. In this case, the probation officer was well aware of the adverse effect of all this on the children, yet two of them were to be in the man's care. Another attempt by a probation officer to get the man to recognize his own violence and his responsibility for it followed the man assaulting his ex-partner and her 'boyfriend' whilst on parole. Other charges were brought: Affray, Unlawful Imprisonment, Possession of an Offensive Weapon. Much of the work consisted of getting the man to admit the offences and to work on the offending behaviour; this included the analysis of violent incidents and how and why he 'reacted' the way he did. The focus seemed to be on the relationship between him and his partner. It appeared that any success was limited.

Finally, the research provided examples of more intensive attempts to deal with the problem. One man was placed on a Probation Order, following conviction for Deception. The problems of alcohol and of violence to his partner were recognised by the probation officer. This was followed by assault on his partner. The probation officer's work was aimed at reducing the man's offending, protecting the partner and providing a home for the child. The understanding of the man's violence was complex: drink, insecurity, violence in his childhood, wanting power and control. The probation officer considered the man learnt something about his responsibility for violence, but still did not see himself as a violent person, and therefore would not do any work to reducing it. During the two year period of the Probation Order, he did manage to get two Section 47 charges of assault on the women dropped or dismissed.

A rather different example of an attempt at intensive work was described by a prison probation officer, working with a man convicted of murder, and serving a life sentence. Their analysis centred on a psychodynamic interpretation of the offence at the time, using the concept of a projected transference. This suggested that the man was not intending to murder this woman, but rather another woman whom he thought deserved to be killed. These two contrasted women were, in the probation officer's scheme of understanding, compared with his ambivalent feelings towards his mother. Despite the clearly gendered nature of this analysis, the violence was constructed in this case at least as a unitary phenomenon, with no distinction between violence to women, children or men. The research was not able to evaluate the appropriateness of this intervention.

There are thus a number of areas of concern that have become apparent in relation to the work of the Probation Service with men who are violent to known women:

1. Some cases showed probation officers' lack of involvement in confirming the problem of the man's violence to known women. Some probation officers were concerned to get the man to recognize

the problem but were unsuccessful or largely so. Rarely did probation intervention work specifically on the problem. When this was
done it was sometimes done so in ways that diverted attention from
the man's responsibility.

2. Thus the difficulties found in Probation Service work are of three
   main kinds:
   (a) avoidance of the problem by the probation officer;
   (b) avoidance of the problem by the man;
   (c) lack of success in intervention, through the man's denial, the
       use of inappropriate approaches, etc.
3. There is a specific need to address the avoidance of the problem by
   probation officers. This is being taken up by the 'Domestic Violence
   Policy and Codes of Practice' that have been produced in recent
   years by the Probation Service. These will clearly need to be followed up and taken up by individual probation officers and teams.
4. There is a need for understanding the complexity of men's violence to known women. It is necessary to go beyond explanations
   that rely solely on 'drink'. There are also dangers of explaining the
   man's violence in terms of 'the relationship'.
5. There is a need for more attention to links between men's violence
   to known women and child protection work. It was unclear how
   this latter system interrelated with officers' work on men's violence
   to known women.
6. There is a need to ensure that developing focused work on men's
   violence to known women is done in away that maintains and
   develops support for women and women's projects. This may
   include court-mandated men's programmes specifically designed
   to counter men's violence.

Men's programmes

There has been a considerable debate over the most appropriate kind
of men's programmes to be developed in relation to men who are violent and abusive to women (Adams, 1988; Caesar and Hamberger,
1989; Edleson and Tolman, 1992; Dankwort, 1992–3). In recent
years, there has been a recognition of the importance of both cognitive–behavioural approaches and feminist/profeminist approaches
that focus on power and control (Pence and Paymar, 1990).
Intervention is not only about stopping physical violence, as if that is
some separate activity; it is about moving away from power and control in all aspects of the man's relations with women. To do that

means presenting positive ways of living that do not reinforce power and control. Such men's programmes may involve structured group sessions, often of a fixed weekly programme, for example, of 14, 16, 20 or 25 weeks. There are also sometimes individual sessions. Some programmes also involve work with partners and women's (partner) groups. Some men's programmes can be a significant and effective initiative, especially when linked to wider educational and political change (Dobash et al., 1996). A crucial issue is the placing of such programmes on a formal court-mandated basis rather than leaving them to voluntary access. Any such development needs to carefully screen out men who have no interest whatsoever in change and who may even use the programme to learn new forms of violence and control.

The origins of these programmes have been various. In North America, the initial forms included shelter adjunct programmes, mental health programmes and self-help programmes (Gondolf, 1985). In addition, there have also been initiatives from anti-sexist men and feminist women, and from within the criminal justice system, in particular the Probation Service. In the UK, most programmes have developed in the late 1980s and early 1990s on a voluntary or part-funded basis. There is, however, increasing interest in court-mandated programmes, in which the man completes attendance at the programme as part of his court sentencing following conviction of a violent offence. Perhaps most importantly, there are major variations in the philosophy, theoretical orientations, and practical methods of different men's programmes. These include psychoanalytic, cognitive-behavioural, systemic, and profeminist (Dankwort, 1992–3).

In profeminist models, part of the task is to educate men, sometimes didactically, on the inaccuracy and oppressiveness of their beliefs and actions – what has been called 'profeminist resocialization' (Gondolf, 1993). Typical methods involve the men describing and analysing their actual violence, abuse and controlling behaviour, and moving away from that power and control and towards more equal relationships. More specific techniques include cost-benefit analysis (of the gains and consequences of violent and abusive behaviour), safety plans (strategies for avoiding violence and abuse), and control logs (diary records of attempts to control partners) (Gondolf, 1993). Some programmes are fixed length; others, particularly those that are voluntary or self-help, are more open-ended. A clear example of this is the Duluth 'Power and Control' model (Pence and Paymar, 1990), in which all aspects of men's power and control over women – physical, sexual, economic, emotional and so on – are confronted and, if possible, changed. That the task of the programmes is to edu-cate, challenge and change the full range of men's behaviour and not only physical violence.

There has been a good deal of interest in the evaluation of the effec-tiveness of men's programmes (for example, Pirog-Good and Stets-Kealey, 1985; Edleson, 1990, Edleson and Syers, 1990). Not surpris-ingly, one of the most difficult questions is the evaluation of different curricula and approaches amongst men's programmes. A recently completed evaluation study of the effectiveness of two men's pro-grammes (CHANGE, Stirling, and the Lothian Domestic Violence Probation Project, Edinburgh), working with a combination of cogni-tive-behavioural methods and a profeminist 'Power and Control' framework, has produced relatively impressive results (Dobash *et al.*, 1996). Importantly, this evaluation used women partners' assess-ment of men's behaviour following intervention. Three months after the imposition of the criminal justice sanction (i.e. men's programme or other sanctions, for example, fines), 20 per cent of the men in the programmes had committed another violent act, while 62 per cent of the men with other criminal justice sanction had done so. After a year, the comparable figures were 33 and 75 per cent respectively. An even clearer differentiation appears when the frequency of vio-lence is considered. After three months, none of the women, whose partner was in the programme reported five or more incidents of viol-ence, while 16 per cent of the women whose partner had other crim-inal justice sanctions did so. After a year, the comparable figures were 7 and 37 per cent. This particular evaluative study fits closely with some US evaluations. For example, Tolman and Bennett (1990) found that 60 per cent of men who complete programmes had not physically assaulted women after six months.

In my own research, men from three programmes with quite dif-ferent philosophies were interviewed. Virtually all the men had some positive remarks about the programme they were in; only one of the 19 men referred to the research from the men's programmes (41 were from other sources) dismissed the experience as a 'complete waste of time' (Hearn, 1998b). However, such responses cannot in themselves be taken as evidence of 'success' in stopping violence. Furthermore, as there are relatively few such groups, they may attract a relatively diverse group of men who can operate in groups and also have the resources to get there. Firm assessments of effec-tiveness need to be treated with caution. Some men enter such groups to rescue failing or failed relationships with a woman. Rescuing the relationship appears to be the main aim for such men; stopping or reducing their violence appears to be the means to an end. Certainly for a substantial proportion there appears to be a reduction or stopping of physical violence whilst they are in the group. However, as one of the group leaders reported, 'What I find with men in the group is that the physical violence stops probably within the first week. They over-compensate then by increasing the verbal, emotional and psychological [violence], because they've nowhere to off-load the tension you see. That takes a long time.' Another group leader considered that for one man, the violence would not have stopped if he had not been involved in the group. More worrying is that for a few men joining such groups can be dangerous: as they can learn or increase their expertise in knowing the particular ways, physically or non-physically, are most harmful and hurtful to the particular woman.

While this research does not provide the material for the evaluation of the effectiveness of men's programmes, it is important to note that these interventions are, first, focused, and second, at least directed to talking about 'effectiveness' and 'degrees of success' in reducing or eliminating violence. Most important, such interventions cannot be evaluated *in general*, as there is a wide variation in the methods and approaches used. To put this more bluntly, it is rather foolish to argue for or against all such men's programmes; the crucial issues are what is the nature of this particular programme, how it deals with women's safety, how is it funded, and with what broader costs and benefits.

In this research, men's programme groups themselves often involved complex dynamics whereby men recognized their similarity with and difference from others' stories and behaviours, and their similarity and difference from others' intentions to change or not to change in the future (Hearn, 1998a). Peer support between men in men's programmes is one way of some men changing their behaviour through a process of mutual re-education (Gondolf, 1984; Saunders, 1989). On the other hand, DeKeseredy (1990) has highlighted the dangers of men gaining peer support for their violence and abuse, and Gondolf (1989, p. xi) has argued that: 'Those batterers in deep denial and resistance may be more likely to respond to the didactic confrontation of the feminist approach.'

The group leaders understood the men's violence in a diverse series of ways: men's upbringing, rejection by parents, father's violence to mothers, the man's desire to control and dominate, overcontrol of his emotions, difficulty in dealing with women's assertion, the company with which the man mixed, as well as psychiatric and addiction problems. The key issues here are that:

1. the man's violence was the focus;
2. the men were seen more as individuals, with different individual histories and 'characters';
3. a mixture of psychological and social reasons for the man's violence was often recognized;
4. there was generally reluctance to explain violence as a function of addiction;
5. there was sometimes an understanding of issues of power, control and domination.

Overall these group interventions can be understood as ways of enhancing men's health and welfare, of sometimes reducing and stopping violence, and sometimes, though not always, assisting women's health and welfare.

General agency policy development

Social work interventions with men need to be located in the context of the full range of agency contacts. Men who have been violent to known women generally have far less contact with agencies than do women who experience such violence. Many men have no or negligible contact with agencies. For some men, it is quite unlikely that, short of murder, they will have much sustained contact with agencies. Even so there is a large amount of agency contact that does take place with men who have been, or are being, violent to known women. Unfortunately this is usually not directly focused on stopping the violence. The problem may be mentioned in passing, other problems may be attended to instead or the violence may be dealt with periodically but not necessarily in a way that is likely to reduce or eliminate it. Then while there is a large amount of agency time and resources devoted to the problem both with women and with men much of the time and resources is not directed in countering men's violence.

More generally, there are general issues concerning the development of agency policy and practice that cross particular agency responses to the problem of men's violence to known women (Hearn, 1995d, 1996e). These include the following:

1. Educating men on what violence is.
2. Dealing with the problem as the responsibility of the statutory sector.

3. Producing clear, general policy statements.
4. Developing public campaigns.
5. Changing the conditions that produce and sustain men's violence.
6. Addressing other oppressions.
7. Developing appropriate and detailed policy and practice.
8. Monitoring, maintaining and improving policy and practice.
9. Working against violence with men in contact in a focused way.
10. Placing issues of power, control and responsibility as central in focused work with men.
11. Developing inter-agency work with men.
12. Making men, men's power and men's violence explicit in agency and inter-agency work.
13. Addressing the need to change men in agencies.
14. Dealing with ambiguous issue of men's support for men.
15. Reaching out to men not in contact with agencies.

While all of these are important, it is necessary to emphasize the importance of attending to and changing men's behaviour in organizations. It is not possible, on the one hand, to work with men against *their* violence and, on the other, to behave in violent and abusive ways as men. Accordingly, developing ways of organising and managing that are non-oppressive, non-violent and non-abusive is a high priority (Hearn, 1996a, p. 113; also see Collinson and Hearn, 1996).

Any innovations in work by men and/or with men has to supplement broader public policy, including consistent police and prosecution policy and practice; inter-agency work with women experiencing violence; improved housing provision for women; and state support for Women's Aid and other projects for women. Men's violence to women represents a clear challenge to the development of agency policy and practice by men and in relation to men. There is thus a need for a national, and indeed transnational commitment against violence.

As the Gulbenkian Foundation Commission Report (1995, p. 18), *Children and Violence*, stressed as its first priority recommendation:

> Individuals, communities and government all levels should adopt a 'Commitment to non-violence', of similar standing to existing commitments to 'equal opportunities'.

The Report (p. 18) continued:

> The aims of the commitment are to work towards a society in which individuals, communities and government share non-violent values and

resolve conflict by non-violent means. Building such a society involves ... consistent disavowal of all forms of inter-personal violence – in particular by opinion-leaders.

Governmental and other policies and strategies should make it clear to boys and men that violence, should advocate policies that encourage men to behave in ways that facilitate women's equality, and emphasis how the realization of such changes depends partly on men in politics and policy-making, and their own understanding of their gendered actions. Mullender (1997, p. 28) has summarized recent initiatives as follows:

> Wife abuse only became a formal international priority in the 1980's during the United Nations' Decade for Women. In 1992, a UN Declaration recognised violence against women and children as a human rights issue, and the UN Platform of Action from the Fourth World Conference on Women, held in Beijing in 1995 ... built upon this by including violence against women as one of its critical areas of concern.

Since the Beijing Conference there have been a number of international follow-up meetings, and the full Conference, 'Beijing Plus Five', takes place in New York in June 2000. In addition, other international initiatives against men's violence to women have included the national responses to the UN to CEDAW (Convention on the Elimination of All Forms of Discrimination Against Women) since its signing in 1979, and more recently positive policy development and facilitation from UNESCO, the Council of Europe, and the European Union.

Conclusion

Men's relationship with social work is only understandable in the context of men's broader position in society, including men's reproduction of violence. Changing men in and through social work hinges on similar principles and politics to changing men more generally throughout society. This has been the focus of some men's, particularly profeminist men's, concerns since Second Wave feminism. Changing men does not just involve the simple adoption of principles by men but recognizing ambivalences, dilemmas and contradictions and working from that reality.

Social work is directly and often indirectly concerned with the problems of men – as the creators of problems, the sufferers of problems, the avoiders of agency contact. In some cases, these three aspects are intimately related to each other. Men's power, men's oppression of others, men's violence, men's experiences of their own personal problems, and the avoidance of agency contact (whether from the care of agencies or the control of agencies) can all be connected to each other. Men who are users or potential users of social work agencies can both maintain patriarchal power and be the dispensable casualties of patriarchy. Men can need both care and control, and also spend much of their time avoiding both. Men who have been violent to known women have both avoided social work at the same time that social work avoided them. There are, however, signs that social work, probation work and men's programmes are all taking the problem of men's violence to women much more seriously than in the past, and are beginning to develop methods for such direct intervention.

Finally, parallel issues around the problem of men persist *within* welfare agencies that deal with men. Not least among these is the question of how do men social workers and social work managers themselves renounce and act against violence, and stop any collusion with it. To address these issues necessitates focused attention by men, the development of an understanding and an analysis of men in the agencies, and the formulation of new policies and practices.

Note and Acknowledgement

1. These research projects were the 'Violence, Abuse and the Stress-coping Process, Projects 1 and 2' on women and men respectively, funded by the Economic and Social Research Council (L 206 25 2003). I am indebted to collaboration with Jalna Itanmer as Director of Project 1, and to Roger Barford, Phil Raws and John Davis for assistance with interviews and discussions on Project 2.

5 Men Probation Officers: Gender and Change in the Probation Service

Jill Annison

This chapter focuses on the historical development of the Probation Service tracing the links with social work through shared training and professional qualifications. The formal split between the training routes for probation officers and social workers in the mid-1990s is then reviewed and investigated from a gendered perspective. A theoretically distinctive approach is applied that draws on the literature of gender and organisations. This points to the need for a gendered analysis to be applied in order to reach an understanding of the extent and full implications of recent changes. Challenges and concerns that are facing the Probation Service and probation officers, particularly in respect of the professional value base and practice interventions with offenders are highlighted. The development of a 'smart macho' organizational culture in the 1990s depends on competitiveness in reaching targets. The individual responses of maingrade probation officers to these changes are discussed in this chapter.

Introduction

The Probation Service in England and Wales has experienced a period of uncertainty and adjustment over the past 20 years, surviving a 'roller-coaster ride' through the progressively hard-line law and order rhetoric in the 1980s and the 1990s. The momentum has been maintained in the transition from the Conservative to the New Labour government, with the inter-acting dynamics of politics, managerialism, administrative processing and public participation coming together to shape new developments in the criminal justice field (James and Raine, 1998).

Many of these changes have also been mirrored in social work and social care fields over the same period, with radical legislation being enacted in relation to work with children and families, and with adults (Hanmer and Statham, 1999). Moreover, issues relating to the assessment of risk and public protection have become of increasing importance for both probation officers and social workers. The responses to these pressures reflect not only the wider political, social and economic transformations but also highlight changing practices within these agencies in the endeavour to cope, understand and respond to the challenges posed by this fast-changing situation (Parton, 1996).

For more than 20 years, until the mid-1990s, probation officers and social workers shared the same generic training background and value base, with some workers (including myself) moving at different points in their careers from one agency to another. However, after several years of critical evaluation, the Home Office decided in 1996 to cease the intake of probation sponsored students to Diploma in Social Work courses. This broke the long-standing link with social work training as the mode of entry to the Probation Service and called into question the ethical, moral and practice principles underpinning probation interventions with offenders.

While this development may seem to fracture the connections with social work and, indeed was designed to do so, the position is in reality more complex. The new Diploma in Probation Studies courses did not commence until late 1998, resulting in a period when vacancies will continue to be filled by candidates with Diploma in Social Work qualifications. These new staff members often have little or no prior experience in a probation setting. There is also a short-fall in the number of probation trainees on the new courses in terms of the current and projected staffing requirements in different probation areas. In any case, it will be many years before probation officers from the new training background predominate within the Service (Williams, 1995). The rationale behind these changes and the potential pressures in this on-going situation will be explored later in this chapter.

These developments have highlighted unresolved tensions relating to the future identity and structure of the organization, lines of accountability, managerial functions, and everyday working practices. While most probation officers have a training background that rested on one-to-one work with offenders within their wider social setting, the Home Office is now emphasizing the centrality of demonstrating probation's effectiveness in reducing offending and protecting the public. Moreover, budgetary constraints and resource allocation attached to interventions that meet these criteria have left little room for manoeuvre for probation management and their front-line staff. The pace of change is being stepped up and enforced via public accountability and threats of financial penalties in a way that has already been experienced within educational and medical spheres.

This chapter therefore identifies key aspects in the past development of the Probation Service, particularly in relation to its position *vis-à-vis* the criminal justice system, its social work base and practice links, and oversight from central and local government. In focusing on more recent changes that have taken place within the organization and impacted on probation practice, it is then possible to consider wider implications, particularly in relation to probation's social work heritage and continuing working relationships with other welfare agencies.

The first section explores past attempts by probation officers to establish recognition of their professional status in carrying out specialized roles and tasks within the criminal justice system. It looks at the twists and turns of this 'professional project' (Macdonald, 1995), which has parallels with endeavours by social workers to establish their professional standing. These issues are then revisited from a gendered perspective in relation to men probation officers. In the past the Probation Service had been predominantly staffed by men probation officers but shifts in the organisational gender balance in the 1990s, and official reaction to these changes, drew attention to what had previously been only implicitly gendered professional identities and work practices. My research analysis and findings point to the crucial importance of acknowledging the embeddedness of gender (Halford *et al.*, 1997) in accounting for the extent and pace of change that is impacting on the Probation Service.

In looking at continuity and change from such a gendered perspective it is possible to extend the explanatory framework and sharpen the analysis of recent developments. The Probation Service is but one organization among many that are facing fundamental overhauls and this analysis is applicable to other state-sponsored agencies. This approach also highlights the potential for comparative studies to be conducted in settings such as social services.

The chapter draws on material from qualitative research that I carried out within three disparate local probation areas in England. Interviews with probation officers integrated and built on earlier secondary quantitative analysis of the composition of the Service (in England and Wales). This had highlighted both change and stability in the recent past in terms of the organizational structure, focusing in particular on the gender stratification in different areas and across the hierarchical grades of the organization.

The changing professional base

The literature on the Probation Service includes detailed histories of the Probation Service (see, for example, King, 1969; Jarvis, 1972; Bochel, 1976; Haxby, 1978). In addition there are studies looking at probation officers and their work (Boswell, 1989), and an in-depth investigation into organisational change within one area of the Probation Service (May, 1991). More recently the focus has shifted onto issues relating to probation practice within a wider criminal justice context (see, for example, May and Vass, 1996: and McIvor, 1996). On an official level Home Office publications have set a clear agenda concentrating on 'effectiveness' (see Home Office, 1998a, b), with further research and evaluation in this area being applied to community penalties (McGuire, 1995; Mair, 1997). However, a gendered analysis of the organizational structures and practices within the Probation Service has hitherto been overlooked. The absence of gender in these accounts and in most policy documents continues to conceal the interaction of gender as 'a significant dynamic in worker–worker, worker–manager or worker-service-user relationships' (Hanmer and Statham, 1999, p. 124).

This omission has been addressed within some elements of practice in probation, such as work in the area of sex offending and with women offenders. However, with the exception of some practice developments in relation to sexual and violent offenders, particularly with regard to domestic violence, there is a danger that 'gender' is seen as being relevant only to women. For example, some studies within Probation showed that aspects relating to wider gender issues were struggling to remain within the mainstream of probation practice (Bensted, et al., 1994). Furthermore, concern has been expressed that:

the neglect, if not outright opposition to the issues arising from a male, heterosexual culture seriously affects the capacity of individual probation officers to deliver a gender-conscious service delivery to clients or even more fundamentally survive and prosper as workers in the organisation.

(Buckley, 1992, p. 57)

These tensions seem to be hidden by the positioning of the Probation Service alongside the police, courts, the Prison Service and the Crown Prosecution Service, within a criminal justice system portrayed as having a gender-neutral organisational framework (Pringle, 1989). The apparent invisibility of the gendered nature of the legal system (MacKinnon, 1989), and the functioning of the Probation Service within it, ties in with Joan Acker's observations concerning the widespread lack of acknowledgement of the implicit gendering of 'a job'. This context serves to reinforce the representation of a 'probation officer' as an 'abstract, bodiless worker' occupying an 'abstract, gender-neutral job' (Acker, 1991, p. 172). In this respect it is possible to view all probation officers as being confined by gendered stereotypes, although these impact on the men and women working within the organization in differential, but inter-related ways (Flax, 1990).

An historical overview

The histories of the Probation Service point out that its roots lie in the role of police court missionaries working under the auspices of the Church of England Temperance Society and other missions and voluntary bodies. The development of probation work was underpinned by the instruction within the 1907 Probation of Offenders Act to advise, assist and befriend offenders (Jarvis, 1972). The transfer to a completely state-sponsored agency finally took place in 1941 but it was not until 1948 that legislation was enacted securing central government's oversight of the Probation Service.

A review of the gender distribution of probation officers over this period uncovers a male/female separation within the ideology of official legislation. This reinforced the 'public/private' divide, with (by implication) male officers supervising male offenders, and (by directive) female officers supervising women and children. The concerns about the inappropriateness of men probation officers supervising women offenders convey undertones of biological determinism and 'natural' views of the responses of men and women. For instance, the 1936 Report of the Departmental Committee on the Social Services in the Courts of Summary Jurisdiction reported:

The Committee was adamant that it was necessary to have a woman probation officer in every area. Apart from the risk incurred in putting a woman on probation to a male officer, a woman, the Committee thought, could deal more effectively and with more freedom with the case of another woman or girl than could a man.

(Bochel, 1976, pp. 127–8).

This ruling remained in place until it was repealed in the Criminal Justice Act 1967, with reverberations of this gender split continuing into the 1970s.

The shift away from the 'saving of sinners' to the assessment and treatment of offenders (May, 1991) was signalled in the influential Morison Committee Report (Home Office, 1962). This gave official endorsement to the role and duties of probation officers within the criminal justice system while emphasizing the value and practice base drawn from social work: the report described a probation officer as 'a professional caseworker, employing, in a specialized field, skill which he holds in common with other social workers' (Home Office, 1962, para.54).

While this report emphasized the linkage with social work it is important to delve beneath the apparent similarities. The literature on the growth of the semi-professions over this period (for example, Etzioni, 1969 and Hearn, 1982) described a hierarchical separation within the organizations, with men dominating the higher managerial posts, but with more women than men at lower levels. This distinction was, and continues to be, replicated within Social Services Departments (Grimwood and Popplestone, 1993), with women constituting 'around two-thirds of all social workers in most industrialized capitalist societies' (Roach Anleu, 1992, p. 25). This differentiation was reflected within the Probation Service in respect of the division between probation officers and the administrative staff, with most clerical positions being filled with women. However, in terms of the probation officers entering the Service, there were more men than women across *all* of the different grades at this time. This preponderance of male staff across all grades of the Service was accounted for in terms of the 'better conditions of service, a flatter organisational hierarchy and arguably a more reliable source of finance from the 'law and order sector'' (Hearn, 1982, p. 194).

Perhaps more surprisingly in view of the growing push towards professional status, while acknowledging the desirability of professional training as a prerequisite for initial entry as a probation officer, it did not press for all candidates to hold a recognized qualification. Nevertheless, in spite of this lack of an official directive concerning training requirements, the tenor of the findings from the Morison Committee Report coincided with wider developments within social work education. Probation training thus became integrated as part of social work courses developed under the auspices of CCETSW (the Central Council for Education and Training in Social Work) in the mid-1970s, with the Home Office relinquishing its active part in this process by the end of the 1970s. The acknowledgement of the need for a maingrade probation officer to hold a Certificate of Qualification in Social Work (CQSW) was finally formalized in the 1984 Probation Rules. While these changes standardised the professional training prior to entry to the Service and thus enhanced the drive towards professionalism (Johnson, 1972), this was not legally enshrined as a statutory requirement – a loophole that enabled the Conservative Government to challenge the social work training route in the mid-1990s.

Throughout the 1970s and into the 1980s claims for professional status by probation officers rested on a foundation of specialized knowledge and expert practice, demonstrated most clearly in the individualized casework form of intervention (for example, Hollis, 1972). However, the practice base of probation work was subjected to critical empirical appraisal and was found wanting. Research was published that was interpreted at the time as showing that 'nothing works' in terms of the impact on re-offending (Martinson, 1974). This brought into common usage a catch-phrase that was consonant with the wider debate concerning crime and dealing with offenders in the late 1970s. In addition the political thrust from the Conservative Government moved issues of 'law and order' centre-stage, with rhetoric focusing on punishment, rather than treatment and welfare (Hudson, 1993). This signalled the first major cracks in the shared underpinning values and practices between probation and social work, although both agencies were facing problems at the front-line raised by the Conservative Government's stark refusal to acknowledge any linkage between social problems and crime (Brake and Hale, 1992).

This ideological shift in central Government policy emphasized individual responsibility for actions, while at the same time demanding that the Probation Service should no longer adopt individualized welfare forms of intervention with offenders. This was aligned with the shift away from clinical diagnosis of need to an emphasis on the assessment of risk posed by offenders (and indeed in relation to situations such as child abuse in other welfare agencies). In this respect the identification of 'high risk' cases also was intended to inform the appropriate allocation of scarce resources (Parton, 1996). Increasingly within Probation the use of standardised actuarial instruments, rather than professional judgement by probation officers, is being encouraged to inform this assessment. For Probation this shift from the welfare approach came to the fore most clearly in the legislative 'just deserts' approach of the 1991 Criminal Justice Act where it was intended that the Service would take a centre-stage role in implementing a twin-track policy. This was envisaged as separating out the violent and 'so serious' offenders for sentences of imprisonment, from the majority of 'serious enough' offenders who would be supervised in the community (Stenson, 1991).

In terms of professional status this seemed to identify areas of expertise in relation to the diagnostic assessment and practice interventions that had to be carried out by probation officers and held open the promise of a further reinforcement of occupational closure dependent on specialised skills (Macdonald, 1995). However, the reality of the limitations on judicial discretion led to the legislative changes within the 1993 Criminal Justice Act. This amending legislation with its punitive overtones allowed the court to take into account all offences committed by the offender (instead of the main offence and one other associated with it), as well as abolishing unit fines. As George Mair pointed out this had serious ramifications for the status of probation officers and for the Service:

> Probation officers are having to modify yet again the way in which they work – particularly in assessing seriousness. A harsher penal climate generally means that probation is no longer seen as occupying centre stage, and cut-backs in expenditure are now planned.
>
> (Mair, 1996, p. 35)

Since then the agenda has moved on further. The Probation Service is now being encouraged by the New Labour Government to demonstrate that it can implement nationally accredited community programmes which are effective in terms of reducing offending, with the suggestion that outcomes will determine resource allocation. Indeed, Lord Williams has stated in an unequivocal way 'the cost of prison is £24,500 a year. The cost of probation is up to £3000. If you get a sensible outcome, there cannot be much argument' (Williams, 1998, cited in Teeside Probation Service publication, 1999).

Over the last 10 years these changes in penal policy have led to ever-increasing demands being made on the Probation Service. However, the expansion in the size of the Service in anticipation of meeting the requirements of the 1991 Criminal Justice Act was followed by an almost immediate down-turn in probation officer staffing levels in the wake of the 1993 Criminal Justice Act and subsequent central Government spending controls. This change of fortunes for the Probation Service is clearly demonstrated by the probation officer staffing levels (all grades) shown in Figure 5.1.

The current situation highlights the recurring tensions for the Probation Service in sustaining the remnants of its traditional social work values and working practices, and in responding to the more recent demands stemming from government-directed penal policy (Arnold and Jordan, 1995). For probation officers who joined the Service motivated by a sense of vocation and an 'occupational desire to help clients' (May, 1991, p. 169) these changes mark a substantial shift in terms of power, discretion and workplace cultures. In the introduction to the book *Probation Values*, Brian Williams suggests that these differing elements can be addressed by drawing on 'social work skills and the humanistic principles which underlie all the caring professions', while at the same time separating these out in probation practice from 'the confronting of offending and offensive behaviour' (Williams, 1995, p. 16). However, this suggestion seems to demand an apparently incompatible dual approach that fails to

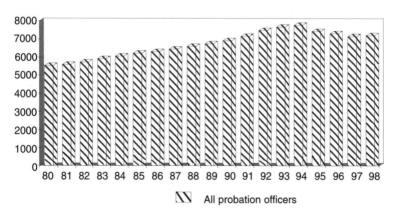

Figure 5.1   National figures of all probation officer staff, 1980–98

Note: 1980–1995 statistics obtained from HM Inspectorate of Probation. 1996–1998 statistics obtained from the Research, Development and Statistics Directorate at the Home Office. The figures are on a full-time equivalent basis.

acknowledge the profound change in the practice value base and the underlying rationale for intervention. The agenda from the Home Office has shifted away from an emphasis on process and relationships. In spite of acknowledging the importance of 'pro-social modelling' (Home Office, 1998b, p. 16), resources are being directed to accredited programmes that stress the uncompromising importance of measurable outcomes. What is often not made explicit is that these approaches are often framed within a certain type of masculinity focusing on: 'confronting, challenging, enforcing, tackling, targeting. This is the language of contact sport and war. It is male language and its objective is to impress, to impress with a demonstration of power' (Cordery and Whitehead, 1992: 30). More recent statements concerning the value base for the Probation Service re-state some traditional values such as 'a strong belief in the capacity of people to change'. However, other 'values' adopt a more combative stance in their expression, as illustrated by the expression that 'effective practice depends upon...an uncompromising stance against the harm caused by crime' (Home Office, 1998b, p. 18).

It is crucial that the pervasiveness of these gendered discourses is incorporated into a conceptualization and explanation of change in Probation (Witz, 1992). The guise of gender neutrality not only masks the full significance of the shift in the underlying value and knowledge base of probation practice but also fails to engage with the gendered social construction of what it is to be a 'probation officer'.

This chapter therefore progresses to investigate and demonstrate the embeddedness of gender within this part of the criminal justice system, extending the understanding of recent developments from such a perspective. This puts in place a gendered analysis of recent changes that is both descriptive and explanatory in reviewing the split from the social work traditions and looking at the current demands facing probation officers in the late 1990s.

Gender and changing times in the Probation Service

The predominance of men probation officers at all grades within the Probation Service throughout most of this century has already been noted and accounted for in terms of its positioning over time as an integral part of the criminal justice system. The application of an analytic framework developed by Franzway *et al.*, (1989) suggests that the Probation Service has increasingly been aligned with the 'coercive apparatus', composed of agencies such as the armed forces, policy, courts and prisons (all with high concentrations of male staff). This is contrasted with its more marginal position in the past between the 'coercive apparatus' and the 'welfare apparatuses', including sectors such as social services, health, education and social security which have more women staff in 'front-line' posts (ibid.). Thus, the increased control being placed on the Probation Service by central Government, together with the changed training arrangements, can be seen as moving Probation away from its long-standing position straddling the two constellations of agencies and towards a more controlling and directive role with offenders. The importance of these developments cannot be over-stated for this is: 'not only a matter of the statistics of the sexual division of labour. There is also a cultural differentiation. The coercive apparatus is "masculinised" in its ideology and practice as well as the composition of its workforce' (Franzway *et al.*, 1989, p. 42).

In my discussions with many of the men (and indeed some of the women) probation officers during my research these gendered expectations were often referred to sarcastically, particularly by those who stressed their social work value base. For instance, Sean, a long-standing probation officer who was working within the family court welfare team in Area 1,[1] commented with heavy irony: 'We're preparing the way. We want good, sensible, firm people – you know, ex-Army officers. But of course, I fit the bill, I'm an ex-serviceman and I can assure my Chief that I'm adaptable to any circumstances!' (Sean, family court welfare team, Area 1).

The gendered structure of the Probation Service thus has a legacy of masculinization that was reinforced by the increasingly aggressive rhetoric concerning law and order throughout the 1980s and into the 1990s. While comments such as those by Sean indicated some resistance to the more invidious elements of stereotypical gender structure and cultures within the Service, they also conveyed an acute awareness of the pervasiveness of these gendered dynamics and discourses. Family Court Welfare teams are situated in an area of work within the Probation Service that has a more ambiguous position in terms of the 'coercive' and 'welfare' dichotomy. It is perhaps not surprising that this element will be moving into a new non-departmental public body to be known as 'The Children and Family Court Advisory Service'. The new

---

[1] All names have been changed to maintain confidentiality, with the local Probation Areas being anonymized as Area 1, Area 2 and Area 3.

organization is expected to combine not only this element of probation work, but also the children's branch of the official solicitor's department and the local authority Guardian ad Litem service (NAPO News, September 1999). Given this new alignment of services it will be interesting to review the gender composition of the staff at the different organizational levels – if the model above holds, it would be expected that the 'front-line' staff would be mainly female.

Given the historical legacy of the predominance of men probation officers, and the established tradition of 'appropriate' aspects of work for those women who did enter the organization, a review of the gender distribution in the recent past revealed a surprising situation. There had been a sharp increase in the number of women probation officers, to the position in 1993 when there was a switch-over, with more women than men probation officers in post in England and Wales (as a whole-time equivalent total of all grades). Figure 5.2 outlines the striking changes in the gender distribution across all probation officer grades between 1980 and 1998.

This shift in the gender balance had been particularly noticeable in Area 2 and was commented upon with some ambivalence by William when I interviewed him:

> I can remember when ... [a female senior probation officer] was the senior, and admittedly there was a vacancy at the time, but going for the

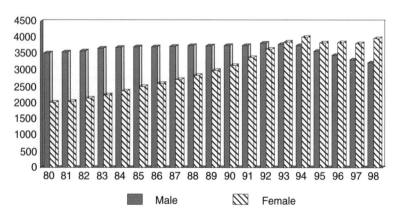

Figure 5.2   Male/female probation officers (all grades), 1980–1998

Note: Information obtained as outlined in Figure 5.1.

Christmas lunch I was the only male out of about 15 people, probation officers and secretaries.

(William, generic community-based team, Area 2)

It would seem that once occupational closure to the Probation Service had been secured via the social work qualification, women had drawn on these educational and vocational credentials to build their professional careers. It can be surmised that this was an unintended consequence of professionalization, with local appointments concealing for a while the wider national picture of gender change in the staffing of the Probation Service. This gendered change is certainly in stark contrast to the masculinized political rhetoric concerning law and order in the mid- to late -1990s.

An overview of the situation at maingrade level

While I discussed these issues with many probation officers at different levels in the organization as part of my research study (Annison, 1998), I am focusing here on the responses of some of the men maingrade officers. This level of the Service is the entry point for most probation officers and this focus provides a specific case study within this chapter to explore some of the current developments and gendered issues reverberating around the Probation Service.

Changes at maingrade level within the Probation Service account most clearly for the shift in the male/female gender balance, with a gradual trend towards more women than men until a clearly noticeable switch-over in 1991. Figure 5.3 outlines this progression.

The actions taken by the then Conservative Government did not directly address the shifting gender balance but, as outlined earlier in this chapter, a review of training was set up. Although it was not an explicit part of its remit, this Government-initiated Review of Probation Officer Recruitment and Qualifying Training (more commonly referred to as The Dews Report [Home Office, 1994]), did target this 'breaching' of the organization by women. The report also addressed concerns about the social work value-base of the Probation Service, reporting statistical information alongside unattributed observations from interviews carried out in the various probation-related locations. A disparaging tone was adopted in this respect:

> We also heard much of the importance of 'social work values' but nothing to suggest these were different from the values of many professions and we noted that this was not a concept embraced by the Home Office.

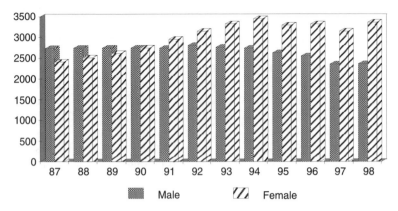

Figure 5.3   Maingrade probation officers, 1987–98

Note: 1987–95 statistics obtained from HM Inspectorate of Probation: 1996–98 statistics obtained from the Research, Development and Statistics Directorate at the Home Office.

> We found this whole sensitive area troubling as we wondered if 'social work values' actually meant that probation officers were expected to think similarly on a range of social and criminal justice issues where a diversity of views would be healthy.
>
> (Home Office, 1994, p. 26)

The interplay of these different discourses, including the assault on the social work ethos and value base within The Dews Report, was further reinforced at official level by Baroness Blatch, at that time Home Office Minister of State responsible for the Probation Service, who stated: 'Although the work of probation officers includes a social work dimension, it is very distinct from that of social workers. The Probation Service is an important part of the criminal justice system and plays a critical role in the corrective punishment of offenders' *Guardian*, 18 October 1995).

A further element was added by the pronouncement in a Home Office memorandum, reported in the *Guardian* (27 June 1994), that future recruitment from ex-police and armed forces personnel (i.e. mainly men) was to be encouraged. This statement also conveyed by inference official preference for a particular kind of heterosexual masculinity within the staffing of the Probation Service.

This political rhetoric, with its gendered dimensions, signalled a clear intention to re-align the role and function of the agency away from its social work foundations, situating its practice more firmly within a community justice framework. It also seemed that this move was being combined with a concerted effort on the part of the Home Office to rein in the increased numbers of women probation officers coming into the Service. While these developments sparked off many comments within the interviews I was conducting there was an overriding sense of resignation in the face of change, as illustrated by Sam's response: 'I get less worked up than I used to... I guess I'm just much more accepting that this is going to be the case now. I used to kick and scream about all that sort of stuff and then I actually realised that it was only me that was getting a bloody nose out of it. And that it didn't change a darn thing' (Sam, family court welfare team, Area 1).

Having highlighted the unrelenting pace of change and the challenges from central government on the probation service and its gendered organizational structure and practices, I now move on to explore responses from some of the male probation officers. I relate their views to issues raised so far and analyse how the changes were impacting on their sense of personal and professional identity.

Becoming and being a man maingrade probation officer

Of the 31 probation officers that I interviewed in-depth during the course of my research, two male probation officers, Sean and William, stood out as embodying the 'vocational' ethos stemming from the traditional foundations of the Service. They had both been appointed in the mid-1970s, having decided to retrain and move on from their initial career choices. They had been influenced to a large degree in making such a transition by their regard for individuals from an earlier generation of probation officers. Each of them spoke of memories of contact with male figures who had 'passed on the mantle' of probation work to them and Sean in particular spoke with feeling about a principal probation officer of a relatively small area (before re-organization in the 1970s), who he described as 'an absolute character'. He reminisced about this local service, which he subsequently joined, as a kind of fraternity where 'you could actually identify, if you like, the founder kind of members of the Probation Service. There was much more a kind of pastoral sort of feel about things then' (Sean, family court welfare team, Area 1).

William voiced similar feelings, describing his colleagues in his first post as being: 'very, very supportive. Although in a sense they were all these sort of independent and autonomous officers, at the same time I thought I was very well cared for' (William, generic community-based team, Area 2). Their view about their personal experiences of the Probation Service and of their places within it conveyed a strong sense of allegiance to the agency and to their work. Neither of them had sought promotion and they each conveyed the impression of accepting their position within a paternalistic form of management (from male chief probation officers), within a discourse of masculinity that exercised power 'in positive ways which enhance subordinates' self-interests' (Collinson and Hearn, 1994, p. 13). These perceptions of the Probation Service had a rather anachronistic feel given the increasing pace of change that was taking place. However, their responses did tally with my experiences in entering the organization in the mid-1970s, when the legacy of 'appropriate' areas of work for men and women still prevailed.

These responses provided an interesting point of contrast with the views expressed by Pete, a probation officer who had entered the Service in the 1980s. While he also demonstrated a deep commitment to his work, thus echoing the vocational foundation of this choice of career, he talked about his approach to being a probation officer as 'bringing a personality to the job within the rules and regulations that the Service has'. He emphasized the satisfaction he gained from his work, even though he bemoaned the move to 'see things reduced to statistics'. The sense of the shifting value base underpinning the types of intervention carried out by the Probation Service seemed troubling to Pete and he lamented the actions to remove the links with social work, particularly given his involvement with people with drug problems. He connected this shift in the focus of probation work with his interpretation of the type of masculinity that this seemed to be demanding. In particular he commented: 'I don't see sergeant majors doing my job without actually having to speak to people about the ins and outs of heroin use and how it affects them... I think we will reinvent the wheel hopefully' (Pete, generic community-based team, Area 1).

Pete reiterated Sean's and William's commitment to a life-long career within the Service (Cockburn, 1990), but seemed to be experiencing difficulty in adapting to the challenges to his autonomy in terms of addressing the requirements of key performance indicators and increased administrative monitoring. Pete was keen to stress to me that he considered that 'most people who are probation officers are very very committed to being probation officers and will walk the extra mile', but wondered what was now involved in being seen as a fully committed organisational member (Mills, 1989). In particular, Pete mused over the difficulties he was experiencing in placing himself as a 'family man':

> This 'business' between the potential conflict between home and office. I still don't think I've fully resolved that after doing this job for about four or five years now. I don't like to take work home, although sometimes I do. I feel tired in this job sometimes. I think overall in this country the employer is asking more and more of people in professional posts – I think it's not just probation. I try to strike that balance in life – that it's there to be enjoyed. It's not all about work though I think. But physically I do find the demands on my time quite... you know, it's demanding I think to be a probation officer.
>
> (Pete, generic community-based team, Area 1)

This sense of insecurity in relation to the inter-connectedness of his personal and professional identity ran through this interview. For Pete there seemed to be concern about whether career progression was linked with organizational expectation of a particular view of masculinity. Most of all, he clearly felt that he was presented with a situation where the demands he was facing were incompatible with his domestic commitments (Collinson and Hearn, 1994).

While acknowledging the sincerity of his viewpoint, this did not match the intensity of feelings expressed by many women, particularly those who were mothers of relatively young children. For example, Pete's comments can be contrasted with those of Nancy:

> You never get rid of the pressure points, you are crucified on them. But yes, I think they were undoubtedly there and I think the job doesn't help. I talked to a friend who was pregnant not so long ago and, you know, you know too much and you read too much in this job, to be mothering at the same time.
>
> (Nancy, generic community-based team, Area 2)

Nevertheless, within the interview with Pete he voiced his awareness of what could be described as the 'gender politics within masculinity' (Connell, 1995, p. 37), connecting this with his wish to hold onto the value base of his social work training against the fast-changing ideological tide within the criminal justice sphere. He referred back to the relevance for him of the traditional care/control dichotomy and was rueful in his comments about the current situation:

> I actually think that we do a good job, but, you know, I don't think that we're on the side of the angels anymore... I think there's a difficult line to

tread now... There are going to be some uneasy alliances here between our traditional role and the victim perspective. It's a challenge, but it could work well... Success in this job is not an easy idea at all.

(Pete, generic community-based team, Area 1)

It was interesting that many of the issues raised by Pete resonated in interviews I had with women probation officers who had entered the Probation Service in the 1980s, raising for all of them problematic areas in respect of 'power, oppression, inequality, identity and self-doubt' (Hearn, 1992a, p. vii). However, all of these officers had come into an organization at a time when, despite the unremitting tide of change, there had been on-going expansion of the Service. The more recent entrants had faced the additional insecurity of cut-backs and potential redundancies, with the likelihood that the prospect of a life-long, continuous career within Probation had all but disappeared (Faulkner, 1995).

The feelings voiced by these long-serving male probation officers contrasted sharply with the responses from Michael, a young black new entrant who I interviewed in the company of two of his female contemporaries in Area 2. As newly appointed probation officers all of these respondents were keen to talk about their reasons for their career choice and to share their perceptions of their prior expectations and their actual experiences of their work. In this respect Michael aligned himself with the two women in expressing some difficulties in adjusting to the uncertain expectations of work as a first-year officer (see Raynor et al., 1994, for discussion of discrepancies in the confirmation process). Nevertheless, Michael was much more focused in identifying the problems at a structural, rather than an inter-personal level.

Michael came across as presenting a very task-centred orientation, meeting the fast-changing situation head-on and looking for career advancement within a set-up that promised meritocratic progression. He seemed to have tuned into the 'smart macho' culture prevalent within the National Health Service and epitomised by the 'new man-agerialism' of the Probation Service. As Maddock and Parkin have pointed out in their research into gender cultures, within this type of organizational setting 'if you work hard and fast and can focus on narrow targets, your gender or ethnic origin is irrelevant' (Maddock and Parkin, 1994, p. 36). However, this implicitly demands a driven, focused approach that privileges work over all other aspects of life, separating the 'public' from the 'private', and potentially carries with it differing gendered implications. In addition, as Connell has stated:

To recognise diversity in masculinities is not enough. We must also recognise the relations between the different kinds of masculinity: relations of alliance, dominance and subordination. These relationships are constructed through practices that exclude and include, that intimidate, exploit and so on. There is a gender politics within masculinity.

(Connell, 1995, p. 37)

This sense that men were now in direct competition with each other, (and indeed with women), in terms of organizational accountability and achievement against measurable outcomes, was rarely addressed directly in my contacts with probation officers, but was apparent as a rumbling undercurrent.

Some gendered observations

The responses by these probation officers illustrate the impact of change in individual and organizational terms. The high levels of stress within the current situation were reported on by many probation officers, particularly relating to increased administrative monitoring and limitations on professional autonomy. These feelings share similarities with the low morale and pressurized working conditions reported regularly by the media within many state-sponsored settings such as the NHS, education and social work. However, I would suggest that the full significance of any of these situations remain unaccounted for unless gendered organizational processes and relationships are also considered.

From their research into equality audits in British public authorities in the early 1990s Maddock and Parkin point to the importance of taking account of gender cultures, suggesting that they are 'not as vague or imprecise as they might first appear' (1994: 29). In this respect the situation within the Probation Service in the 1970s as described by Sean and William would seem to display many of the elements characterized by Maddock and Parkin as a 'gentleman's club' This gender typology fits with the organisational structures at that time of men predominating at all levels of the organizational pyramid. It also concurs with the portrayal of an organizational forum where traditional male and female stereotypes held sway under the benevolent paternalism of male management.

In drawing on these characterizations of gender cultures it is not my intention to convey a sense of progression from one gender culture to another in the development of the Probation Service. The differences between and within local probation areas,[1] and over time, present a far more complex scenario than this. However, this perspective does provide insight into the different gender processes and relationships that cut across each other within organizational settings. In particular the inroads made by women probation officers into the organization in the late 1980s and into the 1990s can be linked to a 'gender blind' approach (Parkin and Maddock, 1995) which had emerged as a response to Equal Opportunity measures. This interpretation can be drawn upon to revisit the public/private dilemma spoken about with such feeling by Pete. It becomes apparent that while this type of organizational culture endeavours to avoid discrimination, it also inadvertently denies the reality of differential outside responsibilities (for some men and many women), as well as gender differences (Parkin and Maddock, 1995).

This in turn comes up against the cultural shift within the organization into the 1990s, described by Maddock and Parkin (1994) as the 'smart macho'. Again on the surface this does not appear to be a gendered culture and in terms of a strict male/female dichotomy this may be so. However, this organizational approach depends on extreme competitiveness to reach performance and budgetary targets – aspects that have been brought to the fore for the Probation Service within the format and requirements of the Home Office's rolling Plans for the Probation Service (see, for example, Home Office, 1995b). The operation of this kind of culture has particular implications for promotion prospects and for the operation of 'new managerialism' within the Service, but extends beyond this to the everyday working practices at all levels for all staff.

Looking forwards

On gaining power in 1997 the Labour Government swiftly reinstated probation officer training, combining a two year degree with a practice-based National Vocational Qualification at Level 4. This approach retains the higher education route into the Probation Service, while adhering to the proposals within The Dews Report (Home Office,

[1] There are currently 54 probation areas in England and Wales but amalgamations will be taking place by April 2001 reducing the number to 42 areas.

1994) to open up entry to a wider range of applicants. These arrangements have been devolved to nine regional consortia, with cohorts of trainee probation officers being appointed locally as employees of each probation area. This severs the link with social work courses in a definitive way and puts in place a contractual relationship between the academic and practice elements within an overall community justice framework.

While holding on to the professional standing arising from the status of pre-entry qualification, this new approach leaves open to question the gendered implications of these changes for individual probation officers, for the status of newly qualified staff, and for organisational cultures in the Service. A profile of the first cohort of trainee probation officers indicated that on a national level 69.7 per cent of the trainees were female, while 30.3 per cent were male (Macnair and McQuillan, 1999). This is hardly the gender turn-about that might have been anticipated in the wake of The Dews Report (Home Office, 1994) and Labour Government's thrusting, masculinized rhetoric of being 'tough on crime and tough on the causes of crime'.

The Home Office continues to emphasise the need for the Probation Service to demonstrate 'effectiveness' and the requirement for individual officers to be 'capable of achieving the required competences' (Home Office, 1998a, p. 9). Directives from the centre have increasingly prescribed the nature of probation intervention, with new National Standards due for implementation in April 2000 further toughening enforcement of community sentences. At the same time nationally accredited programmes are moving the focus away from one-to-one intervention and towards standardised (mainly groupwork) packages. These macho discourses are circumscribing the working structures and practices of probation officers, resurrecting tensions reflected on by probation officers in this chapter, in their attempts to bring about change in complex situations, where offending may be only one element of a cluster of interrelated problems. These issues could augur problems for joint work with Social Services and other welfare agencies.

Within the context of the fast-developing 'What Works' framework the range of interventions carried out by probation officers with offenders is becoming increasingly directed, overseen and scrutinised by the Home Office. These targeted approaches focus on *reducing reoffending* as the key purpose of probation. While this is clearly a laudable aim the overall drive of government policy is moving the Probation Service towards closer alignment with the Prison Service and even further away from its social work roots. The emphasis is shifting towards containment and corrections and it remains to be seen whether probation officers will be able to operationalize community penalties in a constructive way that will encompass the need to address public protection, while at the same time 'embodying and expressing other vital human values as well' (Nellis, 1999, p. 315).

This chapter emphasizes the critical importance of acknowledging the interweaving of gender in reaching an understanding of issues facing probation officers. The Probation Service is one organization among many in the public services that are facing radical overhauls and insights gained from this research point to the scope for comparative analysis to be carried out in other settings. While the focus within this chapter has been on men maingrade officers, the concerns arising from the demands of the 'smart macho' organizational culture (Maddock and Parkin, 1994) have implications for both women and men in relation to the public/private divide in their lives and in the professional value base in their work with offenders. Certainly for many long-serving probation officers the job now bears little resemblance to the vocational profession that they originally joined. What remains to be seen is whether these factors bring about a gender change within the Probation Service, reinstating the post of 'probation officer' as a 'man's job' with all of the implications inherent in such a directive gendered approach.

6 Men and Community Care

Ric Bowl

In this chapter, Bowl takes on the task of writing about the broad area of community care in relation to men. While some writing and research exists on men in relation to child care and the criminal justice system little has been written on men and community care. Bowl describes men as both the receivers of care and as carers. Although men often benefit from community care services, dominant forms of masculinity represent men as 'competent' and 'independent' and exclude the idea of men as carers. Bowl identifies how men in particular cultures and contexts provide care for friends, partners and relatives. He argues that social workers need to challenge dominant stereotypes of men as being, at best, 'reluctant' carers. These practice developments would be encouraged, in Bowl's view, by detailed research on men and community care.

Introduction

My aim in this chapter is to examine the impact of masculinities on community care. I set out to explore the implications of the social construction of masculinity for those who are 'cared for' and those who are engaged in community care, both professionally and as informal carers. Writing a chapter on men and community care is a challenging experience. Challenging because it is impossible not to be aware of the danger of giving nurture to those who would argue that feminist ideas have transformed society to such a degree that men are being short changed and their needs ignored. This idea is manifest in many ways. It is seen in elements of the 'men's literature' whether it be denying men's societal advantages (Baker, 1992; Lyndon, 1992; Farrell, 1993) or positively championing some of the qualities of men's lives that came in for criticism in the 1970s and 1980s (Bly, 1991; Farrell, 1991). The idea that men are being short-changed is also seen in the common sense understanding of many men who feel that, particularly at work, 'the pendulum has swung too far' despite the continuing evidence of the glass ceiling that limits women's progress within their organizations (Martin, 1988; Freeman, 1990; Williams, 1992; Kay and Hagan, 1995; Shaiko, 1996). Closer to home it was seen in the 1980s within social services departments, when work with girls became a focus of attention for many feminist workers. 'What about the boys?' was the refrain, despite the fact that mainstream group work for adolescents had always been and continued to be shaped around boys' needs. It can also be detected in an article by Fisher (1994) which, while usefully reminding us of the existence of a significant body of men carers, mainly spouses, denies the significance of gender in shaping both our expectations and the realities of who provides care and how that is valued by society.

Men's contributions to the debates about community care are in themselves interesting – being predominantly concerned about broad policy issues, management systems or financial costs. There has been relatively little engagement by men in the more micro issues – what it feels like to be a carer, the physical and emotional costs and benefits, the impact of these on carers as people and the implications of this for professional workers. Similarly men social workers who asked 'what about the boys?' in the 1980s were rarely concerned with the precise content or objectives of work with boys. Hence, they did not consider how such work might, to some degree, serve to question the very ideas of masculinity that were often deeply implicated in the reasons these boys became service users of social services departments in the first place. All of which falls in line with one established characteristic of mainstream masculinities – men's preference for the macro, the academic, the rational, their interest in policy-making and their relative discomfort with emotionality and particularly self-analysis.

In this chapter, I have no intention of contesting the view that existing notions of gender fundamentally disadvantage women particularly in the area of community care. Nor would I contest the view that this merits priority in our collective consideration of the implications of community care. Nonetheless we all live gendered lives. Our gender shapes our life opportunities; it shapes our material and emotional experiences; it shapes the way we view others and it shapes their view of us. Therefore I focus both on the social construction of masculinities and its impact upon the provision of community care.

This brings me to the other element of challenge. Community care is a broad almost indefinable concept and much has been written about the contentious nature of both 'community' and 'care'. These controversies, including the continuing belief in 'community' as an almost organic inter-dependence of individuals in one locality that is rarely experienced in practice, are usefully reviewed by Barnes (1997). She also reminds us of the criticism made by some elements of the disability movement that the concept of 'care' implies passive recipients and powerful providers. They would prefer to stress citizen's rights to particular forms of support. Barnes further focuses upon the trend within social policy to see care as a commodity that can be bought and sold – to stress the practical as opposed to the affective component of care. Such a conception of care fails to recognise the link between the 'tending' element of personal care and the 'caring about' element, highlighted in Parker's (1981) analysis. The extent to which this trend itself reflects the influence of mainstream masculinities forms part of the following discussion.

Put together 'Community Care' has been used to describe the development of domestic-scale residential establishments as opposed to huge campus institutions; it has been used to describe the development of domiciliary care delivered to people's own homes; and it has been used to describe informal care provided by spouses, other family members, friends and neighbours. It has also been used to describe a host of different policy initiatives with a wide range of groups of service users and most recently to describe the system of assessment and provision established in social services departments following the NHS and Community Care Act 1990.

My focus will be upon two elements of these disparate meanings. It will be on the informal care provided by spouses, siblings, friends, etc. largely for older people and others with physical disabilities, and on the role of professional workers in supporting that care, predominantly under the auspices of the NHS and Community Care Act 1990. By placing these boundaries around the concerns of this chapter I accept that I am ignoring a range of issues and many acts of support and help that could come under the heading of men and community care. Many of these are explored in other sections of this book, particularly Chapter 7 by Phillips on men and mental health services.

Defining masculinities in the context of community care

First, I intend to revisit briefly the literature on the social construction of masculinities to highlight those elements most pertinent to the discussion of community care. Then in turn I will consider the issues raised first concerning men as clients[1] and informal carers and then men as professional workers within community care.

So what are the features of masculinity that might be relevant to considering men and community care? Writing some time ago (Bowl, 1985) I suggested that isolating the components of masculinity was not easy, that those writing about it often simply assumed we knew what they were talking about without clear definition. I put forward what I described as a 'working view of the inter-related components of masculinity' which drew upon Marxist and feminist macro theory, academic psychological research and the experiential men's literature. I recognize that both my own views and the material and ideological circumstances that nurtured the development of this construct, have undergone some change. Nonetheless, I am happy to argue that it offers an enduring image of mainstream masculinity that remains implanted in the consciousness of many men and women alike. As such this working view offers a useful broad framework on which to hang subsequent discussion of men and community care.

Central to this framework is the notion of men as providers, as 'bread-winners'. This is clearly both important to those men in work (Hood, 1986) but perplexingly is arguably more critical to many out of work (Mattinson, 1988; Willott and Griffin, 1996). The idea of men as 'bread-winners' is underpinned by both notions of independence, relying on yourself rather than others, and competence. The importance of the latter should not be underplayed. Despite Tolson's (1977) assertion that the presence of competent women in the workplace would undermine men's confidence in their assumed superiority over women, experience suggests such confidence remains a characteristic of many men. Certainly whatever their views of the relative competence of women, many men remain reluctant to admit either under-

---

[1] I recognise that those described as 'clients' and 'carers' are all in one sense 'service users' but from here on use the shorthand of 'service users' and 'carers' respectively to refer to these groups of service users with often distinct sets of interests and needs.

developed skills or difficulty in handling regular tasks because of temporary circumstances, such as illness or stress.

Men's assumption of competence can in turn be linked to the concept of 'competitiveness'. Capitalism has always been driven by competitiveness, although this could be seen to be tempered in its impact on the individual by the need for a degree of co-operation between employees within corporate units competing in the market. In recent years the increasing emphasis on performance related pay, individual achievement targets and short-term contracts within our work culture, and the insecurity this brings, must inevitably have reinforced the impact on individual men and placed further emphasis on demonstrating competence and hiding areas of relative weakness.

Mirroring this outward manifestation of men in public is the perception of man as 'master' within his own domestic setting. Whilst it can be convincingly argued that neither the Victorian paterfamilias nor the brutal pre-war working class stereotype described by Young and Willmott (1962) are now seen as acceptable role models, many men still expect the family unit to serve as a refuge from the pain and pressures of public life (Davidoff and Hall, 1987). Men also continue to expect the final authority, show a reluctance to participate in domestic work and often have a circumscribed involvement in the emotional life of the family (Ford, 1985; Henwood et al., 1987). Such detached dominance may be achieved by consensus but there also remains a strong tendency for this to be imposed if necessary by use of intimidation and violence (Pahl, 1985; Mooney, 1993; Bush and Hood-Williams, 1995).

There is very little scope within this perception of men for them to take a major role in 'caring', at least not in the sense of engaging substantially in intimate physical care for, or emotional support and exchange with, other members of the household. They do their caring financially, by providing the material infrastructure that enables the family to survive, and morally, by shaping the rules within which other members of the family develop and grow (Hearn, 1987). Nor should we assume that the advent of the 'new man' has significantly changed this pattern. Lewis and O'Brien (1987), for example, show that, despite some changes in the pattern of involvement of fathers, real parental caring responsibility still rests with women.

A third strand to this mainstream masculinity is what Thompson (1995) refers to as 'emotional restriction'. There is no doubt, for example, that irrespective of their relative advantage, men, like women, do experience difficult life events. They suffer bereavement, separation and divorce, job redundancy and retirement. Indeed relatively recent material changes in society – the 'breakdown' in family structures, increases in life expectancy and the re-structuring of employment – make them all more likely. They also throw doubt onto the continuing relevance of both the 'breadwinner' and 'master' strands of mainstream masculinity which, it has been argued, contributes to higher levels of anxiety and insecurity among men (Hearn, 1987). Yet men are less likely to seek emotional help; despite changes in hospital admission patterns, are less likely to report severe psychological distress and are reluctant to express feelings to other men. Some have rooted this in the taboo on homosexuality and the fear of intimate exchange with other men (Clarke, 1974; Hoch, 1979).

Difficult to separate from this is the protest masculinity that denies the possibility of men engaging in 'feminine behaviours' and figures prominently in our adolescent development. It can also be seen clearly to link to ideas about competence and independence. To talk about issues that trouble us implies weakness and failure – a need for others to help us. Seidler (1994) roots this convincingly in the triumph of a narrow view of reason within modernity. Men have learnt to operate within a framework of problem-solving instrumentality that denies the emotional. Emotions and feelings, rather than being seen as a further source of learning, are seen as a distraction that hinders progress. Feelings like sadness, tenderness, fear, for example, are problematic in the workplace and need to be conquered or disregarded.

Jourard (1974) in particular sees extreme dangers in men's inexpressiveness. It may give rise to men lacking the language to discuss what is happening to them emotionally and ultimately perhaps not perceiving it. This will contribute to less self awareness, less insight and less sensitivity to what may be happening to others. As Seidler (1994, p. 43) puts it:

> Since we learn to discount our emotional needs and desires, learning to treat them as 'irrational' or as interruptions in a rationally directed life, it is hardly surprising that we are deaf to the expressions of others... For many middle-class men it would seem as if life would be much simpler if it could be organised in the rational ways of the office.

Yet men do care!

One of the weaknesses of current theorizing, and indeed what little empirical study there has been about men and masculinity, is that it focuses on particular groups of men – often adolescents, younger fathers, factory and office workers. Where there have been detailed studies of the lives of older men these have focused on redundancy and retirement and the impact of men's identification with work (for example, Crawford, 1973; Phillipson, 1978; Bytheway, 1986). While this research is useful in showing how men are shaped and the expectations and values that will impact upon them throughout their lives, it tends not to emphasize that at particular points in their lives some men are significantly involved in caring.

Fisher (1994) cites the evidence of Office of Population Censuses and Surveys studies which showed over 40 per cent of 'carers' to be men, although he acknowledges their use of a rather broad definition of caring responsibilities that probably leads to this being an over-estimate of those responsibilities. Arber and Ginn's (1995) more detailed analysis of the 1990–91 General Household Survey supports this argument. They identify that even men carers living in the household are less likely to be sole or main carers than women (59 per cent as opposed to 86 per cent) and that men carers outside of the household are likely to spend less time on caring than their female counterparts (22 per cent and 34 per cent respectively providing over 10 hours of care per week). Nonetheless the differences only serve to alert us against over-stating the role of men carers. It remains true that equal proportions of elderly men and women are caring for a disabled spouse and that about 40 per cent of elderly parents being cared for by an unmarried child at home are being cared for by a son (Arber and Ginn, 1995, p. 20).

So as I have argued that mainstream expectations of masculinity tend to lead to the suppression of caring and emotional tendency in men, how can this be reconciled with the existence of a substantial degree of caring by men?

Arber and Gilbert (1989b) provide an argument that is supported by the evidence we have in this area. They propose two ideal types of experience leading to taking on a caring role. This first path is that usually trodden by men carers and is seen as a corollary of the 'life long' experience of living together with someone within the context of a relationship. Hence the relatively high proportion of male spouses and of unmarried sons living with elderly parents who take up caring roles. Women in contrast, while they may also find themselves caring in these circumstances, are also influenced by the socially defined view that caring is a natural part of women's role. Hence where conscious decisions are made about who should provide care, particularly for an older person outside of the home or coming into co-residence for the first time, it is more often daughters and daughters-in-law who accept this role rather than sons.

Of course, not all men have found themselves cut off from the potential to offer nurture and care that is apparently to be denied them by mainstream masculinities. Within the predominant culture there have always been exceptional men who have taken on caring roles, though their history is largely invisible – 'man tends family' doesn't quite have the same appeal to headline writers as 'Hilary conquers Everest'. The life histories of Christian's (1994) 'anti-sexist' men show that several were influenced by fathers who, to different degrees, had taken significant roles in their care and nurture. Indeed the resistance of individual men to the images cast for them holds out hope for those committed to changing masculinities.

Equally importantly other cultures and other masculinities are part of our society. Societal responses to HIV and the concomitant inability or reluctance of many mainstream caring agencies and their workers to respond appropriately, for example, have led to the development of a network of mutual care provision within communities of gay men. This has involved both caring in the psychological sense of sharing pain and emotional distress and providing intimate personal care – both to a degree not associated with mainstream masculinity. There are also a number of different ethnic minority cultures within Britain within which expectations concerning gender participation in caring may be different. A friend who is a Hindu from Gujerat recently recounted his own experiences when his father-in-law suffered a stroke. Local care workers automatically expected that this man's spouse or daughter would take on the main home caring role but such is the separatist male/female culture and associated cross gender taboos concerned with physical caring within this particular community that sons are expected and usually willing to take on this role. In the absence of a son it was the son-in-law who took on this task.

Recent research also demonstrates that one response to the challenge of unemployment has been for men to take on informal caring roles. MacDonald's (1996) interesting study describes how volunteering, including caring for older people has, in part, compensated for the loss of the gender-related identity of men workers in heavy industry on Teesside. Participants in this study talked of gaining fresh insights into themselves which challenged their dependence on an image of themselves as a 'breadwinner'. Nonetheless, it was also clear that this was often seen by them as a holding pattern rather than a new identity. This is mirrored in studies of early retirement where men showed a preparedness to take over domestic and personal care tasks in response to a particular crisis in the household but reverted to more traditional roles when the crisis passed (Cliff, 1993).

Old images and current experiences

The above examples from the experiences of unemployment highlight one of the great contradictions in mainstream masculinity. In many ways traditional images of masculinity are an anachronism – the end of the brief period of full employment in the UK and the growth in non-family households have eroded the relevance of the 'breadwinner' identity; more women at work and the 'feminization' of work as we have moved from heavy industry to service industries have challenged ideas of men's superiority and special competence in the workplace; demographic change means we have more older men no longer in paid employment and who experience the dependency induced by the onset of illness and disability; men are increasingly asked to take their share of domestic and care tasks and some have had to in the absence of alternatives; and increasingly women expect a changed emotional response from men.

Dominant forms of masculinity, that have never been as functional as might be expected (Morgan, 1992), have been in crisis and yet it would be wrong to underestimate their continuing impact on the psyche of men, on their responses to others and of others to them. This 'virtual masculinity' guides film-makers, advertisers and social institutions, however much or little it draws upon the experiences of real men. Connell (1987) describes it as 'hegemonic masculinity' to which other masculinities are subordinate. It has a tendency to absorb these other masculinities and emerge perhaps reshaped but largely unscathed. Certainly one response to the crisis in masculinity has been to re-assert old values as seen in the macho posturing that accompanied the Malvinas and Gulf conflicts and is seen within the political discourse of toughness in 1990's America and in modern media images (Kimmel, 1996).

The tension between the demands of this outdated notion of masculinity and the experiences and desires of individual men is shown in the residual commitment to the 'breadwinner' concept among some of Christian's (1994) 'anti-sexist' men and may have particular implications for men involved in significant caring roles. It may lead to their being isolated from other men and it may contribute to doubt about their own abilities to provide care. This may be further exacerbated if it is this stereotype that dominates the thinking of those they care for and the informal and formal workers with whom

they come into contact. The following section explores the implications of mainstream masculinity for first service users and then
informal and professional providers of community care.

Masculinity and giving and receiving care

Significant numbers of men with physical and learning disabilities
and particularly older men may be the 'clients' of community care
services. How might mainstream masculinity impact upon the experiences of these service users? I would want to focus first upon the
experience of becoming someone who is to be subject to care. Most
men experience care provided by a spouse or mother for extended
periods of their lives and some may, therefore, find little difficulty in
accepting social care provided by formal and informal carers.

However, the care provided within the context of community care
may be of a different nature than that experienced earlier in men's
lives. It may be necessitated by the sudden or accelerating impact of
disability or chronic illness and this may be exacerbated by the
absence of a spouse or parent or by their inability to provide care. For
older men care may then be provided by daughters or sons for whom
they have previously seen themselves as taking responsibility. Such a
perceived role reversal must involve a degree of adjustment.
Alternatively strangers will be brought into the home to perform
routine domestic tasks and/or personal care tasks.

This is in contradiction of two important elements of mainstream
masculinity – it implies dependence rather than independence and it
questions the 'competence' of men service users to perform perhaps
quite simple domestic tasks. Some research evidence suggests domiciliary care services are allocated to men with higher levels of physical capability than the women allocated similar services (Bebbington
and Davies, 1993). Not only does that disadvantage women but also
it gives rise to potentially contradictory experiences for men. They
may appreciate the help, not least because they may be unused,
unskilled or simply unwilling to take up tasks they see as women's
work, but at the same time experience a reinforcement of their lack
of competence and their dependent status. Hence the provision of care
services may in itself undermine a notion of masculinity that is
already potentially challenged by other changes wrought by the
development of disability and dependence – such as the loss of the
'breadwinner' role and the related erosion of the idea of 'mastery' in
the domestic sphere.

The performance of the more intimate personal care tasks raises problems of a different order. Parker (1993) highlights the distressing nature for some couples of intimate spouse care, not least because of its interference in their sexual relationship. Yet for men to accept such care from a stranger may be no less problematic, at least at first. Care from a younger woman contradicts the cross-sex taboo on caring and may also undermine male sexuality, while receiving intimate care from a man crosses the touching taboo and may be resented because of the obsessive dread of homosexuality that haunts mainstream masculinity.

Bereavement will also be an increasingly common experience for older men and this may add further to these other areas of potentially difficult adjustment. The ingredients are present, therefore, for considerable emotional turmoil which men may not be well placed to handle. Nor will they necessarily have the inclination or the language to discuss this with friends, carers or the professionals responsible for assessing their 'needs'. Tannen (1992), for example, focuses on men's concern with status in communication and its importance in limiting their preparedness to ask for help. This again is linked to the notion of male competence. One response may be for men to exaggerate their own coping capabilities, another is to become more private and reserved in times of real crisis (McGill, 1985).

Given continuing evidence about the role of intimidation and violence within the home in sustaining men's perceived dominance, one expected response to the emotional confusion or frustration generated by the experience of dependency and care might also be for some men to re-assert their power and control in this way. The evidence on this is under-developed but certainly there is growing evidence of the extent of male domestic violence within relationships between older couples and evidence of abuse of not only spouses but also other informal and formal carers (Wilson, 1994; Pain, 1995; Aitken and Griffin, 1996).

Masculinity and professional practice

It would be encouraging to think that community care workers engaged with men service users were informed by an analysis of the gendered nature of their lives and that consideration of emotional needs might be at the core of community care assessments. This would be consistent with the arguments made for a more holistic and less resource-bounded approach to the assessment of need by a succession of commentators (Black *et al.*, 1983: Bowl, 1986: Hughes,

1995) both before and since the NHS and Community Care Act 1990.

While the systems of assessment and provision that have been developed since the Act are in the relatively early stages of operation, the signs are hardly entirely positive. Ellis (1993) highlights how community care assessors remain relatively unaware of how their own implicit conceptual frameworks influence assessments and the extent to which particular issues are considered within those assessments. Hughes (1995) similarly draws attention to how assessors' perceptions of the lives of service users and their consequent needs may be distorted by stereotypes. While endorsing the value of life review in exploring the feelings and understandings that shape needs, she remains fearful that the reforms may also 'reduce the scope for professional practice with more complex issues involving, for example, emotional problems, conflicts of interest, conflict, moral dilemma or loss' (Hughes, 1995, p. 12)

These fears are to an extent borne out by the other, as yet limited, research into the changes that have been brought about in assessment and practice. Petch (1996) and Futter and Penhale (1996), for example, highlight how much assessment remains service-constrained and often focused on practical services. Lewis and Glennerster (1996) also report both an increasing focus on higher dependency service users and that care managers are spending less time on counselling and other forms of direct work with service users. Nonetheless, Social Services Departments continue to stress in practice guidance the importance of adopting an anti-discriminatory approach in assessment and service provision.

Such an approach implies recognizing the impact of gender on both the shaping of need and community care workers' responses to it and striving to ensure that this does not prevent appropriate help being provided. This might bring preparedness to look beyond the initial defensive 'hands off, everything is all right' attitude of some men service users that can mask concerns that only become apparent when the facade cracks and emergency help is required. It might also bring a preparedness to facilitate, endorse and work with the expression of emotion by those men and not to see it as an aberration. This would be in contrast to the difficulties encountered by social work students identified by Forster (1996) when they encountered angry, helpless men service users because it contrasted with their expectations of strength, rationality and an action orientation inculcated by their acceptance of a model based on mainstream masculinity.

Such an analysis might also usefully inform work with men carers. First it needs to be recognized that caring per se, by men or by women, can be a physically and emotionally stressful experience. The hours involved, the physical labour, the disrupted sleep patterns can in themselves place a physical burden, perhaps on a carer who is themselves older or may not be physically strong. The time commitment may prevent engagement in social activity and personal interests. There may be financial costs both in employment opportunities lost or expenses incurred. All may exacerbate the emotional costs – the sense of responsibility, guilt, rejection and criticism, particularly if the person being cared for suffers from dementia, even the experience of physical abuse – that may come with the caring role (Askham and Thompson, 1990; Parker, 1990).

Against these stresses must be placed the positive aspects of caring, as to simply focus on disadvantages would be to give a one-sided view of caring and indeed would only serve to devalue the caring role. The paucity of research into the experience of men carers leaves us relatively ill-informed about the balance of disadvantages and advantages to them. Ungerson (1987), Cliff (1993) and MacDonald (1996) all offer evidence of men, both retired and made redundant, gaining a reinforcement of their sense of usefulness similar to that they might expect to gain from a job and, in some cases, approaching it in the same way. Hollingsbee (1995) reports on the sense of satisfaction drawn by men from the challenge of caring for spouses experiencing Alzheimer's Disease. Fisher (1994) suggests that most men carers were able to identify social rewards for caring, such as an improved relationship with the person they are caring for, as well as deriving an enhanced sense of their own personal identities. Ungerson (1987) and Parker (1993) also cite the element of love involved in the motives of male spouse carers, in particular, and the sense they have of repaying their spouses for the lifelong care that they have received.

Yet how does this square with mainstream masculinity? Certainly the evidence of Cliff (1993) and MacDonald (1996) is that, for many men, caring does not fit too well with their perceptions of masculinity and is seen as only a temporary role. And what about sons and son-in -laws who care – how do they experience the role? For men it would appear there is potential for confusion and stress both in the nature of caring itself and in reconciling the role with the expectations with which they are imbued. The men in the study by Hollingsbee (1995), for example, emphasized the feelings of regret and discomfort felt in having to adapt to a role that was new to them.

Accurately assessing the stresses that men carers experience and developing strategies to deal with them may be particularly difficult. Men carers may be reluctant to reveal their difficulties and admit to weaknesses, preferring to maintain the face of competence and coping. Levin et al (1988), for example, suggest that men carers are less likely to report stress arising from the caring role. This is supported by the research of Kay and Applegate, who describe some of the men carers they studied as 'quite adroit at masking the difficulties they are experiencing by presenting a stoic, stiff upper lip to those who are observing or assessing their efforts as carers' (1995, p. 213). A sense of 'coping' was particularly important to the men interviewed by Hollingsbee, who were extremely reluctant to lose control of their caring task. Hence while support was gratefully received it induced guilt. Nor did they gain much from carer support groups and, when they did attend, they tended to derive their support particularly from other *men* who were going through a similar experience. Nonetheless they were happy to share their experiences with the researcher and the research 'demonstrated the need for male carers to have someone with whom they may talk openly; a confidant' (Hollingsbee, 1995, p. 35).

The challenge for professional workers is not to accept that everything is okay simply because care is being provided but to be flexible and open to potential difficulties faced by men carers. This involves recognizing the strengths in men who care but also keeping their emotional experiences on the agenda. It means providing the space for men carers to talk about the frustrations and difficulties of caring including, where appropriate, reflection on how that fits with their view of themselves as men. This may be particularly difficult where it involves a challenge to an image of masculinity to which workers themselves also subscribe.

There may be other problems if workers are too prepared to accept the stereotype that men don't care and, that if they do, it is reluctantly. This can become a self-fulfilling prophecy if it leads to responding in ways that circumscribe men's willingness and ability to provide care. The danger here is in assuming that there are certain areas of caring or certain caring skills that men carers will be almost inevitably unwilling or unable to handle. Kay and Applegate (1995) show that, while tasks requiring intimate physical contact were experienced as more stressful, men carers both undertook and gained satisfaction from the full range of care-giving activities including the provision of social and emotional support. Contrary preconceptions may be quite damaging. Hollingsbee (1995), for example, reports that the men he interviewed were happy to accept help from daughters in emergencies and for occasional respite but none received assistance with personal care and some were particularly concerned that they were being coerced by formal services into accepting relief from the caring role that they did not want.

It is now established that a major caring role involves peaks and troughs, that like many valued activities it is at times a struggle, particularly in the early stages of adapting to the role (Motenko, 1989). A potential pitfall for workers with men carers is to offer inappropriate substitute care at the first sign of difficulty or perhaps simply because of preconceptions about what care men are competent to provide. Such a reaction fails to recognize or encourage the development of new or enhanced caring skills. If this happens, and there is certainly some evidence which suggests that men carers get higher levels of support particularly from the voluntary sector than their female equivalents (Arber and Ginn, 1995), workers will not be facilitating the extension of individual caring skills and indeed the aggregate potential for increased informal care.

What about the issues concerning men as professional workers and community care? What has the foregoing analysis got to say about that? Some commentators have questioned the motives of men's involvement at all in the caring occupations, arguing that men have introduced a notion of professionalisation that has tried to suppress and control emotionality and to see it as entirely separate from the more highly valued rationality and instrumentality (Hearn, 1987). Yet caring occupations inevitably involve the sensual, the emotional. They involve working with people who are angry, confused, grief stricken and frustrated; who may be looking for practical help but also for understanding and a sharing of their pain.

Subscribing 'to a professional code that values "not being emotional" ' (Hearn, 1987, p. 140) must make this a difficult experience for men. Perhaps that is one reason why in the 1960s and 70s men in social work retreated into community work and research and development, why more men are found in probation work and why men are over-represented in social work management, policy-making and academic positions. Community care is an area where men have been relatively conspicuous by their absence, though Arshad (1996) questions whether that balance may be changing with a new emphasis on rational assessment and resource management as being at the heart of community care work.

Certainly there seem to be dangers in men's tendency to endorse and accept male inexpressiveness. Men workers may be particularly reluctant to engage with service users who express emotional needs and be enthusiastic to fall back on the rationality of 'objective' assessment because that is what makes them feel more comfortable. To do so would be detrimental to the quality of assessment within community care and to reinforce the long established tendency, for example, in assessments of the needs of older people to overlook the issues they see as most important in their lives and overstress those to which there is an identifiable practical 'solution'. Just as rational knowledge and emotional experiential knowledge should not be seen as competing mutually exclusive spheres, if we refuse to engage with the emotional life of community care service users, we will only learn part of the story.

Of course it could be that men who select themselves for social work are different – perhaps more 'feminized' – sorts of men. Certainly there is some evidence that that is how they see themselves (Cree, 1996) though the men in her research also described pressure on them to adhere to traditional views of masculine behaviour. My own experience as a social work educator is not encouraging in this respect. Inevitably different men respond in different ways, but it is difficult to detect much difference in the responses of experienced men social workers to those of other men with whom I engage. They appear to value the emphasis on contracts and care plans, prefer to engage with macro analyses of discrimination and service deficiency and to resist analysis of how their own personal practice may fall at least in part within the mould of mainstream masculinity. In particular, few have engaged with the critical feminist literature that has focused upon the role that gender might play in social work interventions nor with the literature on masculinity (a point echoed by Arshad's 1996 survey).

The need for a gendered analysis

In conclusion I want to stress two distinct but related points. First, I have been aware, particularly when writing the latter part of this chapter, about how little we really know about the impact of masculinity on community care in practice. I have tried to bring together the body of theory and empirical observation about masculinities and apply it to a field where it has been little explored and where even the empirical evidence available has been gathered with scant attention to this knowledge and therefore provides little illumination.

Much of what I have written about practice remains speculation. Despite the attention given to feminist theory within social work, we still have too little detailed information about the specific ways in which gender affects the helping process, either from the point of view of helper or helped. I have speculated about the potential influence of concepts of masculinity on how both carers and cared for experience care but we need to explore these issues much further than current evidence allows. We need to know more, for example, about whether men service users and carers find it easy to admit to difficulties that they experience and whether they find it easier or not to share this with men workers. Would they, for example, fear their approbation or benefit from the shared perspective that they offer? We need to know more about the approach of men workers in assessing both men and women. Do they produce a more restricted and bounded assessment and if so how can we challenge that? In the absence of this more detailed knowledge, the danger is that we continue to ignore the impact of gender or that we base our decisions on myths and stereotypes. Neither would serve community care well.

Feminism has given us many lessons and one that cannot be overlooked is that men are gendered individuals too and not the ungendered representatives of humanity (Morgan, 1992). However imperfect our information, there is no excuse for ignoring the impact of masculinity on the exchanges and relationships that make up community care. While it would be wrong to over-emphasize and over-interpret its influence, I hope I have demonstrated that it is important for all of us interested in the role of men in community care not to be guided by a limited stereotype of masculinity. Rather the task is to deconstruct hegemonic forms of masculinity, recognisze the tensions between these forms of masculinity and some men's everyday experience of caring and perhaps even see our engagement with community care as one medium through which we can work towards the development of less oppressive forms of masculinity.

7 Men and Mental Health Services: a View from Social Work Practice

Nigel Phillips

The link between young men and suicide is gaining increased coverage in the media while other aspects of men's mental health, and the services provided, receive little attention. In this chapter, the specifically 'gendered' diagnosis of mental health is discussed. For example, men are under-presented as suffering from depression, whereas men are over-represented in psychiatric diagnoses which involve drug and/or alcohol misuse. Emotional 'inexpressiveness' is often linked to men's depression and suicide, however, in this chapter social isolation and psychological instability are highlighted as key factors in men's mental ill-health. Three case histories are used to describe the varied experiences of men users of mental health services.

Introduction

Discourses about men and mental health have started to be denoted and cautiously explored within the enlarging field of gender studies (e.g. Busfield, 1996). In attempting to write about men, masculinities and mental health in the context of social work practice my aim is to locate this apparently new topic within a framework provided by the practice and management of social work and social welfare.

126

I have worked as a social worker and subsequently as a team manager in the area of mental health social work and have worked with significant numbers of men requiring help and support as a result of experiencing a mental illness or a breakdown in their ability to deal with emotional stress in their lives.

Frequently, though not invariably, the men that the mental health social worker sees are said to be suffering from a mental disorder (diagnosed by a psychiatrist) such as depression, anxiety, or schizophrenia. The role of the social worker, amongst other things, will be to find solutions to problems out of the client's own personal resources where they had previously believed they had none left. The social worker attempts to maximize the client's ability to remain living in the community, or, in circumstances where the client has been admitted to hospital, to restore him to independent living. This will necessitate working not only with the individual man but also with his family and friends. Last, but by no means least, mental health social workers frequently exercise their statutory responsibilities as an Approved Social Worker under the Mental Health Act, 1983. In this role the mental health social worker will, amongst other things, carry out assessments where compulsory admission to a psychiatric hospital may be indicated.

Before examining some of the specific issues to do with male clients and male social workers in the mental health field, it is first necessary to briefly survey what we currently know about men and mental health. The steady stream of thinking and writing which has emerged over the past 20 or so years to establish a critical study of men (Hearn and Morgan, 1990). These studies have concerned themselves with many aspects of men's relationships with women, children, and with other men over a broad range of issues that include sexuality, violence, sexual abuse (directed at children and female partners), and emotional inarticulacy. Underpinning all of this, has been the study of how men as individuals and as groups have reacted to the changing social roles of men (and women) in the post-industrial/post-modern world in which we find ourselves in the late twentieth century.

It is clearly necessary to draw attention to the fundamental role which feminism has played not only in the development of theories about men's practices within a patriarchal society but also in the stimulus given to some men to begin an explicit analysis of these practices. This has encouraged the raising of certain issues intrinsically 'owned' by men, but of vital concern to both men and women, such as how men express their emotions, how men manage their relationships with women and with other men, and in what ways men acquire or negotiate their gender identities and sense of being a man.

While it is not within the scope of this short chapter to systematically address all these issues, nevertheless any attempt to look at men's mental health must pay some attention to these issues since they can potentially tell us much about why some men may become mental health service users or experience psychological distress. In addressing these areas of concern there is also an opportunity for men to improve the quality of their relationships with women, children, and other men as well as advancing a better understanding of their own mental health needs.

While I shall be arguing that the growth of ideas and practices explicitly around men and mental health is thus far relatively undeveloped, nevertheless I intend to show that there are some theoretical developments and numerous practice examples concerned with men as users and providers of mental health services which suggest a way forward in our understanding. I would point out here that such a perspective is neither dismissive of women's experience as mental health service users, nor is it suggesting that men's experience is in some way worse, but rather that there are gender differences and these are worthy of consideration in their own right. At the same time, I would hope to shed light on some related topics such as men and emotional expression, men's self-destructive and addictive behaviours, and men's violence. However, the first question we must ask is what do we currently know about men and mental health? The following is a brief overview of some of the main issues, and the research underpinning them.

Men, depression and emotional expression

Although depression is a universal illness, it is women who are seen more often by health services: a survey of episodes of illness in general practice found that more than twice as many women than men were diagnosed as suffering from depression (Busfield, 1996). There has for some time been much discussion as to the reasons for this (e.g. Penfold and Walker, 1984; Ussher, 1991). While it is outside the scope of this paper to repeat these arguements, it is nevertheless pertinent to note that there are two broad approaches within feminist writing to explaining the over representation of women in psychiatric services (Busfield, 1996).

The first approach arises from the idea that gender is itself embedded in the concept of mental disorder. Dominant constructions of women as 'passive', 'dependant', and 'neurotic' when applied to a discourse of mental disorder inevitably result in more women than men being so diagnosed. The second approach suggests that women's position in society, as a result of such influences as the feminization of poverty, violence by men towards women, sexual abuse and the over-representation of women as carers, may be particularly conducive to 'madness' and 'mental disorder'. In short, as Busfield suggests, there needs to be an emphasis on mental disorder as both social construct and social product.

According to a fact sheet published by the Royal College of Psychiatrists for the Defeat Depression Campaign (Royal College of Psychiatrists, 1996), men are just as likely as women to develop depression but are much less likely to ask for help. The fact that men are far less likely than women to consult doctors across all levels of psychological distress (Goldberg and Huxley, 1992) may be associated with women's greater familiarity with medical consultation for matters connected with gynaecology and pregnancy, but also on account of the fact that women are likely to have greater contact with doctors through their roles as carers, both of children and dependant adults (Thompson, 1995).

But as the leaflet goes on to suggest a more significant reason may be that most men are reluctant to admit that they feel fragile or vulnerable and so are less likely to talk about their feelings with their family, friends or their GP. As Busfield (1996) points out, for men to publicly (or even privately) express certain emotions such as fear, anxiety and misery may be seen as indicative of just such vulnerability and dependence and therefore incompatible with ideas of masculine control and achievement. Notions of men and their sex role socialization have been widely discussed in the literature of men's studies (e.g. Fasteau, 1975). It may suffice to quote from David Cohen's book, *Becoming a Man* (1990):

> Our expressions of any negative feelings get repressed. It's hard to accept them as part of life. Rather they show us up as being less in control than society tells we ought to be. It isn't that feelings are less intense than those of women but that certain feelings are shameful. Triumph and success are splendid. If you have cause for any other feelings – misery, fear, worry – it's best to hide them. Put on the mask. Assume the stiff upper lip.
>
> (Cohen, 1990, p. 85)

However the notion of emotional inarticulacy in men (Bowl, 1985) is not without its critics, some of whom would suggest that the Cohen quotation comes from what one author calls the 'male confessionalist' tendency of men's studies (Cameron, 1992, quoted by Johnson, 1997), in that it presents the idea of men's own emotional torment at not being able to meet a patriarchal society's expectations that not only should men be able to demonstrate power and control, but in so doing appear rational and unemotional (Siedler, 1991). While it is not my intention here to enter into the debate concerning the legitimacy or otherwise of the notion of men's inexpressiveness, nevertheless it is clear from my own practice that men who are mental health service users (along with other men) can and do express themselves emotionally in many different ways, some of which may be deemed as inarticulate.

Thompson (1995) is surely correct in suggesting the more useful term emotional restriction in that what is being described 'is not simply a reluctance to express emotion but, rather a tendency to give vent to a restricted range of emotions', the problem as Thompson points out being that the emotions more readily expressed by men are those which are potentially destructive, for example, anger and aggression. In her survey of the literature on gender and expressiveness, Busfield (1996) suggests that:

> ...the public expression of certain emotions in men (anxiety, fear and misery) is discouraged in many circumstances as indicative of vulnerability and dependence, and as incompatible with ideas of masculinity and the importance attached to control and achievement. In contrast, expressions of rage and anger, which may enhance power and the ability to control others, are not curtailed in the same way.
> (Thompson and Walker, 1989, cited by Busfield, 1996)

If it is the case that men feel they should be self-reliant and refuse to talk about their feelings, there is evidence to suggest that men suffering from depression will attempt to make themselves feel better (or self-medicate) by coming to rely on alcohol and drugs (Meth and Pasick, 1990) as both an obliteration of their misery and as a widely accepted adjunct of masculinity. One study goes further in suggesting that depression and alcoholism are different but equivalent disorders, wherein men are reluctant to admit being depressed or to seek treatment and mitigate this by drinking (Weissman and Klerman 1977, cited by Busfield, 1996). There are a number of studies showing that many treated alcoholics have symptoms of depression, e.g. Tyndel (1974), cited by Busfield (1996).

As far as social work practice is concerned, workers have always been aware of the particular difficulties posed by men service users who are unable to discuss their emotional distress, and are only able to acknowledge depression as a component of their problems via the medium of alcohol. Encouraging men to acknowledge their emotional distress and to pursue less destructive ways of expressing their emotional needs has always formed a major part of social work help for these men. In a later section on men as users of mental health services I will consider some of the routes along which men may have travelled before they become mental health service users and indeed prior to even acknowledging depression as a consequence of often traumatic life events.

Men and severe mental disorder

Since the first Health of the Nation White Paper in 1992 set out primary targets (supposedly to be met by the year 2000) concerned with improving the health and social functioning of mentally ill people and reducing their high rate of suicide, we have increasingly seen the introduction of the term 'severe mental disorder' or 'severe mental illness'. Given the novelty of the term, it would be useful to give some definition, and then move on to look at its possible association with issues of gender.

All definitions of what are primarily psychological constructs remain problematic. Goldberg and Huxley (1992) are among recent writers to criticize the so-called categorical model of mental disorder on the grounds, among others, of lack of robustness of categories, constancy over time and discontinuity between a syndrome and supposed normality. However, as they say, it is hard to see how any alternative model would necessarily fit the data better. The Department of Health guide for practitioners working in mental health services *Building Bridges* (1996) defines people suffering from severe mental illness as individuals who:

1. are diagnosed as suffering from some sort of mental illness (typically schizophrenia or a severe affective disorder);
2. suffer substantial disability as a result of their illness, such as an inability to care for themselves, sustain relationships or work;
3. are currently displaying florid symptoms, or are suffering from a chronic enduring condition;

4. have suffered recurring crises leading to frequent admissions/ interventions;
5. occasion significant risk to their own safety or that of others. (Department of Health, 1996, p. 11)

The inclusion of this last dimension of safety clearly refers to what the same document calls the 'continuing anxiety ... over the care and treatment of severely mentally ill people [where] a number of suicides, homicides and other serious incidents have understandably led to great public and professional concern'. What is being referred to here is the public and media outcry over acts of homicide and self-harming behaviour committed by individuals who were subsequently said to have been suffering from a schizophrenic illness – namely Christopher Cluness, Ben Silcock and others within the short period from 1991 to 1993 (e.g. Ritchie *et al.*, 1994).

An inquiry into 'Homicides and Suicides by mentally ill people' (Royal College of Psychiatrists, 16 January 1996) found among other things that in the UK, 'the suicide rate among mentally ill people was running at more than two a day' (*Guardian*, 16 January 1996), adding to a growing clamour to improve care in the community. Whatever the shortcomings of service provision or breakdowns in professional communication that have been shown up in subsequent inquiry reports, it is the case that all of the individuals concerned are men.

Previous statistics have shown that the diagnostic rates for all forms of mental disorder included a greater number of women in all categories other than that of personality disorder, which in any case accounted for a low rate of admission to hospital (Miles, 1987). The figures quoted by Busfield (1996) emanating from the 1986 study by the Royal College of General Practitioners indicate a similar story. In this survey, taken from GP consultation rates, the only psychiatric diagnostic areas in which men now outnumber women are those related to drug and alcohol misues. While all such statistical material should be evaluated in terms not only of the gender bias of psychiatrists making the diagnosis (Ussher, 1991) but also in regard to the reliability of the diagnostic criteria themselves (Goldberg and Huxley, 1992), there is nevertheless a problem emerging of what might be termed gender perceptions and mental disorder. While men are under-represented in both GP consultation levels and admissions to hospital, those cases which led to public enquiries and attracted much publicity (all of whom were said to be suffering from schizophrenia) were all men.

The answer may lie largely in a greater propensity for men to be violent to themselves as well as others. However, this is not perhaps the whole explanation, and what we may be witnessing is a confluence of media stereotyping of men who suffer from severe mental illness, and a genuine problem of mental health service provider organizations in engaging with men service users. These men may not regard themselves as having a mental health problem or see no efficacy in the services they are being offered (for example they reject taking medication owing to the unpleasantness of the side-effects).

Two of the most widely reported cases (that of Christopher Cluness and Horritt Campbell) were black men suffering from a mental disorder who committed violent and 'inexplicable' crimes. Black men are frequently represented as both violent and criminal (Gilroy, 1987). They are also often pathologized as mentally ill (Fernando, 1991). The combination of violent behaviour and mental ill health all too easily form dominant representations of black men in the mainstream media.

Men and suicide

Considerable media attention was shown with the publication of figures from the Royal College of Psychiatrists (1996) which indicated that more men, and in particular young men, were both attempting and successfully committing suicide. By the age of 20, four times as many men are likely to commit suicide as women; this reduces to a 2:1 ratio by the age of 70. These figures need to be contrasted with those for non-fatal deliberate self-harm where women outnumber men by about two to one. One-third of all successful suicides by men are caused through self-poisoning by car exhaust fumes, while overdoses followed by hanging are the next most common means. Inevitably the very nature of two of these methods leaves little likelihood of a 'second chance'. The different methods used by men and women to attempt suicide may help to explain the higher proportion of men for whom suicide is fatal.

According to the Health of the Nation figures, suicide continues to account for 1 per cent of all deaths annually (5542 deaths in 1992), and has become the second most common cause of death in 15–34 year old males. Prior to the recent Royal College Psychiatrists report, it is known to have risen by 75 per cent in young men (that is, aged 15–24) in the 10 years to 1992. The Health of the Nation: Key Area

Handbook on Mental Illness (1994) recommendations go further in setting a specific target 'to reduce the suicide rate of severely mentally ill people by at least 33 per cent by the year 2000. As practitioners and researchers we need to know more about this apparent male vulnerability.

According to research summarized in Vaughan (1995), there appear to be two constellations of social factors indicated in male suicide, both of which are related to mental illness. The first group tends to be young, male and single, and are characterized by a degree of psychological instability. They are often well-known to the mental health services, possibly having made previous attempts at suicide, and most significantly are likely to have been diagnosed with a severe mental illness such as schizophrenia. The second group are likely to be older men, who are either divorced or widowed. Such individuals are characterized as being somewhat inflexible in outlook and to be poor adjusters to change. They become socially isolated, are prone to self-neglect, and react poorly to significant life events such as illness and disability. If they come into contact with services (and many do not) they are likely to be diagnosed as suffering from severe depression. They resort to suicide as the only solution to their isolation and despair.

While these pen-pictures of men's greater vulnerability to suicide have their utility, there are questions of economic and social changes, which need to be addressed if we are to appreciate the complexity of the issues. The first of these is unemployment. Mary Buck (1997) surveys much of the literature on how men and women differently experience unemployment. This may owe much to the accepted sexual division of labour which identifies men as 'breadwinners' and women as 'carers' (Henwood and Miles, 1987, cited in Buck, 1997). If men are said to suffer particularly from mental distress when unemployed, then perhaps we have to look to the overall benefits of employment, namely 'the provision of money, activity, variety, temporal structure, social contacts, and a status and identity within society's institutions and networks' (Warr, 1982, cited in Buck, 1997).

Buck (1997) suggests that men, who had infrequent social contact outside working hours, when employed, were more likely to become depressed when they subsequently became unemployed. This was correlated by commentators with increasing levels of under- and unemployment among the proportion of the male population regarded by the Registrar General as being unskilled. Since these figures first began to emerge in the 1980s, theories have been put forward concerning links with anomic suicide which was first identified by Durkheim (1952) who regarded it then as a largely a phenomenon connected with a social and spiritual 'rolelessness' exhibited by a number of young men. In the society of Durkheim's time individual rewards and preferment were linked to a man's ability to provide for himself and his family without recourse to public welfare.

No historical deviation should divert us from the problems involved in attempting to focus responsibility for male suicide on any single factor such as unemployment. Charlton *et al.* (cited in Vaughan, 1995) fail to produce any evidence of a direct relationship between changes in unemployment and suicide rates. However, with marital and relationship breakdown it seems we are on somewhat firmer ground. Single, widowed and divorced men have suicide rates which are almost three times greater than those of married men (Vaughan, 1995). Adults whose childhoods were characterized by parental divorce or separation tend to experience higher rates of emotional disturbance, but for an explanation of the gender differ-ence with respect to suicide, we need to return to the issues of indi-vidual men's reluctance to talk about, or display a full range of emo-tions. Jourard (1974) argues that low rates of self-disclosure among men are indicative of an added burden of stress over and above the actual life events concerned, e.g. marital breakdown. He cites Wilhelm Reich's view that being 'manly' implies the necessity to wear a kind of 'psycho-armour' without which the true self would all too easily be revealed in its nakedness and exposed vulnerability (Reich, 1948, cited in Jourard, 1974). Ultimately the final act in the lives of some inexpressive and existentially lonely men is the suicide of a man whom nobody knows.

> He turned on the gas,
> and he went to sleep with the windows closed
> so he'd never wake up to his silent world
> ... and all the people said
> what a shame that he's dead
> but wasn't he a most peculiar man?
>> (Paul Simon, 1966)

Men as users of mental health services

In the light of what I have said above I will now make some gener-al observations about men as users and providers of mental health services. I shall consider not only how men experiencing psychological distress might best be helped (or be facilitated more easily to help themselves, or each other), but I also intend to evaluate the impact on the professional helpers, in this case male social workers in the mental health arena.

I have already said that men do not consult doctors as readily as do women regarding areas of stress in their lives: explanations for this include women's greater contact with doctors and men's reluctance to discuss their emotional lives. Clearly this has serious implications for men's decisions on whether to actively seek out help with personal and family problems, and how to deal with the distress brought about by having a severe depression or even schizophrenia. It has been argued that men clients are far less likely to refer themselves for 'talking treatments' that is, counselling and psychotherapy. Pasick et al., (1990) suggest that 'for most men psychotherapy is the antithesis of masculinity: to enter therapy, men must violate several tenets of the credo of manhood' (p. 47)

I now want to consider some of the experiences more or less unique to men which may cause them to feel depressed (or suicidal) and as a consequence be referred or refer themselves to mental health services. I want to make it clear that I am making no claim that parallel experiences are not suffered by women nor that trauma suffered by men is any more significant in its distorting effect on an individual's life. What I am suggesting is that men's and women's experiences and perceptions are likely to be gendered and therefore qualitatively different.

Let us start with the experiences of childhood. While the 'discovery' in the 1980s of sexual abuse of girls and young women is now well known, it is rather more recently that similar findings have emerged concerning men. It is now widely accepted that boys are sexually abused by adults, peers and siblings (Bolton et al., 1989). In an American study (Finkelhor et al., 1990, cited in Busfield, 1996) of a sample of 2626 adults, 16 per cent of the men (as against 27 per cent of the women) said that they had been sexually abused prior to the age of 18. While much of the reported behaviour concerned unwanted touching, no less than 9.5 per cent of the men they had suffered someone trying or succeeding in having sexual intercourse. The abuse of power together with the distortion of previous relationships of trust associated with child abuse are likely to have damaging consequences for the mental health of these men. Some of the literature surveyed by Bolton et al. (1989) suggests that boys may do worse than girls. They quote Kempe and Kempe (1984) who suggest that:

> Both mother–son and father–son incest leave a boy with such severe emotional insult that emotional growth is often blocked. Some of the boys tend to be severely restricted and may be unable to handle stress without becoming psychotic, while others may have symptoms [of mental ill health] but never be recognized as incest victims.
>
> (Bolton et al., 1995 p. 73)

Such symptoms are likely to include self-directed feelings such as guilt, depression and low self-esteem, as well as other-directed symptoms such as behaviour problems, resentment and aggression (Nielsen, 1983). There is evidence that it is particularly hard for boys (and men) to disclose, both on account of the secrecy involved with ongoing abuse, and because of their reluctance to acknowledge that they can be victims. Dominant constructions of masculinity suggest that boys should be strong and handle adversity without 'crying about it'. To break the secret would be to show signs of weakness.

Therapy for the sexually abused male can only begin with breaking the silence, and thereby acknowledging that 'real men can have feelings', a necessary reversal of the notion that it is 'unmanly' to express feelings (Mangan and Walvin, 1987). If that silence is not broken, then the consequences for the mental health of the abused male are far-reaching. Bolton et al. (1995) suggest that a distortion of interpersonal relationships is the most common result, with some sexual abuse survivors replaying in their adult relationships many of the issues of power and control which characterized their own childhoods. It is not hard to see how for these men depressive illness is a common outcome.

A second case history for men's mental health is that provided by generations of young men who, while knowing they were gay, nevertheless spent a significant part of their adult lives passing as heterosexual. The reason for this as suggested by Coyle and Daniels (1992) is that most people internalize negative social representations of homosexuality, and that the suspicion that one might be gay and that the socially devalued gay/homosexual category has relevance for the self may be a source of considerable distress. In a study of gay identity formation, Coyle (1991, cited in Coyle and Daniels, 1992) showed that 'passing' as heterosexual exerted particular strains, including guilt, dishonesty and estrangement from oneself and others, all of which is likely to prove highly detrimental to psychological well-being.

In his autobiographical memoir, Monette (1992) recalls his own experience of having reached his mid-20s pretending to be 'straight', and with his life containing considerable anguish, deciding to see a psychiatrist, who apparently had some experience in treating 'deviant ' male patients. The notion of healing the sick, as represented by a gay man who has spent some years struggling against his true sexuality having his first consultation with the doctor who intends to 'cure' him of his 'disorder' is consistent with psychiatric orthodoxy since the time of Freud. The above exchange is mainly remarkable on account of the fact that it took place in the early 1970s, though perhaps less remarkable if it is remembered that homosexuality was until the 1970s officially regarded as a mental disorder in the American Psychiatric Association's Diagnostic and Statistical Manual (Spector, 1972, cited in Busfield, 1996).

A positive point emerging from the gay identity study (Coyle, 1991, cited in Coyle and Daniels, 1992) is that where a respondent perceived being gay as holding salient personal advantages, they were less likely to experience anxiety, stress and depression. By the same token, a high degree of involvement in the gay subculture was also associated with a raised level of psychological well-being. Clearly there is an opportunity here for preventative mental health work allowing gay men who are already experiencing psychological distress to have an opportunity to discuss and clarify their ideas on sexuality and self-image. Men who are in the process of negotiating their sexuality might benefit from undertaking the process alongside women who are in the same position *vis-à-vis* a lesbian identity. A group organized on this basis was run with a degree of success in the mental health resource centre where I myself am employed, in spite of some emotional costs for the individuals concerned.

My third case study of men as mental health service users concerns the more general theme of helping men to change through counselling and therapy. Over the past year (1996–97) articles have appeared in the press in relation to stress experienced by men, especially following the Royal College of Psychiatrists report on male suicide (1996). They have ranged from investigative pieces (David Cohen, *Guardian*, 4 May 1996) to outright scepticism and satire on men's ability or willingness to change (Suzanne Moore, *Guardian*, 25 April 1996). Cohen's article, '*It's a guy thing*', picks up themes that he developed in an earlier book (Cohen, 1990) about the intermeshing of personal narrative of men's lives – himself and others – with political and cultural changes. He describes a group of miners who have been made redundant and the ways in which individual men have had to come to terms with change, for example, the man whose wife returns from work to vent her frustration at 'the man behind the ironing board'. Cohen interviews Seidler, the writer on men and therapy, who says:

> The combination of large scale unemployment and feminism has forced men to rethink how they are brought up as men. This is causing deep uncertainty and anxiety [since] it is hard for men to really change because there is an inflexibility built into what it means to be a man. ... We don't realize our relationships are in trouble until it's too late.
>
> (quoted in Cohen, 1996)

On the other hand, Moore (1996) in her article, 'Men behaving sadly', suggests that men are only beginning to experience in their lives what women have always coped with:

> Men feel bad about themselves, about their relationships, about their children, about working too hard or not having any work. In short they feel like us, it's just that women are more likely to seek help ... It is not the silence and suffering of depressed men that is worrying; it's the silences of men who claim that everything is really alright.

If this to some extent represents the views of journalists and media commentators on the issue of male depression and its implications for masculinity, what active steps are men themselves (users of mental health services, sufferers from depression, men who want to change their lives) taking to confront these issues? Critics of certain strands of the men's movement in the United States have suggested that followers of the writer Robert Bly have sought to reassert their masculinity mainly by a tendency to 'retreat into the forest and bang drums, and to smell each other's armpits' (French, 1996). However it must be said that while these mythopoetic men's groups have offered little to men with mental health problems, living in such communities (albeit temporarily) may provide some men with the opportunity to give and receive support from other men.

In a remarkable book that examines the lives and aspirations of a group of men and women who are living in the community and diagnosed as schizophrenic, Barham and Hayward (1995) ask one of their respondents (Ben) about 'facing life alone' when you have a mental health problem. Ben goes on to describe a friend of his (also an ex-psychiatric patient) thus: 'He's very isolated. I go round his house and sometimes he's in quite a mess, he doesn't clean up and things like that. .... But when you're living on your own – I don't think it's unique to mentally ill patients .... it's a bit of laziness really!' (1995, p. 54).

As the authors suggest, the problems Ben describes are neither peculiar to ex- psychiatric patients, nor necessarily a product of mental illness. Rather, they are the kinds of problems faced by single men in general and isolated single men in particular. As Ben further comments: 'Women seem to cope with it better – keeping flats nice and tidy – maybe it's down to the way we were brought up as men' (Barham and Hayward, 1995, p. 54).

While the comments of Barham and Hayward's respondents are largely devoid of gendered content, there are still areas where the 'damaged' status of being a schizophrenic has serious consequences for the man's self-esteem: 'The main side-effect of the medication about which [Sidney] complained was loss of sexual interest and prowess which generated a good deal of anguish in his relationship with his girlfriend' (1995, p. 65).

Ultimately what do we know specifically about men in therapy, or recovering from severe mental illness? There is little available literature but it is possible to draw a sketchy picture the sources that are around. Hazlehurst (1994) describes a men's group that he was involved in running in a psychiatric rehabilitation community. With no experience of mental health issues, he finds himself thrown in at the deep end with only his knowledge of leading men's groups as some kind of compass. Six months later he reviews some of the events in the life of the group:

> I realised that my own fears and fantasies about the men must mirror a common reaction to them; that the labels the psychiatric establishment puts on them over-shadow and devalue their experiences and concerns as men. An example of this was the experience of all of them that the side effects of drugs [medication] on their sex drive are never explained nor do they feel able to ask what they might be.
>
> (Hazlehurst, 1994, pp. 15–16)

The men were free to attend or not as they chose. The group did however provide a safe space with boundaries and there was an agreement to challenge offensive behaviour and attitudes. Within this structure the men were able to make decisions about their involvement:

> It was interesting that the men who made up the core of our group were those who were regarded as the most isolated and who consistently avoided other community meetings ... One of them said that the group was good because for the rest of the time all they talked about with other men in the community was cigarettes and how to get them.
>
> (Ibid., p. 16)

Hazlehurst and his co-worker reflect that they became less directive as discussion began to happen around them rather than through them. The improved communication had enabled the men to improve their relationships with other men in the group and to begin to talk about other important relationships in their lives.

In order to complete my account of men as mental health service users, I shall turn to the notion of men in therapy. As I have already noted, Pasick *et al.* (1990) suggest that 'for most men psychotherapy is the antithesis of masculinity: to enter therapy a man must violate several tenets of the credo of manhood' (p. 152). Thus Allen and Gordon (1990) state that most men resist seeking therapeutic help, and only find their way into therapy as a result of pressure from a spouse, an employer or perhaps a physician. Even when they have come through the door, it seems that for many men there is a barrier to cross since part of being manly is to deny and dissociate from such natural human feelings as fear, sadness and dependency.

It is thus not surprising to find that a primary goals are to help men understand interdependence and connectedness as positive values that anchor a person's life, and to make active choices for change based on an appreciation of past and present events as revealed through therapy (Allen and Gordon, 1990). One particular message that emerges in their discussion of therapy with men is the notion that men feel the need to be in total control of their situation at all times. Allen and Gordon suggest that one of the strategies required to address this issue is for the therapist to adopt what they call more 'male models of communication', which emphasize men's allegedly more active and cognitive approach to the world (p. 150). I would fear, however, that this strategy if followed over enthusiastically by the therapist would tend to maintain men service users' alienation from their feelings, while continuing to support the idea that men remain in control even of their own therapy! This notion of men demonstrating control takes us neatly into my final section in which I shall be looking at how men perform as mental health professionals.

Men as mental health professionals/social workers

What I have to say here is primarily about men who are mental health social workers since that is the area of employment of which I have first hand knowledge. However, these comments should have some relevance for the experiences of men in other mental health professions such as Community Psychiatric Nurses and Occupational Therapists. I will divide my comments into three main areas.

Growth of a managerial culture

Throughout the 1990s writers have been drawing attention to the growth of managerialism, together with a culture of 'auditing' and ever tighter financial control of social services departments. The reasons for this are bound up with the policies of successive Conservative governments of the 1980s and 1990s in pursuit of cutbacks in public spending and attacks on the powers of local government. Pringle (1995) suggests that this more managerial ethos within social work is more consonant with values held by male managers than female ones. His evidence for this comes from other studies such as Hugman (1991) and Davies (1985) who argue that there is a traditional gender distinction between the 'virtuoso' (professional) worker who is more often a man and the 'general' carer, usually a woman.

It is, suggests Hugman (1991) not only men who are more likely occupy the 'virtuoso'/specialist roles as therapists in mental health social work, but they are also far more likely to occupy the managerial roles that supervise the work carried out by a largely female staff with predominantly female service users (also see Christie, 1998a). Hence as Pringle (1995) suggests, it is largely men managers who are enacting the dominance of budgetary control in Care in the Community policies in mental health.

While there is evidence to support Pringle's contention that the ethos of 'male' management is more likely to be in sympathy with the more 'audited' culture of welfare provision (e.g. Eley, 1989), I cannot offer any support from my own experience, both as practitioner and manager, that female workers are likely to be any less motivated to apply for, or less likely to be appointed to, posts in mental health social work. In fact the reverse would appear to be true in that the shortlist for the most recent post for which I was involved in recruitment contained nine names of whom only two were men. As to the notion that the statutory nature of the Approved Social Work role (one of the very few posts within social services departments which local authorities are obliged to provide by the Mental Health Act) is just such a 'virtuoso' role as described by Davies and Hugman, and therefore unlikely to attract female applicants, the opposite would appear to be the case. The figures for entry to the most recent

intake of experienced social workers on Approved Social Work training for a course offered by a consortium in the north of England
reveal that of a total of 53 students, 39 of them were women while
only 14 were men. Smyth (1996) suggests considerable variations between social service departments in the employment of men and women as social
workers. Their survey suggests an equal percentage (15 per cent) of
men and women working as mental health social workers. I would
go further and suggest that in those local authorities where traditional casework and counselling have not been entirely replaced by
care management type work, then mental health work is likely to be
as popular a specialism to pursue for women as for men. This leads
me on to my second point.

Sexual abuse in psycho-therapeutic relationships

We know from surveys of clients receiving psychology and psychotherapy services (and from the admissions of therapists themselves) that an alarming amount of what can only be called sexual
abuse perpetrated upon women has been going on for some years
behind the closed doors of consulting rooms. A survey published in
the United States in 1987 suggested that as many as 15 per cent of
psychotherapists had had sexual contact with a patient (Masson,
1988, p. 224). The fact that this abuse has for so long been hidden
is explicable on account of the psychotherapeutic relationship being
protected by a tradition of confidentiality, such that for a patient to
speak about what has taken place in a session would be seen as a
form of 'acting out' (op. cit., p. 211)

Pringle (1995) tells us that while not all abusing therapists are
male, there are indications that, as with the often systematic abuse
carried out in residential children's homes over many years, men are
far more likely to be implicated than women. Pringle (1995, p. 129)
quotes Ussher (1991) in her view that:

> These men are not aberrations. They do not deviate greatly from men in
> other positions in society. Pathologizing them or ridiculing them conve-
> niently ignores the fact that sexual contact between powerful men and
> powerless women is part of the fabric of our society.

I do not intend to burden the argument further with references to
men residential workers who have abused girls and women in their
care, be they young people, those with learning disabilities or people

with mental health problems, though the examples of individuals such as Frank Beck remain as salutary lessons for social services departments.

There appear to be issues here for men in mental health social work. The first is that they will be offering counselling and support to women (and men) who are regularly or periodically overwhelmed by chronic mental disorders, and therefore vulnerable to predatory professionals. Men social workers in mental health have therefore of necessity to adhere to an ethical prescription that covers all aspects of their personal and professional conduct. In particular they will need to demonstrate anti-sexist role models to their clients so that not only is the notion of abusive male therapists thrown into perspective, but also men in positions of relative power are shown to have a gentle yet expressive side to their nature (Meth and Pasick, 1990) in order to partly counteract the idea that the prevailing norm of men's behaviour remains one of aggression and inarticulateness.

The second issue is that as care managers alongside their women colleagues, they are responsible for monitoring the effectiveness of the therapy they purchase from the private and voluntary sector, and by inference its ethical standards. Men as care managers will increasingly need to confront this issue as the role of social services departments moves further towards an 'enabling' role and away from direct provision of services (Department of Health, White Paper, 1997). There is so far no indication that a change of government is likely to reverse this trend.

Gendered roles in responding to violence

The third issue is that it tends to be men who are expected (by managers and by some women colleagues) to take a lead in dealing with situations of actual or potential violence originated by that small number of mental health service users (male and female) who are seen to pose a threat to themselves or others when they are actively mentally disordered. Thus, in Approved Social Work practice, there are widely followed (usually informal) procedures in many social work teams regarding male workers going out on certain kinds of referral where there is some identifiable risk of violence, sexual harassment or generally unpredictable behaviour posed by the client being assessed. I am not thereby suggesting that it is inappropriate for men to take the lead in these situations, but rather that men practitioners themselves need to beware of reinforcing gender stereotypes in providing statutory services to individuals suffering from a severe mental disorder.

The growth of managerialism, abuse perpetrated by social workers and therapists, and a predisposition to identify men social workers as more liable to deal with risk situations are, in their different ways, examples of the need for both practitioners and their managers in mental health social work to recognise important gender issues in both the structures responsible for providing services, and in the nature of the services themselves.

Conclusion

I would first state that this has of necessity been no more than a quick survey of the landscape that constitutes 'men and mental health'. In the future there clearly needs to be more thinking devoted to what have tended to become peripheral themes i.e. the mental health needs of men service users and men working as therapists, counsellors and social workers.

While the evidence is not entirely clear, it is nevertheless possible to summarize that for most mental health problems the figures suggest that women outnumber men in terms of both GP consultations and referrals to specialist services in the community, and admissions to inpatient services in psychiatric units. This holds good across a range of widely accepted, though not unquestioned, diagnostic categories based on a medical model. However, if the figures for personality disorder, alcohol and drug misuse are included, the position of men within the context of mental health needs becomes more visible.

Among the other questions remaining to be looked at are the different ways in which men deal with distress, and the impact that cultural constructions of masculinity and femininity have on the diagnosis of mental disorders. Why it is that men with mental disorders are far more likely than women to be seen as posing a threat to themselves and others when they fail to engage with services such as clinics, medication and day centres. A further question that needs to be addressed relates to why there appear to be a disproportionate number of black men who are being diagnosed as suffering from mental health problems that are seen as dangerous to themselves and others.

Finally, a great many more questions remain to be asked about the needs of men who use and who provide mental health services, and whether more gender-specific services that attempt to address issues such as men's relative inexpressiveness are the way forward. As to whether men who are mental health professionals should be the best people to work with male clients of the service, the case remains unproven except to state the particular value of male role models. Such staff who are men will need to be actively anti-sexist and be perceived to facilitate problem solving in ways that are non-aggressive and allow male clients to be mutually supportive of each other in the groups or community settings that form part of their rehabilitation from depressive illness or severe mental disorder. If men collude with other men around perpetuating gender stereotypes, then perhaps it is the mental health professionals who need to proactively expose this collusion across a range of situations and processes.

8 Men and Masculinities in Social Work Education

Viviene E. Cree

Social work education in the UK is largely based within institutions of higher education in which men are over-represented as lecturers and senior academics. Social work courses challenge gendered hierarchies by seeking to promote anti-sexist policies and practices. Evidence from research presented in this chapter suggests that men social work students recognize that they are entering a non-traditional occupation for men and describe themselves as non-traditional men because of their professional commitment to care for others. Cree argues that the 'non-traditional' orientation of men social work students may encourage the development of anti-sexist practice. Building on this potentially optimistic view of men social workers, suggestions are made for the development of a gender-aware social work curriculum.

Introduction

This chapter explores some of the complexities that are at the heart of any consideration of men and masculinities in social work education. It begins with a broad discussion of higher education in general and social work education in particular and goes on to discuss the position of men as social work students. Finally, strategies for creating positive work around men and masculinities in social work education are presented.

My perspective in writing this chapter is best described as critical post-modern (Cree, 2000a). It comes from a recognition that people's lives continue to be structured by inequalities and oppression, including those based on gender, but that we also inhabit a number of different, potentially contradictory and changing identities, and hence a number of different and possibly ambiguous positions in relation to power. My interest in men and masculinities thus comes partly from the wider feminist project to attempt to build a more equal society; to confront unequal power relations in society and seek to change them (Cavanagh and Cree, 1996). It also reflects a post-modern appreciation of contingency, resistance and the inevitability of change (Cree, 1995).

Definitions

I will use the word 'masculinities' in its plural form in recognition that there are different ways of expressing masculinity in society. The Women's Liberation Movement of the 1970s has been criticized from within and outside for its essentialist position in relation to women and men's behaviour and attributes (Grant, 1993). More specifically, the idea that 'all men are rapists' has been experienced as deeply offensive to many men and to some women. Yet the difficult questions remain. Why is it that it is men who perpetrate most sexual abuse? Why do men allow other men to control their partners through violence and intimidation? Why do men continue to hold positions of authority even in women-centred occupations such as social work and nursing? Finally, how should women and men locate themselves in addressing these questions? These questions suggest that there needs to be a distinction between hegemonic masculinity and masculinities in the 'real worlds' of men's lives.

Kimmel (1990, p. 100) sets down ideological 'rules of masculinity' against which men have conventionally judged themselves:

(a) No sissy stuff: avoid all behaviours that even remotely suggest the feminine.
(b) Be a big wheel: success and status confer masculinity.
(c) Be a sturdy oak: reliability and dependability are defined as emotional distance and affective distance.
(d) Give 'em hell: exude an aura of manly aggression, go for it, take risks.

What is described here is *normative*, hegemonic masculinity. This is not to suggest that other kinds of masculinity do not exist. Instead, other forms of masculinity are judged in relation to this idealized picture. Edwards (1994) picks up this theme. He explores the ways in which, historically, gay men have always been portrayed as 'the other': as weak, effeminate and somehow undermining of masculine identity. The response of some gay men in the 1960s was to exaggerate their effeminacy. By the 1970s and 1980s an alternative option available to young gay men was to play out 'macho' themes in an over-stated masculine presentation. As Edwards suggests, 'gay men could be "real" men too' (p. 116).

In recent years, the subject of men and masculinities has been explored by a vast number of writers. As MacInnes (1998) states, 'every man and his dog is writing a book on masculinity' (p. 1). Some writers have been sympathetic to the feminist cause (e.g. Brittan, 1989; Brod, 1987; Connell, 1987, 1995; Hearn, 1987; Hugman, 1991; Pease, 1999, 2000), others directly in opposition to it (e.g. Bly, 1991; Lyndon, 1992; Thomas, 1993). Those who are anti-feminist in their approach blame women for men's emotional shortcomings: men have been castrated by women (mothers, partners and others) and need to get together with other men to find their 'true self' or 'inner man'. Pro-feminist men reject this analysis, arguing that women's oppression is far more fundamental and damaging than any so-called 'crisis in masculinity'. They set out to explore the seeming disjuncture between hegemonic masculinity and men's varied life-experiences. Brittan (1989) argues that although there may *seem* to be endless numbers of ways of 'being a man', this variation does not undermine male domination. He continues: 'Masculinism is the ideology that justifies male domination. As such it is the ideology of patriarchy' (p. 4). Hugman (1991) agrees. He suggests that patriarchy, although it is internally divided by racism and class, is shared to some degree by all men: 'Masculinity, socially constructed maleness, is structured around the exercise of this power' (p. 190).

As a feminist seeking to work from an anti-oppressive position, I acknowledge that there are different ways of being a man in British society, and hence in Mac an Ghaill's (1996) words, 'multiple masculinities'. However, this does not detract from the experience of patriarchal structures and the power of individual men. It is this complex reality which provides the foundation for an analysis of men and masculinities in social work education.

Men and masculinities in higher education

Any exploration of men and masculinities in social work education must begin with the acknowledgement that higher education institutions are traditionally bastions of male privilege. Universities in particular are male-centred in their organization, their teaching and their knowledge base: women have referred to themselves as 'outsiders in the sacred grove' (Aisenberg and Harrington, 1988). Research into gender at work conducted by the Association of University Teachers illustrates how deep-seated and continuous these systems are: men have *always* occupied the senior and management posts within universities (Association of University Teachers, 1991, 1994).

Women are not of course the only excluded group within higher education. Gay men and lesbian women, working-class people, those with a disability and those from black or minority ethnic groups have also experienced discrimination in terms of employment and career advancement (Witz, 1993). The outcome of this exclusionary process is that white, middle-class, presumed heterosexual men have traditionally controlled higher education and set standards for its teaching.

At the level of individual disciplines, there seems to be more variability. Departments such as social work and nursing have always had a higher level of women in positions of authority. Women make up 55 per cent of departmental heads in Departments of Social Work in Scotland, while at the same time being under-represented in the ranks of senior lecturers (Lloyd and Degenhardt, 1996).

It is difficult to gauge how long it will take for the imbalance in employment patterns to change. The women who have broken through the 'glass ceiling' find themselves in a very male environment. Some universities and colleges have argued that short-lists for senior positions should always include women. While this may seem to be a step in the right direction, it may also be more cynically viewed as an excuse for inaction: if this mechanism is in place then it absolves decision-makers of responsibility for exploring more wide-ranging changes.

When it comes to the content of education, feminist writers have pointed out that academic knowledge which is presented as neutral and non-gendered is often based on white Western, male, heterosexist assumptions and perspectives. In a ground-breaking text, Spender (1981) pointed out that men have 'taken themselves as the starting point, defined themselves as central, and then proceeded to describe the rest of the world in relation to themselves (p. 24).'

Women, when they do get a mention, are commonly presented as the exception to the rule, compared and contrasted with the male 'norm', whether this is in studies of social class, crime and deviancy, or human development, to name just three (Cree, 1997). But the issue is more complex still. Although 'man' has been the subject of much academic writing, men themselves have conventionally been very little explored and little theorized, leading to a position where the differences between men, as well as those between women and men have been under-researched and largely non-theorized (Hearn, 1987).

Men and masculinities in social work education

It is widely accepted that men in social work education (as in social work practice) wield a disproportionate amount of structural and organizational power. Although social work as a profession is predominantly carried out *by* women who are working *with* women, those in positions of seniority in the worlds of social work education and practice have been largely middle-class, white men (Abramovitz, 1985; Howe, 1986; La Valle and Lyons, 1993). The Scottish situation looks superficially better, given the comparatively high numbers of women who are Professors of Social Work. But this advantage is more than compensated by the large numbers of men at senior level as compared with women who are part-time, on fixed term contracts and at basic grade level (Lloyd and Degenhardt, 1996).

Social work education's regulating body in the UK, the Central Council for Education and Training in Social Work (CCETSW), has displayed little interest or concern in the issue of gender inequality in social work education. More than this, official statements on social work education have shown little reference to gender. CCETSW's Diploma in Social Work, although ethical in its underpinnings, betrays a conservative approach to social work's wider function. The stated purpose of social work illustrates this point. Social workers have to 'balance the needs, rights, responsibilities and resources of people with those of the wider community, and provide appropriate levels of support, advocacy, care, protection and control' (p. 16). The two key words in this passage are 'balance' and 'appropriate'. There is no question of changing society or challenging welfare policies. Social workers are undoubtedly 'fixers' not 'revolutionaries', to use Howe's (1987) terminology. Given that the wider purpose of social work is defined in such a cautious manner, it is unsurprising that the Diploma has little to say about sexism, gender oppression or even sexuality. The Equal Opportunities statement which prefaces the document does mention 'gender', as does a later section on social work knowledge. But there is no mention of sexism, heterosexism or anti-sexism. Broad entreaties that students should learn how to 'counter unfair discrimination, racism, poverty, disadvantage and injustice in ways appropriate to the situation and their role' (p. 9) are not translated into plans for action, and certainly not in the context of gender discrimination.

In spite of this, I believe that there is room for manoeuvre in terms of challenging sexism and changing masculinities. First, agencies (academic institutions and practice agencies) should be informed of the Equal Opportunities statement and urged to make changes (including making attempts to eliminate gender discrimination and sexism/heterosexism) in keeping with the ethos behind this statement. Second, social work programmes should be encouraged to teach students about gender, gender discrimination and homophobia, sexism and heterosexism as part of their commitment to building a knowledge base around oppression and discrimination. Thirdly, individual students should be invited to explore issues of sexuality, gender and oppression as it affects them personally: in line with the value requirement that they should 'identify and question their own values and prejudices, and their implications for practice' (CCETSW, 1995, p. 18).

Men and masculinities and social work students

While CCETSW may have paid little attention to men's differential power in social work education and practice, both men and women students are aware of the significance of gender in social work. Moreover, men coming into social work education do so in the knowledge that their promotion prospects are higher than those of women and that their career paths as a result may be quite different. Taylor's (1994) research found that women and men social work students *know* that their promotion prospects are likely to be affected by their gender: the women expected to be discriminated against; the men did not. This finding echoes results of my own illuminative study of first-year social work students from 4 programmes in Scotland (Cree, 1996). Here I discovered that the students whom I interviewed (35 in total) acknowledged that men's promotion prospects were higher than those of women, often adding the rider 'not that I think that is right' (ibid., p. 80).

This finding merits further consideration and investigation. Do men come into social work because they see it as a good bet in terms of securing a management post and an easy promotion ladder? Kadushin's (1976) early research into men in social work offers a more circumspect explanation of this phenomenon. He notes that men move quickly into positions where there will no longer be an incongruence between their personal and professional sense of self; they move into administrative and management posts so that they can spend more time with men and with masculine modes of being while working in what is a 'women's profession'.

My research study introduces a different, though not entirely oppositional explanation. Although the women and men students whom I interviewed rejected the idea that social work is a 'women's profession', they were nevertheless aware that for women, a career choice in social work was conventional, whereas for men, a decision to become a social worker was to a degree 'going against the grain'. This held potential advantages for men in social work: they felt freer and at the same time more visible, hence more likely to be noticed and to be praised for attitudes and behaviour routinely expected of women (Cree, 1996, p. 80). Williams' (1993) study of men in female-dominated professions amplifies this point. She argues that masculinity is a boon for men in women-centred occupations, because 'qualities associated with men are more highly regarded than those associated with women even in predominantly female jobs' (p. 3).

The implications for men in social work education are clear. Not only are men likely to achieve attention because of their smaller numbers, they are also likely to be rewarded for 'caring' qualities (sensitivity to others, compassion, ability to express feelings and emotions) which are taken for granted in women. But there is another dimension here. Research suggests that men are routinely valued more highly than women: in situations where men and women are in more equal in numbers and the topic is not regarded as conventionally 'feminine', men still receive unequal attention. For example, studies of gender in the school classroom demonstrate that boys receive more attention in the form of more praise and more reprimands; that teachers select topics which they think will interest boys; that they perceive boys as more active learners than girls; that boys' work is graded more highly than that of girls (Skelton, 1993). Those of us who are teachers in social work education, whether women or men, must be aware of these gendered dynamics and set out to control them, for example, by introducing systems of anonymous marking of written assignments and by seeking to encourage and credit the contributions of women students whenever possible.

Returning to my study, there is another important aspect of men's explanations for choosing social work as a career. Just as the students were aware that a career in social work was unconventional for men, so they saw themselves as unconventional men. They saw themselves as more in touch with their 'female sides', closer to women friends than to men, and not afraid to value in themselves what are conventionally seen as 'feminine' qualities. Analysis of results of carrying out Bem's Androgyny test with men and women students supported this identification with attributes commonly held to be 'feminine' (Cree, 1996, pp. 81–3).

Investigations of men in non-traditional settings (men who are nurses, teachers and house-husbands) suggests that there may be a connection between men's willingness to take on caring responsibilities and their own experiences of being nurtured by their parents. Some studies have highlighted relationships with mothers as of key significance (Chusmir, 1990). Others have argued that relationships with fathers (absent and present) are more important (Rosenwasser and Patterson, 1984–5). I asked all the students whom I interviewed to share with me their understandings of their reasons for becoming social workers. Some did indeed choose to explain their career-choice in terms of childhood or family background: they described an experience of loss in childhood, of caring for a relative, or of growing up with a parent or significant adult who was heavily involved in community or church activities. For other students, experiences and choices made in adulthood were seen as the major influences. Many students (both women and men) were attracted to social work because they saw it as a 'people-centred' occupation where it was anticipated that personal job satisfaction would be high. Some students defined their decision to enter social work principally in career terms, describing social work as a reasonably well-paid job with good career prospects. Significantly, the kinds of explanations students gave were not divisible on the basis of gender. Men and women were equally likely to stress childhood relationships, career and/or personal satisfaction as motivating factors for choosing social work as a career. But just as importantly, women students were much more likely to have had previous experience in being primary carers themselves (caring for children or older relatives) than men students.

The realisation that there are men who see themselves as different and who are keen to think about this offers scope for new approaches for changing masculinities in social work education. It suggests that it may be possible for women to engage with men in the pro-feminist aim of challenging discrimination and gender oppression in society. But it is important to underpin any developmental work (personal and institutional) with the acknowledgement that social work education is inevitably influenced by the conventional sexist, heterosexist and patriarchal assumptions and structures of wider society. It is a truism that students who are men are likely to gain from the very systems which they may seek to challenge and change.

Strategies for change

This section will explore strategies for working to explore men and masculinities in social work education through developments in the knowledge-base (theory and research), social work practice (in skills' teaching in academic institutions and work with service-users on placement) and values and attitudes throughout social work programmes.

Social work knowledge-base

I have already argued that academic knowledge has historically been focused at men and men's concerns. Social work knowledge has been criticized for its inherent sexism and for its acceptance of traditional gendered ideology (Brook and Davis, 1985; Dominelli and McLeod, 1989; Hanmer and Statham, 1988; Hudson, 1985; Wilson, 1977). Whether we are talking about work with children and families, criminal justice or community care, the reality is the same: we live in a sexist society and as a result, social work knowledge reflects and preserves that sexism. Hale (1984) points out that gendered assumptions about individuals and families are at the root of social work assessments and subsequent interventions. Because the woman is viewed as the 'key person in maintaining the functioning of the family', she may be held to be responsible not just for her own behaviour but for that of her partner, her children, her parents, and even her neighbours (p. 169).

But social work knowledge is not *only* sexist; this is not the only or even the primary reason for its existence (Cree, 1995). Some concepts within social work may at times work against standard assumptions about men and women's behaviour. Social work's emphasis on the individual 'client' and 'client self-determination' has always allowed for the possibility of a decision being made which may not be considered the 'normal' one in terms of conventional, sexist wisdom. Hence social workers have supported women who wish to leave abusive partners; to find residential accommodation for older or sick relatives; and to give up children for adoption.

In addition, social work knowledge is not static: it is constantly changing as it mediates with new ideas and practices. The development of feminist social work and black perspectives in social work have fundamentally challenged social work theory and practice. Assessment of the impact of feminism on mainstream social work ranges from the potentially optimistic (e.g. Kearney and Le Riche, 1993; Phillipson, 1992; Thompson, 1995) to the deeply pessimistic (e.g. Carter, Everitt and Hudson, 1992). My view is that while the more extensive claims of feminism may have indeed been relegated to the margins, there is undoubtedly a level at which the general aims of the anti-discriminatory and anti-sexist agenda have become accepted within the social work enterprise. There are also specific instances of a feminist approach becoming 'mainstreamed', for example, in criminal justice work with violent offenders.

There are different ways in which social work education might take forward the project to build a knowledge-base which is both anti-sexist and pro-feminist. At the broad level, social work educators must explore the experience of women and men in all their diversities and seek to adopt models which are inclusive and which are strongly rooted in an analysis of gender oppression. The systemic approach of Thompson (1997) provides a useful starting-point. Thompson presents a picture of three concentric circles: the personal is surrounded by the cultural which in turn is enclosed by the structural. Effective social work practice is premised on an ability to understand and make use of these inter-connected systems.

Starting with the personal, social work students must have the opportunity to reflect on the effects of gender socialization on themselves and those with whom they are working (e.g. Hugman, 1991; MacInnes, 1998; Mackie, 1987; Phillips, 1993). They must learn about the very diverse ways of being men and women – about men and women from different ethnic and class backgrounds, ages, cultures and histories, gay men, lesbian women and 'straight' men and women, trans-sexual and trans-gendered men and women (e.g. Pease, 1999; Whisman, 1996). They should hear about research into men who are not typically 'masculine' in their behaviours and attitudes, such as men who care for others (e.g. Arber and Gilbert, 1989a; Fisher, 1994; Russell, 1983; see Chapter 6 of this book). They should also find out about the structural context within which these sexualities are expressed. They should learn about discrimination and oppression in society (e.g. Brittan and Maynard, 1984; Connell, 1987; Hearn, 1987); about domestic violence and child sexual abuse (e.g. Kelly, 1988; Waterhouse, 1993; see also Chapters 2 and 4 of this volume); about men and crime (e.g. B. Campbell, 1993; Hudson, 1988; Naffine, 1987). They should consider the impact of unemployment on men's lives (e.g. Roberts, 1995) and the high rate of men's suicide (see Chapter 7 of this book). All of this is central to mainstream social work knowledge and practice.

Social work practice

A discussion of men and masculinities is not only a matter for academic theory. Students also need to develop skills to enable them to work in practice with women and men. As I have outlined already, social workers have been criticised in the past for failing to engage with men, even in situations where the main concern is a man's behaviour (as offender, abuser, parent or person seeking help). This may be because women service users are perceived to be more approachable and less intimidating than male service users. Men carry the threat of violence, sexual harassment, rape and other sexual violence even when this threat is not transferred into action (Stanley, 1984, p. 201). Social work students, men and women alike, may also find it easier to discuss feelings and powerful emotions with women: the difficulties which many men experience in expressing feelings have been well-documented (Hugman, 1991; Phillips, 1993; Scher et al., 1987).

Social work students must be given the opportunity to learn new ways of communicating. For men, this will mean practising listening to others: being prepared to look at feelings and let go of any stereotypically male urge to 'score points' competitively and be in control. For women, the task will be about finding ways of challenging men while still maintaining personal safety. Some of this work can be carried out in skills' classes in the academic institution. Students working in single-sex and mixed-sex groupings with the aid of video recording equipment can role-play scenarios where they try to confront or counsel another person of the same and different sex. Placement also offers limitless scope for advancing anti-sexist and pro-feminist social work practice. As well as the skills-development through actual work with service-users, students can reflect on their practice through the use of learning logs, process recordings and case vignettes, building up a deeper analysis of the impact of gender on their work.

The failure rate of men on social work placements suggests that this work should be given urgent priority. Although there has not yet been systematic research on men who fail social work courses, colleagues in Scotland have been aware that men disproportionately fail in social work education. It is suggested that male students who pass their academic written assignments fail practice studies and practice placements largely because of an inability to look at their use of self in social work practice (Lloyd and Degenhardt, 1996). This highlights the importance of social work education striving to address the cultural production of masculinities and to extend men's ways of behaving and relating to others.

Values and attitudes

While the knowledge and skills of social work education are important, the process of examining values and attitudes is equally so. As well as learning in an intellectual sense about oppression and discrimination in society, students (men and women) must be faced with the personal impact of oppression and discrimination. Sexism, racism and homophobia do not exist only at a structural level. Students should be invited therefore to examine the ways in which gender and sexuality are socially constructed and experienced at the individual level. They need to look at themselves as men/women and their relationships with those in their lives (loved-ones, partners, children, parents, friends) so that they can begin to unpack and examine their relationships with service users. If this groundwork is not undertaken, students may find themselves meeting their own needs for love and acceptance, or control and domination through their work. Or, just as problematic, they may adopt double standards, expecting attitudes and behaviour of service users which they do not live up to in their own lives.

This draws on a feminist concern for consciousness-raising: what Hudson (1985) refers to as a 'method of helping women to reflect upon their experiences as women and to name previously private experiences' (p. 651). For women, consciousness-raising has a dual purpose: it allows them to explore their shared experience of oppression while at the same time admitting the unique quality of their lives and experiences. Men in social work education would benefit from the chance to do some of this work themselves: to explore the interconnections between their personal biographies and their common experiences as men. For Thompson (1995), this work starts with an exploration of what he calls the 'costs of sexism', widely understood by women but often not fully appreciated in the context of men.

These include emotional and sexual restriction, reluctance to seek help, role stereotyping, competitiveness and the need to 'prove oneself', violence and aggression, crime and delinquency, restricted relationships, stress, 'bad faith'/'inauthentic' existence and the oppression of women (pp. 464–9).

But the work cannot end here. If men getting together with men simply results in men anguishing about their condition (and for some men this has included a suggestion that they suffer oppression equally to women) then the wider objective of working towards a fairer and more equal society will not be reached. Men in social work education must begin to look at ways forward: at how they can take their commitment to gender equality and anti-sexism out into the world of work. Phillipson (1992) suggests two approaches for teaching equality practice which will develop critical awareness, provide factual information and help the development of strategies for alternative practice (p. 45). The first approach proposes distinguishing between 'explanation' (the 'why' questions) and 'expression' (the 'how' questions): why does oppression exist and how does it feel to be oppressed and to oppress others? Both questions must be addressed so that students can begin to understand experiences from the inside. The second approach makes the case for 'perspective transformation', a process of unlearning, re-framing and change, based on the work of Paulo Freire (1972). Phillipson suggests that this might be achieved by helping students to unravel their beliefs and ideologies and try out new ways of behaving.

Work with men on values and attitudes might be usefully carried out in the context of single-sex groups. Male youth leaders and male social work educators have begun to do this with some measure of success (e.g. Bowl, 1985; Boyle and Curtis, 1994; Lloyd, 1990). But there is a strong argument for the continuing presence of women and of a woman's perspective in work with boys and men. Bailey and Cox's (1993) investigation into different ways of examining gender in the classroom found that men in single-sex groups sometimes failed to address the issues: they simply did not talk about them. Hainsworth (1996) takes this further, arguing that without a woman's presence it is all too easy for men to forget the power which they hold.

As social work educators (women and men), we can encourage students to explore the choices open to them in a number of ways, by encouraging them to begin this process in group and in individual settings and in our role as lecturers, tutors and practice teachers. We may also wish to model a different kind of relationship by co-working with a different-sex colleague to jointly lead routine social work teaching as well as specific sessions which directly focus on the subject of sexuality, gender, masculinity and femininity.

There are two final issues relating to values and attitudes which merit further discussion: the notion of commonalities and issues of power in the learning environment. I will examine each in turn.

The idea of a shared commonality with service users or 'clients' has been a major source of debate and disagreement between feminist social workers. Some have perceived the notion of commonalities (that is, shared experience as women and common experience of oppression) as central to their work with women in social work and fundamental to the creation of trusting, equal and sharing relationships with women service users (e.g. Brook and Davis, 1985; Dominelli and McLeod, 1989; Hanmer and Statham 1988). Others, (e.g. Wise 1995) have been highly critical of this perspective, asserting that commonality is impossible given the reality of statutory power and control within social work. Hudson (1989) also rejects the idea of homogeneity amongst women, stressing that women are a heterogeneous group and that other social divisions maintain the power of some women at the expense of others, for example, black women, older women, lesbian women.

A similar debate has recently been played out by men in social work, though in practice it has proved difficult territory for men to enter. While male social work students may be happy to explore the 'costs of masculinity' (Bowl 1985) or even the 'costs of sexism' (Thompson 1995), do male social work students *want* to explore their commonalities with men who abuse children or are violent to their partners? Pringle (1995) does not shrink from naming the destructive sides of masculinities. He argues nonetheless that it *is* possible for male social workers and service users to build on their common experience as men. He envisages this within the context of anti-oppressive practice: social workers and service users forming alliances to push for change within welfare organizations. Translated into the context of social work education, this may mean students working with each other and with service users (on placement) or with interested staff members (in either academic or practice institutions) to push the frontiers of work on gender issues, confronting such concerns as homophobia, structural inequality, men's violence, institutional sexism and sexual harassment.

A discussion about values and attitudes would not be complete without a consideration of the importance of power in the learning environment: institutional power as well as gender-based power. One of the biggest potential obstacles to learning in any learning situation is the assessment process (Cree, 2000b). Students are constantly aware (whether in the classroom or in placement) that their knowledge, skills and values are on display and that their work is assessed, formally and informally. This can inhibit experimentation or risk-taking by students. Staff members working with students on issues of sexuality must be clear about boundaries and confidentiality, and set out expectations and 'rules' for the group at the beginning of any session. They must also recognize that learning may throw up particular difficulties for some students who may need time and support after the session is over.

Power is also apparent in the more intimate dynamics of the tutor-student or practice teacher-student relationship. Educational research has shown that men in authority may be more supportive of women and more confrontational of men (Weiner and Arnot, 1987). As a woman tutor I am aware that it is easy to get drawn into a maternal role in the tutorial relationship and to play either the nurturing, supportive mother or the angry, punishing mother (Berne, 1964). Tutors and practice teachers have what Phillipson (1992) refers to as 'role power': power by virtue of their role as assessor and mediator of learning. When role power comes together with class and 'race' power, as in the scenario of a white middle-class female tutor/practice teacher working with a black working-class male student, then a discussion of power must be central to the working relationship. The tutor or practice teacher should also look to find other ways of supporting the student, for example, through a self-help group or through individual consultancy or mentoring for the student.

One useful way of conceptualizing the relationship between women in positions of power and men in less powerful roles is that of 'critical engagement'. As feminist researchers interviewing violent men, Cavanagh and Lewis (1996) sought to build open communication with men, while at the same time not being seen to condone their behaviour or attitudes. Their solution was the idea of 'critical engagement': a way of questioning without alienating men, engaging with them 'with an open mind and a feminist perspective' (p. 185). Transferred to the social work education environment, critically engaging with men students is likely to take the form of listening to, and encouraging them to try out less conventionally 'masculine' ways of behaving. It will also mean confronting and challenging them in the classroom and tutorial group, particularly when men always ask the questions in the classroom, dominate small group discussion, or 'hide' behind tasks and actions in their work with service-users on placement. Men cannot, however, be the sole target of critical energies. Social work educators must also encourage women students to take on leadership roles within the student group, to value their opinions and beliefs and to try out different ways of behaving with each other, with men students and with service users. In sum, educators must be constantly on guard against gendered assumptions and look for opportunities to expand the repertoire of skills which are held by both women and men.

A way forward

There can be no neutral response to the issues raised in this chapter. By doing nothing we maintain the status quo with all its inequalities, its gender stereotyping and its potential destructiveness for women and men. It is vital that we take up the challenge to work positively with men (in all their diversities) in social work education. There are many productive ways to achieve this at the level of knowledge, skills and values, in individual and in group settings. The following themes must be central in this work.

Personal change is not enough

An examination of men and masculinities in social work education has to be about more than men finding their inner selves or discovering the 'wild man' within, as sections of the 'Men's Movement' might seem to advocate. There has to be a connection between personal change and feminism and the wider political struggle for gender equality and equality across other structures of oppression. The personal is (and must be) political, if change is going to have any impact. Segal (1990) puts this succinctly:

> Personal change is important. But beneath and beyond possibilities for personal change lies the whole web of interconnecting social, economic and political practices, public policies, welfare resources and understandings of sexuality which actually confer power upon men.
>
> (p. 294)

Making connections

Men and women who are seeking to work on sexuality and gender issues in social work education should make connections with each other, so that they do not become isolated and disheartened by the lack of institutional backing for their enterprise. This may mean men meeting other men, or men networking with women's groups. It may also mean making connections with others who are working on different areas of oppression, such as 'race' and ethnicity, age or disability.

Women must be involved

Cavanagh and Cree (1996) stress that it is not enough to encourage men to do this work themselves. This does not, of course, mean that it is solely women's responsibility to change men or that there is no place for men working together to discern their masculinities. But women's experience must stay firmly on the agenda, otherwise existing power imbalances may not be challenged or changed. Canaan and Griffin (1990) assert that feminists must continue to point out 'how men's analyses omit or distort certain key features of our experience with, and understanding of men and masculinity' (p. 207).

Men are not a homogeneous group

Although men may seem to occupy a position of advantage in society and hegemonic masculinity continues to exert power over institutions and individuals, not all men benefit equally from this. Gay men, black men, poor men, disabled men and older men continue to experience marginalization and discrimination in society. Moreover, while men (and women) are both targets and creators of discourses around sexuality, these discourses are themselves contradictory and changing.

Men who are students in social work education, while potentially dominant in terms of conventional expectations of gender role, are likely to share feelings of powerlessness with their women colleagues as they are subjected to scrutiny and assessment. They may have a commitment to professional caring that is non-traditional in terms of gender stereotypes. Men's greater visibility in social work education (caused by their smaller numbers), may bring them additional pressures, both positive and negative. The ambiguities and complexities that are fundamental to the experiences of men in social work offer the possibility of working towards a greater understanding of men and masculinities in social work education and a more enlightened social work practice.

Bibliography

Abramovitz, M. (1985) 'Status of women on faculty and status of women's studies in Israeli schools of social work', *Social Work Education*, 4(3), 3–6.

Acker, J. (1991). 'Hierarchies, jobs, bodies: a theory of gendered organisations', in J. Lorber and S. A. Farrell (eds), *The Social Construction of Gender*, London: Sage, pp. 162–79.

Adams, D. (1988) 'Treatment models of men who batter: a profeminist analysis', in Y. Kersti and B. Michele (eds), *Feminist Perspectives on Wife Abuse*, Newbury Park, Ca: Sage, pp. 176–99.

Adams, J. (1996) 'Lone fathers: still a problematic status?', *Practice*, 8 (1), 15–26.

Adams, R. (1996) *Social Work and Empowerment*, 2nd edn, Basingstoke: Macmillan, pp. 195–209.

Ahmad, B. (1990) *Black Perspectives in Social Work*, Birmingham: Venture Press.

Aisenberg, N. and Harrington, M. 91988) *Women of Academe. Outsiders in the Sacred Grove*, Cambridge, Mass: University of Massachusetts Press.

Aitken, L. and Griffin, G. (1996) *Gender Issues in Elder Abuse*, London: Sage.

Allen, J. and Gordon, S. (1990) 'Creating a framework for change', in R. Meth and R. Pasick (eds), *Men in Therapy*, New York: Guilford Press.

Annison, C. J. (1998) *Probing Probation: Issues of Gender and Organisation within the Probation Service*, Unpublished PhD thesis, University of Plymouth.

Arber, S. and Gilbert, N. (1989a) 'Men: the forgotten carers', *Sociology*, 23 (1), 111–8.

Arber, S. and Gilbert, N. (1989b) 'Transitions in caring: gender, life course and care of the elderly', in B. Bytheway, T. Keil, P. Allat and A. Bryman (eds), *Becoming and Being Old: Sociological Approaches to Later Life*, London: Sage.

Arber, S. and Ginn, J. (1995) 'Gender differences in informal caring', *Health and Social Care in the Community*, 3, 19–31.

Archer, J. (ed.) (1994) *Male Violence*, London: Routledge.

Armstrong, L. (1996) *Rocking the Cradle of Sexual Politics: What Happened When Women Said Incest*, London: The Women's Press.

Arnold, J. and Jordan, B. (1995). 'Beyond befriending or past caring?: Probation values, training and social justice', in B. Williams (ed.) *Probation Values*, Birmingham: Venture Press.

Arshad, R. (1996) 'Building fragile bridges: educating for change', in K. Cavanagh and V.E. Cree (eds), *Working with Men: Feminism and Social Work*, London: Routledge, pp. 147–69.

Askham, J. and Thompson C. (1990) *Dementia and Home Care: a Research Report on a Home Support Scheme for Dementia Sufferers*, Mitcham: Age Concern England.

Association of Chief Probation Officers, (ACOP) (1992/1996) *Position Statement on Domestic Violence*, London: ACOP.

Association of University Teachers (1991) *Pay at the Top of the University Ladder*, London: AUT.

Association of University Teachers (1994) *Long Hours, Little Thanks*, London: AUT.

Badgett, M. V. L. and King, M. C. (1997) 'Lesbian and gay occupational strategies', in A. Gluckman and B. Reed (eds), *Homo Economics: Capitalism, Community, and Lesbian & Gay Life*, New York: Routledge, pp. 73–86.

Bailey, S. and Cox, P. (1993) 'Teaching gender issues on social work courses', *Social Work Education*, 12 (1), 19–35.

Baker, A. (1992) *Naked at Gender Gap: a Man's View of the War Between the Sexes*, New York: Birch Lane Press.

Barham, P. and Hayward, R. (1995) *Relocating Madness*, London: Free Association Books.

Barker, R. W. (1994) *Lone Fathers and Masculinities*, Aldershot: Avebury.

Barnes, M. (1997) *Care, Communities and Citizens*, London: Longman.

Bauman, Z. (1991) *Modernity and Ambivalence*, Cambridge: Polity Press.

Bauman, Z. (1992) *Intimations of Postmodernity*, London: Routledge.

Bebbington, A. and Davies, B. (1993) 'Efficient targetting of community care: the case of the home help service', *Journal of Social Policy*, 22, 3, 373–91.

Beaumont, B. (1995) 'Managerialism and the Probation Service', in B. Williams (ed.), *Probation Values*, Birmingham: Venture Press.

Beck, U. (1992) *Risk Society: Towards a New Modernity*, Cambridge: Polity.

Benedict, M. I., Zuravin, S., Brandt, D. and Abbey, H. (1994) 'Types and frequency of child maltreatment by family foster care providers in an urban population', *Child Abuse and Neglect*, 18, 577–85.

Bensted, J. Wall, R. and Forbes, C. (1994) 'Cyberpunks, Ronnie Biggs and the culture of masculinity', *Probation Journal*, 41 (1), 18–22.

Berne, E. (1964) *Games People Play*, New York: Grove Press.

Berry, P. (1987) 'Life as a gay worker', *Community Care*, 25 June, vi–vii.

Beveridge, W. (1942a) *Social Insurance and Allied Services*, Cmnd.6404, London: HMSO.

Beveridge, W. (1942b) *Children's Allowances and the Race, Pillars of Security*, London: Allen and Unwin.

Black, J. et. al. (1983) *Social Work in Context*, London: Tavistock.

Bly, R. (1991) *Iron John: a Book About Men*, Shaftesbury: Element Books.

Bochel, D. (1976) *Probation and After-Care: Its Development in England and Wales*, Edinburgh: Scottish Academic Press.

Bolton, F.G., Morris, L.A. and MacEachron, A.E. (1989) *Males at Risk: the Other Side of Child Sexual Abuse'*, Newbury Park, Ca.: Sage.

Boswell, G. (1989) *Holding the Balance Between Court and Client*, Social Work Monograph, Norwich: University of East Anglia.

Bowker, L., Arbitell, M. and McFerron, J. R. (1988) 'On the relationship of wife beating and child abuse', in Y. Kersti and B. Michele (eds), *Feminist Perspectives on Wife Abuse*, Newbury Park, Ca.: Sage, pp. 158–74.

Bowl, R. (1985) *Changing the Nature of Masculinity: a Task for Social Work?*, Norwich: University of East Anglia BASW.

Bowl, R. (1986) 'Social work with old people' in C. Phillipson and A. Walker (eds), *Ageing and Social Policy: a Critical Assessment*, Aldershot: Gower.

Bowlby, J. (1951) *Maternal Care and Mental Health*, Geneva: World Health Organisation.

Boyle, R. and Curtis, K. (1994) *Breaking the Chain*, Edinburgh: Pilton Youth Programme.

Bradley, H. (1993) 'Across the great divide: the entry of men into "Women's Jobs"', in C.L. Williams (ed.), *'Women's Work', Men in Nontraditional Occupations*, Newbury Park, Ca.: Sage, pp. 10–27.

Brake, M. and Hale, C. (1992) *Public Order and Private Lives: the Politics of Law and Order*, London: Routledge.

Briere, J., Smiljanich, K. and Henschel, D (1994) 'Sexual fantasies, gender, and molestation history', *Child Abuse and Neglect*, 18, 131–7.

Briggs, A. (1961) 'The Welfare State in historical perspective', *Archives of European Sociology*, 11, 221–58.

Brittan, A. (1989) *Masculinity and Power*, Oxford: Blackwell.

Brittan, A. and Maynard, M. (1984) *Sexism, Racism and Oppression*, Oxford: Basil Blackwell.

Brod, H. (ed) (1987) *The Making of Masculinities*, London: Allen and Unwin.

Brook, E. and Davis, A. (1985) *Women, the Family and Social Work*, London: Tavistock.

Brown, C. (1981) 'Mothers, fathers and children: from private to public patriarchy', in L. Sargent (ed.), *Women and Revolution: the Unhappy Marriage of Marxism and Feminism*, New York: Maple, pp. 239–67.

Bryson, L. (1992) *Welfare and the State. Who Benefits?*, Basingstoke: Macmillan.

Buck, M. (1997) 'The price of poverty: mental health and gender', *Critical Social Policy*, 50, 17 (1), 79–97.

Buckley, K. (1992) 'Heterosexism, power and social policy', in Senior, P. and Woodhill, D. (eds), *Gender, Crime and Probation Practice*, Sheffield: Pavic.

Burnham, D., Boyle, J., Copsey, M., Cordery, J., Dominelli, L., Lambert, J., Smallridge, M., Whitehead, V. and Willis, S. (1990) 'Offending and masculinity: working with males', *Probation Journal*, 37(3), 106–11.

Busfield, J. (1996) *Men, Women and Madness: Understanding Gender and Mental Disorder*, Basingstoke: Macmillan.

Bush, T. and Hood-Williams, J. (1995) 'Domestic violence on a london housing estate', *Home Office Research and Statistics Department Research Bulletin*, 37, 11–18.

Bytheway, B. (1986) 'Making way: the disengagement of older workers' in C. Phillipson, M. Bernard and P. Strang (eds), *Dependency and Interdependency in Old Age: Theoretical Perspectives and Policy Alternatives*, London: Gower.

Caesar, P.L. and Hamberger, L.K. (eds) (1989) *Treating Men Who Batter*, New York: Springer.

Cameron, D. (1992) *Feminist and Linguistic Theory*, 2nd edn, Basingstoke: Macmillan.

Campbell, A. (1993) *Out of Control: Men, Women and Aggression*, London: Pandora.

Campbell, A. and Muncer, S. (1994) 'Men and the meaning of violence', in J. Archer (ed.), *Male Violence*, London: Routledge, pp. 332–51.

Campbell, B. (1993) *Goliath: Britain's Dangerous Places*, London: Methuen.

Campbell, B. (1995) 'Old fogeys and angry young men: a critique of communitarianism', *Soundings*, 1 pp. 47–64.

Campbell, B. (1997) 'Metaphorically speaking: communities in crisis', *Community Care*, 12–18 June, 20–1.

Canaan, J. E. and Griffin, C. (1990) 'The new men's studies: part of the problem or part of the solution?', in J. Hearn and D. Morgan (eds), *Men, Masculinities and Social Theory*, London: Unwin Hyman.

Carabine, J. (1998) 'New Horizons? New Rights? Postmodernising social policy and the case of sexuality', in J. Carter (ed.), *Postmodernity and the Fragmentation of Welfare*, London: Routledge, pp. 121–35.

Carrigan, T., Connell, B. and Lee, J. (1985) 'Toward a new sociology of masculinity', *Theory & Society*, 14 (5), 551–604.

Carter, P. (1993) 'The problem of men: a reply to Keith Pringle', *Critical Social Policy*, 38, 100–5.

Carter, P., Everitt, A. and Hudson, A. (1992) 'Malestream training?: women, feminism and social work education', in M. Langan and L. Day (eds), *Women, Oppression and Social Work: Issues in Anti-Discriminatory Practice*, London: Routledge, pp. 112–28.

Cavanagh, K. and Cree, V.E. (eds) (1996) *Working with Men: Feminism and Social Work*, London: Routledge

Cavanagh, K. and Lewis, R. (1996) 'Interviewing Violent Men', in K. Cavanagh and V. E. Cree (eds), *Working with Men. Feminism and Social Work*, London: Routledge, pp. 87–112.

Central Council for Education and Training in Social Work (CCETSW) (1989) *Requirements and Regulations for the Diploma in Social Work, Paper 30*, London: CCETSW.

Central Council for Education and Training in Social Work (CCETSW) (1995) *Assuring Quality in the Diploma in Social Work – 1, Rules and Requirements for the DipSW, Revised Paper 30*, London: CCETSW.

Chandler, T. (1993) 'Working with fathers in a family centre', *Working With Men*, 4, 11–13.

Chandler, T. and Dennison, M. (1995) 'Should men work with young children?,' in *The Abuse of Children in Day Care Setting*, Leicester: NSPCC Training.

Charlton, J. *et al* (1993) 'Suicide deaths in England and Wales', *Population Trends*, Spring, 71.

Christian, H. (1994) *The Making of Anti-sexist Men*, London: Routledge.

Christie, A. (1998a) 'Is social work a non-traditional occupation for men?', *British Journal of Social Work*, 28 (4), 491–510.

Christie, A. (1998b) 'A comparison of arguments for employing men as child care workers and social workers in Denmark and the UK', *Social Work in Europe*, 5 (1), 2–17.

Christie, A. (1998c) '"Balancing gender" as men social workers', *Irish Social Worker*, 16 (3), 4–6.

Chusmir, L. C. (1990) 'Men who make Non-traditional Career Choices', *Journal of Counseling and Development*, Sept./Oct., 69, 11–16.

Clarke, D. (1974) 'Homosexual encounter in all-male groups,' in J. H. Pleck and J. Sawyer (eds), *Men and Masculinity*, New Jersey: Prentice-Hall.

Clarke, J. (ed.) (1993) *A Crisis in Care?: Challenges to Social Work*, London: Sage.

Clarke, J. (1996) 'Public nightmares and communitarian dreams: the crisis of the social in social welfare', in S. Edgell, K. Hetherington and A. Warde (eds), *Consumption Matters*, Oxford: Blackwell, pp. 66–91.

Cliff, D. (1993) 'Health issues in early male retirement,' in S. Platt, H. Thomas, S. Scott and G. Williams (eds), *Locating Health: Sociological and Historical Explanations*, Aldershot: Avebury.

Cockburn, C. (1990) 'Men's power in organisations: "Equal Opportunities" intervenes', in J. Hearn and D. Morgan (eds), *Men, Masculinities and Social Theory*, London: Unwin Hyman.

Cohen, D. (1990) *Becoming a Man*, Routledge: London.

Cohen, D. (1996) 'It's a guy thing', *Guardian*, 4 May.

Cohen, S. (1985) 'Anti-semitism, immigration controls and the welfare state', *Critical Social Policy*, 13 (5), 73–92.

Collier, R. (1994) 'Child support, class subversion, crass scapegoating', *Achilles Heel*, 17 autumn, 18–21.

Collier, R. (1995) *Masculinity, Law and the Family*, London: Routledge.

Collinson, D. and Hearn, J. (1994) 'Naming men as men: implications for work, organisation and management', *Gender, Work and Organisations*, 1(1), 1–23.

Collinson, D. L. and Hearn, J. (eds) (1996) *Men as Managers, Managers as Men: Critical Perspectives on Men, Masculinities and Managements*, London: Sage

Connell, R. W. (1987) *Gender and Power: Society, the Person and Sexual Politics*, Oxford: Blackwell.

Connell, R. W. (1989) 'Cool guys, wimps and swots: the interplay of masculinity and education', *Oxford Review of Education*, 15 (3), 291–303.

Connell, R. W. (1995) *Masculinities*, Cambridge: Polity Press.

Cordery, J. and Whitehead, A. (1992) '"Boys don't cry"', in P. Senior and D. Woodhill (eds), *Gender, Crime and Probation Practice*, Sheffield: Sheffield City Polytechnic PAVIC Publication.

Cornwall, A. and Lindisfarne N. (eds) (1994) *Dislocating Masculinity: Comparative Ethnographies*, London: Routledge.

Coyle, A. (1991) 'The construction of gay identity', PhD thesis, University of Surrey.

Coyle, A. and Daniels, M. (1992) 'Psychological well-being and gay identity,' in D. Trent and C. Reed (eds), *Promotion of Mental Health*, vol. 2, Aldershot: Avebury.

Crawford, M. (1973) 'Retirement: a rite de passage', *Sociological Review*, 21, 447–61.

Cree, V. E. (1995) *From Public Streets to Private Lives. the Changing Task of Social Work*, Aldershot: Avebury.

Cree, V. E. (1996) 'Why do men care?,' in K. Cavanagh and V. E. Cree (eds), *Working With Men: Feminism and Social Work*, London: Routledge, pp. 64–86.

Cree, V. E. (1997) 'Surviving on the inside: reflections on being a woman and a feminist in a male academic institution', *Social Work Education*, 16 (3), 37–60.

Cree, V. E. (2000a) *Sociology for Social Workers and Probation Officers*, London: Routledge.

Cree, V. E. (2000b) 'The Challenge of Assessment', in V. E. Cree and C. Macaulay. (eds) *Transfer of Learning in Vocational and Professional Education*, London: Routledge.

Cree, V. and Cavanagh, K. (1996) 'Men, masculinism and social work', in K. Cavanagh and V. E. Cree (eds), *Working With Men: Feminism and Social Work*, London: Routledge, pp. 1–8.

Dale, J. (1986) 'Feminists and development of the welfare state: some lessons from our history', *Critical Social Policy*, 6 (1), 57–65.

Dankwort, J. (1992–93) 'Violence against women: varying perceptions and intervention practices with woman abusers', *Intervention* (Quebec), 92, 34–49.

D'Arcy, M. and Gosling, P. (1998) *Abuse of Trust: Frank Beck and the Leicestershire Children's Home Scandal*, London: Bowerdean.

Davidoff, L. and Hall, C. (1987) *Family Fortunes*, London: Hutchinson.

Davis, E., Kidd, L. and Pringle, K. (1987) *Child Sexual Abuse Training Programme for Foster Parents with Teenage Placements*, Barkingside: Barnardos.

Davies, M. (1985) *The Essential Social Worker*, Aldershot: Wildwood House

Dawson, G. (1994) *Soldier Heroes: British Adventure, Empire and the Imagining of Masculinities*, London: Routledge.

DeKeseredy, W. S. (1990) 'Male peer support and woman abuse: the current state of knowledge', *Sociological Focus*, 23 (6), 129–139.

Department of Health (1992) *Choosing with Care: The Report of the Committee of Inquiry into the Selection, Development and Management of Staff in Children's Homes (Warner Report)*, London: HMSO.

Department of Health (1996) *'Building Bridges': a Guide to Inter-agency Working*, London: HMSO.

Department of Health (1997) *White Paper on the Future of Social Services*, London: HMSO.

Department of Health (2000) *Lost in Care: Report of the Tribunal of Inquiry into the Abuse of Children in Care in the Former County Council Areas of Gwynedd and Clwyd since 1974 (Waterhouse Report)*, London: The Stationery Office.

Dodd, C. (1995) 'Should men work with children', *Nursery World*, 21 Sept.

Dobash, R. E. and Dobash, R. (1992) *Women, Violence and Social Change*, London: Routledge.

Dobash, R., Dobash, R., Cavanagh, K. and Lewis, R. (1996) *Research Evaluation of Programmes for Violent Men*, Edinburgh: The Scottish Office Central Research Unit.

Dominelli, L. (1988) *Anti-Racist Social Work*, Basingstoke: Macmillan.

Dominelli, L. and McLeod, E. (1989) *Feminist Social Work*, Basingstoke: Macmillan.

Driver, E. and Droisen, A. (eds) (1989) *Child Sexual Abuse: Feminist Perspectives*, Basingstoke: Macmillan.

Durkheim, E. (1951) *Suicide*, New York: The Free Press.

EC Network on Childcare (1993) *Men as Carers*, Brussels: European Commission.

EC Network on Childcare (1996) *A Review of Services for Young Children in the European Union 1990–1995*, Brussels: European Commission.

Edleson, J. L. (1990) 'Judging the success of interventions with men who batter,' in D. Besharov (ed.), *Family Violence: Research and Public Policy Issues*, Washington, DC: AEI Press.

Edleson, J. L. and Syers, M. (1990) 'The relative effectiveness of group treatment with men who batter', *Social Work Research and Abstracts*, 26, 10–17.

Edleson, J. L. and Tolman, R. (1992) *Intervention for Men Who Batter: an Ecological Approach,*. Newbury Park, Ca: Sage.

Edwards, J. (1998) 'Screening out men: or "has mum changed her washing powder recently?"', in J. Popay, J. Hearn and J. Edwards (eds), *Men, Gender Divisions and Welfare*, London: Routledge, pp. 259–86.

Edwards, S. S. M. (1989) '*Policy Domestic Violence*, London: Sage.

Edwards, T. (1994) *Erotics and Politics*, London: Routledge.

Eley, R. (1989) 'Women in management in social services departments,' in C. Hallett (ed.) *Women in Social Services Departments*, Brighton: Harvester Wheatsheaf.

Ellis, K. (1993) *Squaring the Circle:User and Carer Participation in Needs Assessment*, York; Joseph Rowntree Foundation.

Entwistle, N. (1987) 'A model of the teaching-learning process', in J. T. E. Richardson, M. W. Eysenck and D. W Piper (eds), *Student Learning*, Milton Keynes: The Society for Research into Higher Education, Open University Press.

Etherington, K. (1995) *Adult Male Survivors of Childhood Sexual Abuse*, London: Pitman Publishing.

Etzioni, A. (1993) *The Spirit of Community: Rights, Responsibilities, and the Communitarian Agenda*, New York: Crown.

Etzioni, A. (ed.) (1969) *The Semi-Professions and Their Organization*, London: Collier-Macmillan.

Etzioni, A. (1995) 'The responsive communitarian platform: rights and responsibilities', in A. Etzioni (ed.), *Rights and the Common Good: the Communitarian Perspective*, New York: St Martin's Press, pp. 11–23.

Fairclough, N. (1992) *Discourse and Social Change*, Cambridge: Polity.

Faludi, S. (1991) *Backlash: the Undeclared War Against Women*, London: Chatto and Windus.

Fanshell, D. (1990) *Foster Children in Life Course Perspective*, New York: Columbia University Press.

Farrell, W. (1991) 'We should embrace traditional masculinity,' in K. Thompson (ed.), *To Be a Man: in Search of the Deep Masculine*, Los Angeles: Jeremy Tarcher.

Farrell, W. (1993) *The Myth of Male Power*, New York: McGraw-Hill.

Fasteau, M. (1975) *The Male Machine*, New York: Dell.

Faulkner, D. (1995) 'Continuity and change in the Probation Service', *Vista*, 1 (1), 36–43.

Fawcett, B., Featherstone, B., Hearn, J. and Toft, C. (eds) (1996) *Violence and Gender Relations: Theories and Interventions*, London: Sage.

Ferguson, H., Gilligan, R. and Torode, R. (eds) (1993) *Surviving Childhood Adversity*, Dublin: Social Studies Press.

Fernando, S. (1991) *Mental Health, Race and Culture*, Basingstoke: Macmillan.

Ferris, D. (1977) *Homosexuality and the Social Services: the Report of an NCCL Survey of Local Authority Social Services Committees*, London: National Council for Civil Liberties.

Finch, J. and Groves, D. (eds) (1983) *A Labour of Love*, London: Routledge & Kegan Paul.

Finkelhor, D., Hotaling, G., Lewis, I. A., and Smith, C. (1990) 'Sexual abuse in a national survey of men and women,' in *Child Abuse and Neglect*, 14, 19–28.

Finkelhor, D., Williams, L. M. and Burns, N. (1998) *Nursery Crimes: Sexual Abuse in Day Care*, Newbury Park, CA: Sage Publications.

Finkelhor, D. (1986) *A Sourcebook on Child Sexual Abuse*, Los Angeles: Sage.

Finkelhor, D. (1991) 'The scope of the problem' in K. Murray and D.A. Gough (eds.) *Intervening in Child Sexual Abuse*, Edinburgh: Scottish Academic Press. pp. 9–17.

Fisher, D. (1994) 'Adult sex offenders' in T. Morrison, M. Erooga and R. C. Beckett (eds.) *Sexual Offending Against Children*, London: Routledge, pp. 1–24.

Fisher, M. (1994) 'Man-made care: community care and older male carers', *British Journal of Social Work*, 24 (6), 659–80.

Flax, J. (1990) 'Postmodernism and Gender Relations in Feminist Theory', in L. J. Nicholson (ed) *Feminism/Postmodernism*, London: Routledge.

Ford, A. (1985) *Men*, London: Weidenfeld & Nicolson.

Forster, J. (1996) 'Helping men to cope with marital breakdown' in K. Cavanagh and V. E. Cree *Working With Men*, London: Routledge.

Foucault, M. (1977) *Discipline and Punish: the Birth of the Prison (translated from the French by A. Sheridan)*, London: Allen Lane.

France, A. and Wiles, P. (1997) 'Dangerous futures: social exclusion and youth work in late modernity', *Social Policy and Administration*, 31 (5), pp. 59–78.

Franzway, S., Court, D. and Connell, R. W. (1989) *Stalking a Claim Feminism, Bureaucracy and the State*, Cambridge: Polity Press.

Fraser, E. and Lacey, N. (1993) *The Politics of Community: a Feminist Critique of the Liberal-Communitiarian Debate*, New York: Harvester Wheatsheaf.

Fraser, N. (1987) 'Women, welfare and the politics of needs interpretation', *Thesis Eleven*, 17 pp. 88–106.

Fraser, N. (1994) 'After the family wage: gender equality and the welfare state', *Political Theory*, 22 (4), pp. 591–618.

Freedland, J. (1997) 'Master race of the Left', *The Guardian*, 30 August 1–2.

Freeman, S. J. M. (1990) *Managing Lives: Corporate Women and Social Change*, Amherst: University of Massachusetts Press.

Freire, P. (1972) *Pedagogy of the Oppressed*, London: Penguin.

French, S. (1996) 'Silence of the lads', *The Guardian*, 17 April.

Futter, C. (1996) 'Needs-led assessment: the practitioner's perspective' in J. E. Phillips and B. Penhale (eds) *Reviewing Care Management for Older People*, London: Jessica Kingsley.

Gershick, T.J. and Miller, A.S. (1995) 'Coming to terms. Masculinity and physical disability in D. Sabo and D. F. Gordon (eds) *Men's Health and Illness*, Thousand Oaks, Ca: Sage.

Giddens, A. (1991) *Modernity and Self-Identity: Self and Society in the Late Modern Age*, Cambridge: Polity Press.

Giddens, A. (1994) *Beyond Left and Right: The Future of Radical Politics*, Cambridge: Polity.

Giddens, A. (1998) *The Third Way: the Renewal of Social Democracy*, Cambridge: Polity Press.

Giddens, A. (1999) *Reith Lecture Number Four: 'Family'*, *http://news.bbc.co.uk/hi/english/static/events/reith_99/week4/week4.htm*

Gillespie, T. and Lupton, C. (eds) (1995) *Working with Violence*, Basingstoke: Macmillan.

Gilroy, P. (1987) *There Ain't No Black in the Union Jack*, London: Hutchinson.

Goldberg, D. and Huxley, P. (1992) *Common Mental Disorders: a Bio-social Model*, London, Routledge.

Gondolf, E. (1984) *Batters Anonymous: Self-help Counselling for Men Who Batter Women*, San Bernardino, Ca.: BA Press.

Gondolf, E. (1985) *Men Who Batter: an Integrated Approach for Stopping Wife Abuse*, Holmes Beach, Fl: Learning Publications

Gondolf, E. (1989) 'Foreword' in P. L. Caesar and L. K. Hamberger (eds), *Treating Men Who Batter: Theory, Practice and Programmes*, New York: Springer, pp. ix–xiii.

Gondolf, E. (1993) 'Male batterers', in R. L. Weisberg (eds), *Family Violence: Prevention and Treatment*, Newbury Park, Ca.: Sage.

Gonsiorek, J. C. (1994) 'Assessment of and treatment planning and individual psychotherapy for sexually abused adolescent males', in J. C. Gonsiorek, W.H. Bera and D. Le Tourneau (eds), *Male Sexual Abuse: a Trilogy of Intervention Strategies*, Thousand Oaks, Ca.: Sage, pp. 1–110.

Gonsiorek, J. C., W. H. Bera and D. Le Tourneau (1994) *Male Sexual Abuse: a Trilogy of Intervention Strategies*, Thousand Oaks, Ca.: Sage.

Grant, J. (1993) *Fundamental Feminism: Contesting the Core Concepts of Feminist Theory*, London: Routledge.

Grant, L. (1998) 'Wedded to the children', *Guardian*, 7 April, p. 8.

Grimwood, C. and Popplestone, R. (1993) *Women, Management and Care*. London: Macmillan.

Grubman-Black, S. D. (1990) *Broken Boys/Mending Men: Recovery from Childhood Sexual Abuse*, Blue Ridge Summit, Pa.: Tab Books.

Gulbenkian Foundation Commission Report (1995) *Children and Violence*, London: Calouste Gulbenkian Foundation.

Hainsworth, G. (1996) 'Working with boys', in K. Cavanagh and V.E.Cree (eds), *Working With Men: Feminism and Social Work*, London: Routledge, pp. 170–80.

Hale, J. (1984) 'Feminism and social work practice' in B. Jordan and N. Parton (eds) *The Political Dimensions of Social Work*, Oxford: Blackwell.

Halford, S., Savage, M. and Witz, A. (1997) *Gender, Careers and Organisation*, Basingstoke: Macmillan.

Halsey, A.H. (1993) 'Introduction', in N. Dennis and G. Erdos (eds), *Familes Without Fatherhood*, London: IEA Health and Welfare Unit, pp. 1–6.

Hanmer, J. (1990) 'Men, power and the exploitation of women', in J. Hearn and D. Morgan (eds), *Men, Masculinities and Social Theory*, London: Unwin Hyman, pp. 21–42.

Hanmer, J. (1995) *Patterns of Agency Contacts with Women Who Have Experienced Violence from Known Men*, Bradford: Violence, Abuse and Gender Relations Research Unit, University of Bradford.

Hanmer, J. (1996) 'Women and violence: commonalities and diversities', in B. Fawcett, B. Featherstone, J. Hearn and C. Toft (eds), *Violence and Gender Relations: Theories and Interventions*, London: Sage, pp. 7–21

Hanmer, J. (1998) 'Out of control: men violence and family life' in J. Popay, J. Hearn, and J. Edwards, (eds), *Men, Gender Divisions and welfare*, London: Routledge, pp. 128–46

Hanmer, J. and Statham, D. (1988) *Women and Social Work: Towards a Woman-Centred Practice*, Basingstoke: Macmillan.

Hamner, J. and Statham, D. (1999) *Women and Social Work: Towards a Woman-Centre Practice*, 2nd edn, Basingstoke: Macmillan.

Hanmer, J., Hearn, J., Dillan, C., Kayani, T. and Todd, P. (1995) *Violence to Women from Known Women: Policy Development, Interagency Approaches and Good Practice*, Bradford: Violence, Abuse and Gender Relations Research Unit, University of Bradford.

Harder, M. and Pringle, K. (eds) (1997) *Protecting Children in Europe: Towards a New Millennium*, Aalborg: Aalborg University Press.

Harlow, E. (1996) 'Gender, violence and social work organizations', in B. Fawcett, B. Featherstone, J. Hearn and C. Toft (eds), *Violence and Gender Relations. Theories and interventions*, London: Sage, pp. 61–71.

Harlow, E., Hearn, J. and Parkin, W. (1995) 'Gendered noise: organisations and the silence and din of domination', in Itzin, C. and Newman, J. (eds), *Gender, Culture and Organizational Change. Putting Theory into Practice*, London: Routledge, pp. 89–105.

Haxby, D. (1978) *Probation: a Changing Service*, London: Constable.

Hazlehurst, M. (1994) 'Men's group in a mental health community', *Working with Men*, 4, 14–16.

Hearn, J. (1982) 'Notes on patriarchy, professionalisation and the semi-professions', *Sociology*, 16 (2), 184–202.

Hearn, J. (1987) *The Gender of Oppression: Men, Masculinity and the Critique of Marxism*, Brighton: Wheatsheaf Books.

Hearn, J. (1990) '"Child abuse" and men's violence', in Violence Against Children Study Group' (ed.), *Taking Child Abuse Seriously: Contemporary Issues in Child Protection Theory and Practice*, London: Unwin Hyman, pp. 63–85.

Hearn, J. (1992a) *Men in the Public Eye: the Construction and Deconstruction of Public Men and Public Patriarchies*, London: Routledge.

Hearn, J. (1992b) 'The personal, the political, the theoretical: the case of men's sexualities and sexual violences', in D. Porter (ed.), *Between Men and Feminism*, London: Routledge, pp. 161–81.

Hearn, J. (1995a) 'Changing men, changing managements: social change, social research and social action', in M. J. Davidson and R. Burke (eds), *Women in Management – Current Research Issues*, London: Paul Chapman, pp. 192–209.

Hearn, J. (1995b) *'It Just Happened': A Research and Policy Report on Men's Violence to Known Women*, Bradford: Violence, Abuse and Gender Relations Research Unit, University of Bradford.

Hearn, J. (1995c) *Patterns of Agency Contacts with Men who have been Violent to Known Women*, Bradford: Violence, Abuse and Gender Relations Research Unit, University of Bradford.

Hearn, J. (1995d) 'Policy implications for agency and interagency working with men' in J. Hanmer, J. Hearn, C. Dillon, T. Kayani and P. Todd (eds), *Violence to Women from Known Men: Policy Development, Interagency Approaches and Good Practice*, Bradford: Violence, Abuse and Gender Relations Research Unit, University of Bradford, pp. 18–23

Hearn, J. (1996a) 'Men's violence to known women: historical, everyday and theoretical constructions by men', in B. Fawcett, B. Featherstone, J. Hearn and C. Toft (eds), *Violence and Gender Relations: Theories and Interventions*, London: Sage, pp. 22–37.

Hearn, J. (1996b) 'Men's violence to known women: men's accounts and men's policy developments', in B. Fawcett, B. Featherstone, J. Hearn and C. Toft (eds), *Violence and Gender Relations: Theories and Interventions*, London: Sage, pp. 99–114.

Hearn, J. (1996c) 'Is masculinity dead?: a critique of the concept of masculinity/masculinities', in M. Mac an Ghaill (ed.), *Understanding Masculinities: Social Relations and Cultural Arenas*, Buckingham: Open University Press, pp. 202–17.

Hearn, J. (1996d) 'The organization(s) of violence: men, gender relations, organizations and violences', in B. Fawcett, B. Featherstone, J. Hearn and C. Toft (eds), *Violence and Gender Relations: Theories and Interventions*, London: Sage, pp. 39–60.

Hearn, J. (1996e) 'Men talking about violence: agency responses to violence', *Peace at Home*, Conference, Institute of Public Policy Research.

Hearn, J. (1998a) 'Men will be men: the ambiguity of men's support for men who have been violent to known women', in J. Popay, J. Hearn and J. Edwards (eds), *Men, Gender Divisions and Welfare*, London: Routledge, pp. 147–80.

Hearn, J. (1998b) *The Violences of Men*, London: Sage.

Hearn, J. (1998c) 'The welfare of men?', in J. Popay, J. Hearn and J. Edwards (eds), *Men, Gender Divisions and Welfare*, London: Routledge, pp. 11–36.

Hearn, J. (1999) 'It's time for men to change', in J. Wild (ed.), *Working with Men for Change*, London: Taylor & Francis, pp. 5–15.

Hearn, J. and Morgan, D. (eds) (1990) *Men, Masculinities and Social Theory*, London: Unwin Hyman.

Hearn, J. and Parkin, W. (1987) *'Sex' at 'Work': the Power and Paradox of Organisation Sexuality*, Brighton: Wheatsheaf; 2nd edn, Hemel Hemstead: Harvester Wheatsheaf (1995)

Helm, M., Pringle, K. and Taylor, R. (eds) (1993) *Surviving Sexual Abuse*, Barkingside: Barnardos.

Henwood, F. and Miles, I. (1987) 'The experience of unemployment and the sexual division of labour' in D. Fryer and P. Ullah (eds) *Unemployed People: Social and Psychological Perspectives*, Buckingham: Open University Press.

Henwood, M., Rimmer, L. and Wicks, M. (1987) *Inside the Family: Changing Roles of Men and Women*, London: Family Policy Studies Centre.

Hester, M., Kelly, L. and Radford, J. (eds) (1996) *Women, Violence and Male Power: Feminist Activism, Research and Practice*, Buckingham: Open University Press.

Hicks, S. (1996) 'The "last resort"? Lesbian and gay experiences of the social work assessment process in fostering and adoption', *Practice*, 8(2), 15–24.

Hicks, S. (1997) 'Taking the risk?: assessing lesbian and gay carers', in H. Kemshall and J. Pritchard (eds), *Good Practice in Risk Assessment and Risk Management 2: Protection, Rights and Responsibilities*, London: Jessica Kingsley, pp. 27–39.

Hill, M. (1993) *The Welfare State in Britain: a Political History since 1945*, Aldershot: Edward Elgar.

HMSO (1992) *Choosing With Care: the Report of the Committee of Inquiry into the Selection, Development, and Management of Staff in Children's Homes*, London: HMSO.

Hoch, P. (1979) *White Hero, Black Beast*, London: Pluto.

Hollingsbee, I. (1995) 'Elderly male carers for Alzheimer's demented spouses', *Inprint*, Avon and Gloucester College of Health, 3,1, 32–35.

Hollis, F. (1972) *Casework: a Psychosocial Therapy*, 2nd edn, New York: Random House.

Home Office (1962) *Report of the Departmental Committee on the Probation Service (The Morison Committee)*, Cmnd. 1650, London: HMSO.

Home Office (1966) *Trends and Regional Comparisons in Probation (England and Wales)*, London: HMSO.

Home Office (1984) *Probation Service in England and Wales: Statement of National Objectives and Priorities*, London.

Home Office (1991) *Criminal Justice Act*, ch. 53, London: HMSO.

Home Office (1993) *Criminal Justice Act*, ch. 36, London: HMSO.

Home Office (1994) *Review of Probation Officer Recruitment and Qualifying Training (The Dews Report)*, London.

Home Office (1995a) *National Standards for the Supervision of Offenders in the Community*, London.

Home Office (1995b) *The Probation Service: Three Year Plan for the Probation Service (1996–1999)* London.

Home Office (1997) *Crime (Sentences) Act*, London: HMSO..

Home Office (1998a) *Strategies for Effective Offender Supervision (Report of the HMIP What Works Project)*, London.

Home Office (1998b) *Evidence Based Practice: a Guide to Effective Practice*, London.

Hood, J. C. (1986) 'The provider role: its meaning and measurement', *Journal of Marriage and the Family*, 48, 349–59.

Hood, J. C. (ed.) (1993) *Men, Work and Family*, Newbury Park, Ca.: Sage.

Horn, W. F. and Bush, A. (1997) 'Fathers and welfare reform', *The Public Interest*, 129 Autumn, 38–49.

Howe, D. (1986) 'The segregation of women and their work in the personal social services', *Critical Social Policy*, 15, 21–36.

Howe, D. (1987) *An Introduction to Social Work Theory*, London: Wildwood House.

Howe, D. (1994) 'Modernity, postmodernity and social work', *British Journal of Social Work*, 24 (5), 513–32.

Hudson, A. (1985) 'Feminism and social work. resistance or dialogue?, *British Journal of Social Work*, 15, 635–55.

Hudson, A. (1988) 'Boys will be boys: masculinism and the juvenile justice system', *Critical Social Policy*, 21, 30–48.

Hudson, A. (1989) 'Changing perspectives: feminism, gender and social work' in M. Langan and P. Lee (eds), *Radical Social Work Today*, London: Unwin Hyman, pp. 70–96.

Hudson, B. (1993) *Penal Policy and Social Justice*, Basingstoke: Macmillan.

Hughes, B. (1995) *Older People and Community Care: Critical Theory and Practice*, Buckingham: Open University Press.

Hugman, Richard (1991) *Power in Caring Professions*, Basingstoke: Macmillan.

Hunt, P. (1994) *Report of the Independent Inquiry into Multiple Abuse in Nursery Classes in Newcastle upon Tyne*, Newcastle upon Tyne: City Council of Newcastle upon Tyne.

Hunter, M. (1990) *Abused Boys: the Neglected Victims of Sexual Abuse* New York: Fawcett Columbine.

Irving, K. (1996) 'Unwanted attention: the risks of using publicity in adoption and fostering', *Child Abuse Review*, 5(5), 356–61.

Jacobs, J. A. (1993) 'Men in female-dominated fields: trends and turnover,' in C. L. Williams (ed.), *Doing 'Women's Work', Men in Nontraditional Occupations*, Newbury Park, Ca.: Sage, pp. 49–63.

Jacobs, S. (1985) 'Race, empire and the welfare state: council housing and racism', *Critical Social Policy*, 13 (5), 6–28.

James, A. and Raine, J. (1998) *The New Politics of Criminal Justice*, London: Longman.

Jarvis, F. V. (1972) *Advise, Assist and Befriend: a History of the Probation and After-Care Service*, London: NAPO.

Jeffreys, S. (1990) *Anticlimax: a Feminist Perspective on the Sexual Revolution*, London: The Women's Press

Jensen, J. J. (1996) *Men as Workers in Child Care Services*, Brussels: European Commission.

Johnson, Sally (1997) 'Theorizing language and masculinity: a feminist perspective,' in S. Johnson and U. H. Meinhof (eds), *Language and Masculinity*, Oxford: Blackwell.

Johnson, T. (1972), *Professions and Power*, Basingstoke: Macmillan.

Jourard, S. M. (1974) 'Some lethal aspects of the male role,' in J. H. Pleck and J. Sawyer (eds) *Men and Masculinity*, New Jersey: Prentice-Hall.

Kadushin, A. (1976) 'Men in a woman's profession', *Social Work*, 21 (6), 440–7.

Kay, F. M. and Hagan, J. (1995) 'The persistent glass ceiling: gendered inequalities in the earnings of lawyers', *British Journal of Sociology*, 46, 2, 279–310.

Kay, L. W. and Applegate, J. S. (1995) 'Men's style of nurturing elders' in D. Sabo and D. F. Gordon (eds), *Men's Health and Illness*, Thousand Oaks, Ca.: Sage, pp. 205–21.

Kearney, P. and Le Riche, P. (1993) 'Looking at the ordinary in a new way: the applications of feminist thinking to a post-qualifying social work course', *Social Work Education*, 12 (2), 19–28.

Kelly, L. (1988) *Surviving Sexual Violence*, Cambridge: Polity Press.

Kelly, L. (1991) 'Unspeakable acts: women who abuse', *Trouble and Strife*, 21, 13–20.

Kelly, L. (1996) 'When does the speaking profit us?: reflections on the challenges of developing feminist perspectives on abuse and violence by women', in M. Hester, L. Kelly, J. Radford (eds), *Women, Violence and Male Power: Feminist Activism, Research and Practice*, Buckingham: Open University Press, pp. 34–49.

Kelly, L., Regan, L. and Burton, S. (1991) *An Exploratory Study of the Prevalence of Sexual Abuse in a Sample of 16–21 Year Olds*, London: Polytechnic of North London.

Kempe, R. and Kempe, C. (1984) The Common Secret: Sexual Abuse of Children and Adolescents, New York: Freeman.

Kidd, L. and Pringle, K. (1988) 'The politics of child sexual abuse', *Social Work Today*, 20(3), 14–15.

Kimmel, M. (1990) 'After fifteen years: the impact of the sociology of masculinity on the masculinity of sociology', in J. Hearn. and D. Morgan
(eds), *Men, Masculinities and Social Theory*, London: Unwin Hyman,
pp. 93–109.

Kimmel, M. (1996) *Manhood in America: a Cultural History*, London: Free
Press.

King, J. (ed) (1969) *The Probation and After-Care Service*, 3rd edn, London:
Butterworth.

Kitzinger, C. and Perkins, R. (1993) *Changing Our Minds: Lesbian Feminism
and Psychology*, London: Onlywomen Press.

Kitzinger, C. and Perkins, R. (1996) 'Shrinking lesbian feminism: the dangers
of psychology for lesbian-feminist politics', in L. Harne and E. Miller (eds),
All The Rage: Reasserting Radical Lesbian Feminism, London: The Women's
Press, pp. 31–51.

La Valle, I. and Lyons, K. (1993) 'Gender differences in social workers' career
paths', *Women's Link*, 3, 2.

Leonard, P. (1997) *Postmodern Welfare: Reconstructing an Emancipatory
Project*, London: Sage.

Leonard, P. and McLeod, E. (1980) *Marital Violence: Social Construction and
Social Service Response*, Coventry: University of Warwick.

Levin, E., Sinclair, I. and Gorbach, P. (1988) *Families, Services and Confusion
in Old Age*, Aldershot: Gower.

Lew, M. (1988) *Victims No Longer: Men Recovering from Incest and Other Sexual
Child Abuse*, New York: Harper & Row.

Lewis, C. (1985) *On Becoming a Father*, Buckingham: Open University Press.

Lewis, C. and O'Brien, M. (eds.) (1987) *Reassessing Fatherhood: New
Observations on Fathers and the Modern Family*, London: Sage.

Lewis, G. (1997) 'Welfare settlements and racialising practices', *Soundings*,
(4), 109–19.

Lewis, J. (1992) 'Gender and the development of welfare regimes', *Journal of
European Social Policy*, 2 (3), 159–73.

Lewis, J. and Glennerster, H. (1996) *Implementing the New Community Care*,
Buckingham: Open University Press.

Liddle, A. M. (1993) 'Gender, desire and child sexual abuse: accounting for
the male majority', *Theory, Culture and Society*, 10, 103–26.

Liddle, A. M. (1996) 'State, masculinities and law', *British Journal of
Criminology*, 36 (3), 361–80.

Lloyd, S. and Degenhardt, D. (1996) 'Challenges in working with male social
work students,' in K. Cavanagh and V. E. Cree (eds) *Working with Men.
Feminism and Social Work*, London: Routledge, pp. 45–63.

Lloyd, T. (1990) 'Cornerstones of boys' work', *Working with Men*, 10, Oct.

Lyndon, N. (1992) *No More Sex War: the Failures of Feminism*, London:
Sinclair-Stevenson.

Lyons, K., La Valle, I. and Grimwood, C. (1995) 'Career patterns of qualified
social workers: discussion of a recent survey', *British Journal of Social
Work*, 25 (2), 173–90.

Lyotard, J. (1984) *The Post-modern Condition: a Report on Knowledge,*(transla-
tion from the French by G. Bennington and B. Massumi), Manchester:
Manchester University Press.

Mac an Ghaill, M. (ed.) (1996) *Understanding Masculinities*, Buckingham: Open University Press.

MacAskill, E. and White, M. (1997) 'The fight for the family', *Guardian*, 3 Apr. 1.

MacDonald, K. M. (1995) *The Sociology of the Professions*, London: Sage

MacDonald, R. (1996) 'Labours of love: voluntary working in a depressed local economy,' *Journal of Social Policy*, 25 (1), 19–38.

MacInnes, J. (1998) *The End of Masculinity*, Buckingham: Open University Press.

MacKinnon, C. (1983) 'Feminism, marxism, method, and the state: towards a feminist jurisprudence', in S. Harding (ed.), *Feminism and Methodology*, Buckingham: Open University Press, pp. 135–56.

MacKinnon, C. A. (1989) *Toward a Feminist Theory of the State*, London: Harvard University Press.

MacNair, I. and McQuillan, T. (1999) *Recruitment and Selection of Trainee Probation Officers. Monitoring Data – Preliminary Comparative Analysis*, Birmingham: Midlands Training and Assessment Consortium.

Mackie, M. (1987) *Constructing Women and Men. Gender Socialisation*, New York: Holt, Rinehart & Winston.

Maddock, S. and Parkin, D. (1994) 'Gender cultures: how they affect men and women at work', in Davidson, M. J. and Burke, R. J. (eds), *Women in Management. Current Research Issues*, London: Paul Chapman, pp. 29–40.

Mair, G. (1996) 'Developments in probation in england and wales, 1984–1993', in McIvor, G. (ed.), *Working with Offenders*, London: Jessica Kingsley.

Mair, G. (ed.) (1997) *Evaluating the Effectiveness of Community Penalties*, Aldershot: Avebury.

Mama, A. (1989) *The Hidden Struggle: Statutory and Voluntary Sector Responses to Violence Against Black Women in the Home*, London: The London Race and Housing Research Unit.

Mangan, J. and Walvin, J. (1987) *Manliness and Morality: Middle Class Masculinity in Britain and America, 1800–1940*, Manchester: Manchester University Press.

Marsh, C. and Arber, S. (eds) (1992) *Families and Households*, Basingstoke: Macmillan.

Marsh, P. (1987) 'Social work and fathers', in C.Lewis and M.O'Brien (eds), *Reassessing Fatherhood: New Observations on Fathers and the Modern Family*, London: Sage, pp. 183–96.

Marsiglio, W. (1995) *Fatherhood: Contemporary Theory, Research, and Social Policy*, Thousand Oaks, Ca.: Sage.

Martin, S. E. (1988) 'Think like a man, work like a dog, act like a lady: Occupational dilemmas of policewomen,' in A. Statham, E. M. Miller and H. O. Mauksch (eds), in *The Worth of Women's Work: a Qualitative Synthesis*, Albany: State University of New York Press.

Martinson, R. (1974) 'What works?: questions and answers about prison reform', *The Public Interest*, No. 35, Spring, 22.

Marshall, J. (1995) *Woman Managers: Moving On: Exploring Career and Life Choices*, London: Routledge.

Masson, J. (1988) *Against Therapy*, London: Collins-Fontana

Mattinson, J. (1988) *Work, Love and Marriage: the Impact of Unemployment*, London: Duckworth.

May, T. (1991) *Probation: Politics, Policy and Practice*, Buckingham: Open University Press.

May, T. (1994) 'Probation and community sanctions', in Maguire, M., Morgan, R. and Reiner, R. (eds) *The Oxford Handbook of Criminology*, 1st edn, Oxford: Clarendon Press.

May, T. and Annison. J. (1998) 'The de-professionalisation of Probation Officers', in Abbot, P. and Meerabau, L. (eds) *The Sociology of the Caring Professions*, 2nd edn, London: Taylor & Francis.

May, T. and Vass, A. A. (eds.) (1996) *Working with Offenders: Issues, Contexts and Outcomes*, London: Sage.

Maynard, M. (1985) 'The response of social workers to domestic violence,' in J.Pahl (ed.), *Private Violence and Public Policy*, London: Routledge & Kegan Paul, pp. 125–41.

McColl, A. (1991a) 'Violent men on probation', *Working with Men*, Feb. 10–1.

McColl, A. (1991b) 'Working with violent male offenders', *Working with Men*, Sept. 4–5.

McFadden, E. J. (1984) *Preventing Abuse in Foster Care*, Michigan: Eastern Michigan University.

McFadden, E. J. and Ryan, P. (1991) 'Maltreatment in family foster homes: dynamics and dimensions', *Child and Youth Services*, 15, 209–31.

McGill, M. E. (1985) *The Report on Male Intimacy*, New York: Harper and Row.

McGuire, J. (ed.) (1995) *What Works: Reducing Re-offending*. Chichester: John Wiley & Sons.

McIvor, G. (ed.) (1996) *Working with Offenders*, London: Jessica Kingsley.

McMullen, R. J. U. (1990) *Male Rape*, London: Gay Men's Press.

McNeil, M. (1991) 'Making and not making the difference: the gender politics of Thatcherism', in S. Franklin, C. Lury and J. Stacey (eds), *Off-Centre: Feminism and Cultural Studies*, London: Harper Collins, pp. 221–40.

McWilliams, M. and McKiernan, J. (1993) *Bringing It Out in the Open: Domestic Violence in Northern Ireland*, Belfast: HMSO.

Mendel, M. P. (1995) *The Male Survivor: the Impact of Sexual Abuse*, Thousand Oaks, Ca.: Sage.

Meth, R. and Pasick, R. (eds) (1990) *Men in Therapy*, New York: Guildford Press.

Miles, A. (1987) *The Mentally Ill in Contemporary Society*, Oxford: Blackwell.

Millar, J. (1996) 'Women, poverty and social security', in C. Hallett (ed.), *Women and Social Policy: an Introduction*, London: Prentice-Hall/Harvester Wheatsheaf, pp. 52–64.

Mills, A. J. (1989) 'Gender, sexuality and organization theory', in J. Hearn, D. L. Sheppard, P. Tancred-Sheriff and G. Burrell (eds) *The Sexuality of Organization*, London: Sage.

Milner, J. (1992) 'Avoiding violent men: the gendered nature of child protection policy and practice', in H. Ferguson, R. Gilligan and R. Torode (eds), *Surviving Childhood Adversity*, Dublin: Social Studies Press, Trinity College Dublin, pp. 179–89.

Milner, J. (1993) 'A disappearing act: the differing career paths of fathers and mothers in child protection investigations', *Critical Social Policy*, 38, 13, 48–63.

Milner, J. (1996) 'Men's resistance to social workers', in B. Fawcett, B. Featherstone, J. Hearn and C. Toft (eds), *Violence and Gender Relations. Theories and Interventions*, London: Sage, pp. 115–29.

Mirrlees-Black, C. (1994) *Estimating the Extent of Domestic Violence: Findings from the 1992 BCS*, Home Office Research Bulletin No. 37, London: Home Office Research and Statistics Department.

Mitchell, R and Hodson, C. (1983) 'Coping with domestic violence: social support and psychological health among women', *American Journal of Community Psychology* 11 (6), pp. 629–54.

Monette, P. (1992) *Becoming a Man: Half a Life Story*, New York: Abacus Books.

Mooney, J. (1993) *The Hidden Figure: Domestic Violence in North London*, London: Islington Council.

Mooney, J. (1994) *The Prevalence and Social Distribution of Domestic Violence: an Analysis of Theory and Method*, unpublished PhD, Middlesex University.

Moore, S. (1996) 'Men behaving sadly', *Guardian*, 25 April.

Morgan, D. H. J (1992) *Discovering Men*, London: Routledge.

Motenko, A. (1989) 'The frustrations, gratifications and well-being of dementia care-givers,' *The Gerontologist*, 29, 157–65.

Mullender, A. (1997) *Rethinking Domestic Violence: the Social Work and Probation Response*, London: Routledge.

Mullender, A. and Morley, R. (eds) (1994) *Children Living with Domestic Violence*, London: Whiting & Birch.

Murray, C. (1990) *The Emerging British Underclass*, London: IEA Health and Welfare Unit.

Murray, C. (1994) *Losing Ground: American Social Policy, 1950–1980*, New York: Basic Books.

Naffine, N. (1987) *Female Crime*, London: Allen & Unwin.

NAPO News, Sept. 1999, Issue 112, p. 1.

Nellis, M. (1995) 'Probation Values for the 1990s', *Howard Journal*, 34 (1), 19–43.

Nellis, M. (1999) 'Towards "the Field of Corrections": Modernising the Probation Service in the Late 1990s', *Social Policy and Administration*, 33 (3), 302–23.

Newburn, T. and Mair, G. (eds) (1996) *Working with Men*, London: Russell House Press.

Newman, J. (1995) 'Making connections: frameworks for change', in Itzin, C. and Newman, J. (eds) *Gender, Culture and Organizational Change. Putting Theory into Practice*, London: Routledge, pp. 273–86.

Nielsen, T. (1983) 'Sexual abuse of boys: current perspectives', in Personnel and Guidance Journal, 62, cited in Bolton *et al.* (1989).

Oakley, A. and Rigby, A. S. (1998) 'Are men good for the welfare of women and children?', in J. Popay, J. Hearn and J. Edwards (eds), *Men, Gender Divisions and Welfare*, London: Routledge, pp. 101–27.

O'Brien, M. and Penna, S. (1998) *Theorising Welfare: Enlightenment and Modern Society*, London: Sage.

O'Hagan, K. (1997) 'The problem of engaging men in child protection work', *British Journal of Social Work*, 27 (1), 25–42.

O'Hagan, K. and Dillenburger, K. (1995) *The Abuse of Women within Child Care Work*, Buckingham: Open University Press.

Owen, C., Campron, C. and Moss, P. (eds) (1998)) *Men as Workers in Slovicks for Young Children: Issues of a Mixed Workforce Gender*, London: Institute of Education.

Pahl, J. (1985) *Private Violence and Public Policy*, London: Routledge & Kegan Paul.

Pain, R. H. (1995) 'Elderly women and fear of violent crime: the least likely victims?: a reconsideration of the extent and nature of risk', *British Journal of Criminology*, 35 (4), 584–98.

Parker, G. (1990) *With Due Care and Attention: a Review*, London: Family Policy Studies Centre.

Parker, G. (1993) *With This Body: Caring and Disability in Marriage*, Buckingham: Open University Press

Parker, G. and Seymour, J. (1998) 'Male carers in marriage: re-examining the feminist analysis of informal care', in J. Popay, J. Hearn and J. Edwards (eds), *Men, Gender Divisions and Welfare*, London: Routledge, pp. 181–95.

Parker, R. (1981) 'Tending and social policy,' in E. M. Goldberg and S. Hatch (eds), *A New Look at the Personal Social Services*, London: Policy Studies Institute.

Parkin, D. and Maddock, S. (1995) 'A gender typology of organizational culture', in Itzin C. and Newman J. (eds) *Gender, Culture and Organizational Change. Putting Theory into Practice*, London: Routledge.

Parton, N. (1996) 'Social theory, social change and social work: an introduction', in N. Parton (ed.), *Social Theory, Social Change and Social Work*, London: Routledge, pp. 4–18.

Pascall, G. (1997a) *Social Policy: a New Feminist Analysis*, London: Routledge.

Pascall, G. (1997b) 'Women and the family in the British welfare state: the Thatcher/Major legacy', *Social Policy and Administration*, 31 (3), 290–305.

Pasick, R., Gordon, S. and Meth, R. L. (1990) 'Helping men to understand themselves,' in R. Meth and R. Pasick (eds), *Men in Therapy*, New York: Guilford Press.

Pease, B. (1999) 'Deconstructing masculinity – reconstructing men', in B. Pease and J. Fook (eds) *Transforming Social Work Practice*, London: Routledge.

Pease, B. (2000) 'Researching profeminist men's narratives. Participatory methodologies in a postmodern frame', in B. Fawcett, B. Featherstone, J. Fook and A. Rossiter (eds) *Practice and Researh in Social Work. Postmodern Feminist Perspectives*, London: Routledge.

Pence, E. and Paymar, M. (1990) *Power and Control: Tactics of Men Who Batter: an Educational Curriculum*, Duluth, Mn.: Minnesota Program Development.

Penfold, P. and Walker, G. (1984) *Women and the Psychiatric Paradox*, Buckingham: Open University Press.

Penna, S. and O'Brien, M. (1996) 'Postmodernism and social policy: a small step forwards?' *Journal of Social Policy*, 25 (1), pp. 39–61.

Petch, A. (1996) 'New concepts, old responses: assessment and care management pilot projects in Scotland', in J. E. Phillips and B. Penhale (eds), *Reviewing Care Management for Older People*, London: Jessica Kingsley.

Philp, M. (1979) 'Notes on the form of knowledge in social work', *Sociological Review*, 27 (1), 83–111.

Phillips, A. (1993) *The Trouble with Boys*, London: Pandora.

Phillipson, C. (1978) *The Experience of Retirement: a Sociological Analysis*, PhD thesis, Durham University.

Phillipson, J. (1992) *Practising Equality. Women, Men and Social Work*, London: CCETSW.

Pirog-Good, M. A. and Stets-Kealey, J. (1985) 'Male batterers and battering prevention programs: a national survey', *Response*, 8, 8–12.

Pollard, P. (1994) 'Sexual violence against women,' in J. Archer (ed.), *Male Violence*, London: Routledge, pp. 170–94.

Potts, D. (1996) *Why Do Men Commit Most Crime?: Focusing on Masculinity in a Prison Group*, Wakefield: West Yorkshire Probation Services/HM Prison Service.

Pringle, K (1990) *Managing to Survive*, Barkingside: Barnardos.

Pringle, K. (1992) 'Child sexual abuse perpetrated by welfare personnel and the problem of men', *Critical Social Policy*, 36, 4–19.

Pringle, K. (1993) 'Gender issues in child sexual abuse committed by foster carers: a case study for the welfare services?,' in H. Ferguson, R. Gilligan and R. Torode (eds), *Surviving Childhood Adversity*, Dublin: Social Studies Press, pp. 245–256.

Pringle, K. (1994) 'The problem of men revisited', *Working with Men*, 2, 5–8.

Pringle, K. (1995) *Men, Masculinities and Social Welfare*, London: UCL Press.

Pringle, K. (1996) 'Protecting children against sexual abuse: a third way?,' paper presented at conference on 'Human services in crisis: national and international issues', Fitzwilliam College, University of Cambridge, September.

Pringle, K. (1997) *Children and Social Welfare in Europe*, Buckingham: Open University Press.

Pringle, K. (1998) 'Men and child care,' in J. Edwards, J. Hearn and J. Popay (eds), *Men, Gender Divisions and Welfare*, London: Routledge, pp. 312–36.

Pringle, R. (1989) *Secretaries Talk. Sexuality, Power and Work*, London: Verso.

Queer Press Collective (eds) (1991) *Loving in Fear: an Anthology of Lesbian and Gay Survivors of Childhood Sexual Abuse*, Toronto, Ontario: Queer Press.

Rattansi, A. (1994) 'Western racisms, ethnicities and identities in the 'postmodern' frame', in A. Rattansi and S. Westwood (eds), *Racism, Modernity and Identity*, Cambridge: Polity Press, pp. 15–86.

Raynor, P. (1984) 'National purpose and objectives: a comment', *Probation Journal*, 31 (2), 43–7.

Raynor, P., Roberts, S., Thomas, L. and Vanstone, M. (1994) 'The experience of Confirmation', *Probation Journal*, 41 (4), 193–7.

Reason, P. and Hawkins, P. (1988) 'Storytelling as inquiry', in P. Reason, (ed.), *Human Inquiry in Action*, London: Sage.

Reich, W. (1948) 'Character Analysis', New York: Orgone Press.

Riley, D. (1983) *War in the Nurseries: Theories of the Child and Mother*, London: Virago.

Ritchie J. *et al.* (1994) *The Report of the Inquiry into the Care and Treatment of Christopher Clunis*, London: HMSO.

Roach Anleu, S. L. (1992). 'The professionalisation of social work? A case study of three organisational settings'. *Sociology*, Vol. 26, No. 1, pp. 23–43.

Roberts, J. (1998) 'Fathering trust', *Community Care*, (1217), 16–17.

Roberts, K. (1995) *Youth and Employment in Modern Britain*, Oxford: Oxford University Press

Rosenthal, J. A., Motz, J. K., Edmonson, D. A. and Groze, V. (1991) 'A descriptive study of abuse and neglect in out-of-home placement', *Child Abuse and Neglect*, 15, pp. 249–60.

Rosenwasser, S. M. and Patterson, W. (1984–85) 'Nontraditional Male: Men with Primary Childcare/Household Responsibilities', *Psychology and Human Development*, I (2), pp. 101–11.

Royal College of Psychiatrists (1996) *Defeat Depression Campaign, Depression in Men Factsheet*, 16 Jan., London: Royal College of Psychiatrists.

Rubin, L. B. (1983) *Intimate Strangers: What Goes on in Relationships Today, and Why*, New York: Harper and Row.

Russell, G. (1983) *The Changing Role of Fathers* Buckingham: Open University Press.

Rutter, M. (1972) *Maternal Deprivation Reassessed*, London: Penguin Books.

Ruxton, S. (1992) '*What's **He** Doing at the Family? The Dilemmas of Men Who Care for Children*, London: National Children's Home.

Ruxton, S. (1993) 'Caution! Men at work', *Community Care*, Feb. 11, 20–2.

Ruxton, S. (1994) 'Men – too dangerous to work with children?', *Working with Men*, 1, 16–20.

Ryan, T. and Walker, R. (1985) *Making Life Story Books*, London: British Agencies for Adoption & Fostering.

Salisbury J. and Jackson, D. (1996) *Challenging Macho Values*, London: Falmer Press.

Salter, A. C. (1988) *Treatment of Sexual Offenders and Their Victims*, Los Angeles: Sage.

Saunders, D. G. (1989) 'Cognitive and behavioural interventions with men who batter: application and outcome,' in P. L. Caesar and L. K. Hamberger (eds), *Treating Men Who Batter: Theory, Practice and Programs*, New York: Springer, pp. 77–100.

Scher, M., Stevens, M., Good, G., and Eichenfield, G.A. (1987) *Handbook of Counseling and Psychotherapy with Men*, California: Sage.

Segal, L. (1990) *Slow Motion: Changing Masculinities, Changing Men*, London: Virago Press.

Seidler, V. (ed.) (1991) *The Achilles Heel Reader*, London: Routledge.

Seidler, V. J. (1990) 'Men, feminism and power' in J. Hearn and D. Morgan (eds) *Men, Masculinities and Social Theory*, London: Unwin Hyman.

Seidler, V. J. (1994) *Unreasonable Men: Masculinity and Social Theory*, London: Routledge.

Shaiko, R. G (1996) 'Female participation in public interest non-profit governance: yet another glass ceiling?', *Nonprofit and Voluntary Sector Quarterly*, 25 (3), 302–20.

Skeggs, B. (1993) 'Theorizing masculinity', *Jyväslaylän Yuopisto – Nykykulttuurin Tutkimusyksikkö*, 39, 13–36.

Skelton, C. (1993) 'Women and education,' in D. Richardson, and V. Robinson, (eds), *Introducing Women's Studies*, Basingstoke: Macmillan.

Smith, D. (1996) 'Social Work and Penal Policy', in McIvor, G. (ed.) (1996) *Working with Offenders*, London: Jessica Kingsley.

Smith, L. (1989) *Domestic Violence: an Overview of the Literature*, Home Office Research Study 107, London: HMSO.

Smyth, M. (1996) *Qualified Social Workers and Probation Officers*, London: HMSO.

Sone, K. (1993) 'Coming out at work', *Community Care*, no. 987, 7 Oct. 28–19.

Sone, K. (1994) 'Hurt minds', *Community Care*, 17 Mar.

Spector, M. (1972) 'Legitimating homosexuality', *Society*, 14, 52–6.

Spender, D. (1981) *Men's Studies Modified*, Oxford: Pergamon Press.

Stanley, L. (1984) 'How the social science research process discriminates against women' in S. Acker and D. W. Piper (eds) *Is Higher Education Fair to Women?*, Guildford: SRHE and NFER–Nelson.

Stanley, L. and Wise, S. (1993) *Breaking Out Again: Feminist Ontology and Epistemology*, London: Routledge.

Statham, R. (1992) 'Towards managing the Probation Service', in R. Statham and P. Whitehead (eds) (1992), *Managing the Probation Service. Issues for the 1990s*, Harlow: Longman.

Stenson, K. (1991) 'Making sense of crime control', in K. Stenson and D. Cowell (eds) *The Politics of Crime Control*, London: Sage.

Stoltenburg, J. (1990) *Refusing to be a Man*, London: Fontana.

Stone, K. (1993) 'Coming out at work', *Community Care*, No. 987, 7 October, pp. 18–19.

Stone, K. (1994) 'Hurt minds', *Community Care*, 17 March.

Swain, K. (1986) 'Probation attitudes to battered women: apathy, error and avoidance?', *Probation Journal*, 33(4), 132–4.

Tannen, D. (1992) *You Just Don't Understand: Women and Men in Conversation*, New York: Morrow.

Taylor, C. (1994) 'Is gender inequality in social work management relevant to social work students?', *British Journal of Social Work*, 24, 157–72.

Teeside Probation Service (1999) Quote from speech made by Lord Williams, Home Office prisons and probation minister in 1998, quoted in *Facts and Figures*, 4th edn.

Thomas, D. (1993) *Not Guilty: Men, the Case for the Defence*, London: Weidenfeld & Nicolson.

Thompson, N. (1993) *Anti-Discriminatory Practice*, Basingstoke: Macmillan; also 2nd edition (1997).

Thompson, N. (1995) 'Men and anti-sexism', *British Journal of Social Work*, 25, pp. 459–75.

Thompson, L. and Walker A. J. (1989) 'Gender in families: men and women in marriage: work and parenthood', *Journal of Marriage and the Family*, 51, pp. 845–71.

Tolman, R. M. and Bennett, L. W. (1990) 'A review of quantitative research on men who batter', *Journal of Interpersonal Violence*, 5, 87–118.

Tolson, A. (1977) *The Limits of Masculinity*, London: Tavistock.

Trotter, J. (1997) 'The failure of social work researchers, teachers and practitioners to acknowledge or engage non-abusing fathers: a preliminary discussion', *Social Work Education*, 16 (2), 63–76.

Tyndel, M. (1974) 'Psychiatric study of 1000 alcoholic patients' *Canadian Psychiatric Association Journal*, 19, 21–4.

Ungerson, C. (1987) *Policy Is Personal: Sex, Gender and Informal Care*, London: Tavistock.

Ussher, J. (1991) *Women's Madness: Misogyny or Mental Illness?*, London: Harvester Wheatsheaf.

Utting;, W. (1997) *People Like Us*, London: The Stationery Office.

Vaughan, P. (1995) *Suicide Prevention*, Birmingham: PEPAR Publications.

Vogel, C. and Pahl, J. (1993) 'Social and economic change and the organisation of money within marriage', *Work, Employment and Society*, 7 (1), 71–95.

Wallbank, J. (1997) 'The campaign for change of the Child Support Act 1991: reconstituting the "absent" father', *Social and Legal Studies*, 6 (2), 191–216.

Walton, R. G. (1975) *Women in Social Work*, London: Routledge & Kegan Paul.

Ward, L. (1997) 'Blair tries to end vicious circle', *Guardian*, 9 Dec., p. 8.

Warr, P. (1982) 'Psychological aspects of employment and unemployment', *Psychological Medicine*, 12, 7–11 (cited in Buck, 1997).

Waterhouse, L. (1993) *Child Abuse and Child Abusers*, London: Jessica Kingsley.

Weiner, G. and Arnot, M. (1987) *Gender Under Scrutiny: New Inquiries in Education*, London: Open University/Hutchinson.

Weissmann, M. M. and Klerman, G. L. (1977) 'Sex differences and the epidemiology of depression', *Archives of General Psychiatry*, 34 98–111.

Westwood, S. (1996) ''Feckless fathers': masculinities and the British state', in M. Mac an Ghaill (ed.), *Understanding Masculinities*, Buckingham: Open University Press, pp. 21–34.

Whisman, V. (1996) *Queer by Choice. Lesbians, Gay Men and the Politics of Identity*, London: Routledge.

White, V. (1995) 'Commonality and diversity in feminist social work', *British Journal of Social Work*, 25, 143–56.

Williams, B. (ed) (1995) *Probation Values*. Birmingham: Venture Press.

Williams, C. L. (1992) 'The glass escalator: hidden advantages for men in the "female" professions', *Social Problems*, 39 (3), 253–67.

Williams, C. L. (1993) *Doing 'Women's Work': Men in Nontraditional Occupations*, Newbury Park, Ca.: Sage.

Williams, F. (1989) *Social Policy: a Critical Introduction*, Cambridge: Polity Press.

Williams, F. (1994) 'Social relations, welfare and the post-Fordist Welfare State?', in R. Burrows and B. Loader (eds), *Towards a post-Fordist Welfare State?*, London: Routledge, pp. 49–73.

Williams, F. (1998) 'Troubled masculinities in social policy discourses: fatherhood', in J. Popay, J. Hearn and J. Edwards (eds), *Men, Gender Divisions and Welfare*, London: Routledge, pp. 63–97.

Williams, L. S. and Villemez, W. J. (1993) 'Seekers and finders: male entry and exit in female-dominated jobs' in C. L. Williams (1993), *Doing 'Women's Work': Men in Nontraditional Occupations*, Newbury Park, Ca.: Sage, pp. 64–90.

Willott, S. and Griffin, C. (1996) 'Men, masculinity and the challenge of long-term unemployment', in M. Mac an Ghaill (ed.), *Understanding masculin-*

ities: social relations and Cultural Arenas, Buckingham: Open University Press pp. 77–92.

Wilson, E. (1977) *Women and the Welfare State*, London: Tavistock.

Wilson, G. (1994) 'Abuse of elderly men and women among clients of a community psychogeriatric service', *British Journal of Social Work*, 24, 681–700.

Wilson, M. (1996) 'The CHANGE Men's Programme', in K. Cavanagh and V. E. Cree (eds), *Working with Men. Feminism and Social Work*, London: Routledge, pp. 28–44.

Wise, S. (1990) 'Becoming a feminist social worker,' in L. Stanley (ed.) *Feminist Praxis: Research, Theory and Epistemology in Feminist Sociology*, London: Routledge, pp. 236–49.

Wise, S. (1995) 'Feminist ethics in practice', in R. Hugman and D. Smith (eds), *Ethical Issues in Social Work*, London: Routledge, pp. 104–19.

Wise, S. and Stanley, L. (1990) 'Sexual harassment, sexual conduct and gender in social work settings', in P. Carter, T. Jeffs and M. Smith (eds), *Social Work and Social Welfare Yearbook, 2*, Buckingham: Open University Press, pp. 14–28.

Witz, A. (1992) *Professions and Patriarchy*, London: Routledge.

Witz, A. (1993) 'Women at work', in D. Richardson and V. Robinson (eds), *Introducing Women's Studies*, Basingstoke: Macmillan.

Wright, C. (1996) 'Sexuality, feminism and work with men,' in K. Cavanagh and V. E. Cree (eds), *Working With Men: Feminism and Social Work*, London: Routledge, pp. 128–46.

Young, M. and Willmott, P. (1962) *Family and Kinship in East London*, Harmondsworth: Penguin.

Index